WINTER

WINTER

·····································

Five Windows on the Season

ADAM GOPNIK

Quercus

First published in Canada and the United States in 2011 by
House of Anansi Press Inc.

First published in Great Britain in 2012 by
Quercus
55 Baker Street
7th Floor, South Block
W1U 8EW

This book was originally published in Canada as part of the
Massey Lectures Series, co-sponsored by the Canadian Broadcasting
Corporation, Massey College in the University of Toronto, and House
of Anansi Press. The series was created in honour of the Right
Honourable Vincent Massey, former governor-general of Canada, and
was inaugurated in 1961 to provide a forum for radio where major
contemporary thinkers could address important issues of our time.

A CIP catalogue record for this book is available
from the British Library

HB ISBN 978 1 78087 444 9
EBOOK ISBN 978 1 78087 446 3

Text design: Ingrid Paulson
Typesetting: Alysia Shewchuk

Printed and bound in Great Britain by Clays Ltd. St Ives plc

For Gudrun Bjerring Parker

Filmmaker, feminist, lover of the world,
woman of the north,
who raised and loved and nurtured and then
let go of my own true love,
and, knowing too well how Demeter felt, never let her heart
grow cold to the borrower.

CONTENTS

"Our envelope, as I have called it, the cultural insulation that separates us from nature, is rather like (to use a figure that has haunted me from childhood) the window of a lit-up railway carriage at night. Most of the time it is a mirror of our own concerns, including our concern about nature. As a mirror, it fills us with the sense that the world is something which exists primarily in reference to us: it was created for us; we are the centre of it and the whole point of its existence. But occasionally the mirror turns into a real window, through which we can see only the vision of an indifferent nature that goes along for untold aeons of time without us, seems to have produced us only by accident, and, if it were conscious, could only regret having done so."

— Northrop Frye, *Creation and Recreation*

AUTHOR'S NOTE

PART OF THE pleasure of the Massey Lectures, I've learned, is that they are published parallel with their delivery. This is a gift to the speaker, since it means that much of the work is done before the touring starts, and, for the hopelessly dilatory lecturer, the business of last-minute note-making becomes less frantic and wearing. But it's also a challenge to those of us who have gained something over the years by being late with work, and whose practice has been to speak from notes, or even memory — partly, I suppose, as a stunt, but at least as a stunt like skydiving, albeit skydiving without a parachute and in desperate search of a haystack, *must be one somewhere down there.* What is lost in lucidity is made up for by bravado.

Given that a lecture ought to be spoken, and that eventually I would speak these, I wanted for these essays a tone different from my well-varnished usual stuff, but that would still "work" for a reader as writing. I had, then, the idea of delivering a series of mock-Masseys the year before the real ones — five improvised living room lectures in the winter of 2010, one on each subject, supported by the cheer of wine and caffeine. These chapters are based on transcripts of those living room lectures, which I have, with some expert help, ironed and pressed and manicured and trimmed, but not, I think, entirely robbed of at least some of their spoken sound. I have eliminated the more irksome tics — all the "in facts" and "actuallys" and "so, basically" that occur more often than we know, and fear — but I haven't entirely cured, or tried to cure, the slightly ragged and excited edges of the performance. (Spoken sentences, I've discovered, have a natural three-part rhythm: a statement, its expansion, and then its summary in simpler form.) These chapters are meant to sound vocal, and I hope that some of the sound of a man who has boned up on a subject — in several cases, *just* boned up — and is sharing the afternoon's enthusiasm with an evening's friends is still in place. I mention all this lest the reader think, experiencing the breathless rattle and crash of some of these sentences, that I simply did not notice that they sounded the way they sounded, or else for some reason was trying to create from scratch the sound of speech on the page, and failing at that.

These are, then, the amended transcripts of lectures I once gave, designed to be the vocal templates of lectures I have yet to deliver. If there are paradoxes in this enterprise, it seems to suit the subject — which is, really, why winter, a season long seen as a sign of nature's withdrawal from grace, has become for us a time of human warmth.

So I have first and most to thank my listeners — Patty and Paul, Ariel and Alec and David, Becky and Emily, Leland and Aimee, and of course Martha and Luke and Olivia and even Butterscotch, who sat and chewed and wondered why — for bearing with me. There are more people thanked at the back of the book, but without those ears, it wouldn't even have a front.

A. G.
New York
June 2011

ONE

ROMANTIC WINTER
The Season in Sight

I RECALL MY first snowstorm as though it were yesterday, though it was, as it happens, November 12, 1968. The snow began to fall just after three o'clock. I was home from school, in an apartment at the old Expo site of Habitat '67, above the St. Lawrence River, where my family had moved only months before.

I had seen snow in America, of course, as a younger child in Philadelphia, but *that* snow was an event, a once-a-year wonder. *This* snow introduced itself — by its soft persistence and blanketing intensity, its too-soon appearance in the calendar (mid-November!) and the complacency with which everyone seemed to accept that too-soonness — as something that would go on for months and envelop a world. I stood behind the thin picture window that looked onto the terrace and I watched the first outline the world beyond, falling so it first italicized the plants and trees and the lights, drawing small white borders around them, and then slowly overwhelming them in drifts and dunes. I knew that I had crossed over into a new world — and that world was the world of winter.

When I think back to my youth in Montreal, I still think first of winter. I think about cold, of course. I recall moments of walking in cold so bitter that your ears seemed to have turned into ice. (What had happened to my hat? What happens to the hats of all Canadian kids? They are lost to some vast repository of wool that will one day be recovered and used to re-clothe the sheep of the world.) Pain, certainly, and a sort of strange fugue state, wandering in what had *looked* like a big city street hours before but now, at ten below zero on the old scale, seemed as strange and abandoned and polar as any ice pack.

But above all, my memories are of serenity. My memories are of a rare feeling of perfect equanimity — standing on top of Mount Royal in the middle of Montreal on cross-country skis at five o'clock on a February evening, and feeling a kind of peace, an attachment to the world, an understanding of the world, that I had never had before. This emotion has never left me. My heart jumps when I hear a storm predicted, even in the perpetual *grisaille* of Paris; my smile rises when cold weather is promised, even in forever-forty-something-Fahrenheit New York. Gray skies and December lights are my idea of secret joy, and if there were a heaven, I would expect it to have a lowering violet-gray sky (and I would expect them to spell *gray* g-r-e-y) and white lights on all the trees and the first flakes just falling, and it would always be December 19 — the best day of the year, school out, stores open late, Christmas a week away.

Yet loving winter can seem, in the very long perspective of history, perverse. Of all the natural metaphors of existence that we have — light versus dark, sweet against bitter — none seems more natural than the opposition of the seasons: warmth against cold, spring against fall, and above all, summer against winter. Human beings make metaphors as naturally as bees make honey, and one of the most natural metaphors we make is of winter as a time of abandonment and retreat. The oldest metaphors for winter are all metaphors of loss. In classical myth, winter is Demeter's sorrow at the abduction of her daughter by Death. In almost every other European mythology it is the same: winter is hard and summer is soft, as surely as sweet wine is better than bitter lees.

But a taste for winter, a love for winter vistas — a belief that they are as beautiful and seductive in their own way, and as essential to the human spirit and the human soul as any summer scene — is part of the modern condition. Wallace Stevens, in his poem "The Snow Man," called this new feeling "a mind of winter," and he identified it with our new acceptance of a world without illusions, our readiness to live in a world that might have meaning but that doesn't have God. A mind of winter, a mind *for* winter, not sensing the season as a loss of warmth and light, and with them hope of life and divinity, but ready to respond to it as a positive, and even purifying, presence of something else — the beautiful and peaceful, yes, but also the mysterious, the strange, the sublime — is a modern taste.

Now, *modern* I mean in the sense that the loftier kinds of historians of ideas like to use the term, to mean not just right here and now but also the longer historical period that begins sometime around the end of the eighteenth century, breathes fire from the twin dragons of the French and Industrial Revolutions, and then still blows cinder-breath into at least the end of the twentieth century, drawing deep with the twin lungs of applied science and mass culture. An age of growth and an age of doubt, the age in which, for the first time in both Europe and America, more people were warmer than they had been before, and in which fewer people had faith in God — a period when, at last, the nays had it.

My subject is the new feelings winter has provoked in men and women of those modern times: fear, joy, exhilaration, magnetic appeal and mysterious attraction. Since to be modern is to let imagination and invention do a lot of the work once done by tradition and ritual, winter is in some ways the *most* modern season — the season defined by absences (of warmth, leaf, blossom) that can be imagined as stranger presences (of secrets, roots, hearths). This new idea of winter races from the Gothic landscapes of the German Romantics to the lyrical snowfalls of the Impressionists, and from the city Christmas parables of Charles Dickens to the iceberg visions of Lawren Harris, and right on to Nat King Cole singing "Baby, It's Cold Outside." The mystique, the romance of winter is with Scott at the Pole as he eats his last "whoosh" and with Charlie Chaplin in the Yukon as he eats his own shoe.

I won't claim for these chapters anything like encyclopedic completeness, only an essayist's idiosyncrasies: these are five windows among many more that we could open on the history of the winter mind. Yet though these chapters will not be hostage to a reductive thesis, they will hum, I hope, a recurrent theme. That theme is simply defined. Winter's persona changes with our perception of safety from it — the glass of the window, as I sensed in that November snowstorm, is the lens through which modern winter is always seen. The romance of winter is possible only when we have a warm, secure indoors to retreat to, and winter becomes a season to look at as much as one to live through. For Henry James the two happiest words of nineteenth-century bourgeois civilization were "summer afternoon." The answering two words that haunted the imagination of that same culture were "winter evening."

And I hope to make a larger point, larger even than helping you see that these two worlds — the world of the safe window and the world of the white wilderness outside — always in the end merge and become one in the modern mind. That is that there is a humane purpose to watching winter that is found simply in the acts of naming and describing. Winter *is* hard; the cold *does* chill; Demeter *is* mourning. And we oppose that threat with the quiet heroism of comfort. Central heating, double-paned windows, down coats, heated cars. But we also oppose the threatening blank bitterness of winter just by looking at it, and by saying what it's like. The first thing that the earliest polar explorers did was to name the ice shelves and coasts — naming them after their patrons and their patrons' moms — and then the very next thing the very next group of explorers did was to change the names, naming those same things after kaisers and their daughters. Names are the footholds, the spikes the imagination hammers in to get a hold on an ice wall of mere existence.

The Adamic act, one might call it — not in light of this speaker but of that first Adam, whose entry-level job was to name the animals, calling a bear a bear and a snake a snake and then, in the last, expelled extreme, a lady a lady. Giving the animals names is to call them out of mere existence into mind. That act is the thing that makes the world humane. It gives structure and meaning to natural events that in themselves contain none. And it's not just names in the literal sense that do this work; categories, insights, microscopic photographs, and meteorological predictions, concepts, distinctions — all work together to give a sweeter shape to what before was only scary. In the past two hundred years we have turned winter from something to survive to something to survey, from a thing to be afraid of to a thing to be aware of. It's through the slow crawl of distinctions, differentiations, and explanations that the world becomes . . . well, never *manageable*, but recognizable, this place we know. The conquest of winter, as both a physical fact and an imaginative act, is one of the great chapters in the modern renegotiation of the world's boundaries, the way we draw lines between what nature is and what we feel about it. We see and hear and sense in winter emotional tones and overtones that our great-great-grandfathers and grandmothers did not. I hope to describe some of those newly made maps of winter feeling and tell you stories about the people — foolish and greedy and sometimes inspired — who redrew them.

THE BITING STRINGS and breathless beauty of Vivaldi's "Winter," from his *Four Seasons* of 1725, is a place to begin — though the more knowing of you probably cringe and grimace a little when you hear that name. Could anything be more inexorably middle-brow than *this*? Yet sometimes repetition can dull us to true greatness. (I suspect that if Vivaldi's *Seasons* were dug out of a chest today and performed by a suitably sniffy German original-instruments group on a suitably obscure European label, it might be more easily recognized as the masterpiece it is.) Vivaldi's "Winter" still sounds a clarion call. It's among the very first artic-ulations of an entirely new attitude about what winter is and offers. Vivaldi apparently wrote a poem for each of the four sea-sons. The one he wrote for winter describes all the harshness of winter, yet it ends in the same spirit as the music, saying "Ahh, what a scintillating time!" He wrote:

To shiver, frozen, amid icy snow
In the bitter blast of a horrible wind;

To run constantly stamping one's feet;
And to feel one's teeth chatter on account of the excessive cold;
To spend restful, happy days at the fireside
While the rain outside drenches a good one hundred
To walk on the ice,
And with slow steps to move about cautiously
For fear of falling;
To go fast, to slip and fall down;
To go on the ice again and run fast
Until the ice cracks and opens up;
To hear coming out of the iron gates
Sirocco, Boreas and all the winds at war:
That's winter! but of a kind to gladden one's heart.

This is one of the early intimations we have in modern times of there being something specifically pleasure-giving, pleasure-seeking, about winter. A Venetian winter — of the kind that Vivaldi, with his all-girl orchestra at the Pietà who first played this piece, knew — is not exactly a Whitehorse winter. But it is more biting than one might expect, as any December visitor to Venice knows, and the decision to embrace it, to embroider it, to make it a musical subject as pleasing as any other is a moment to "gladden one's heart."

Now, while I said my subject is not winter as a physical fact but rather winter as a poetic act — winter in mind rather than winter in matter — nonetheless those subjects raise a simple question: What *is* winter? Why do we have winter? What is its reality? So, with Vivaldi's sharp strumming still in our ears, let me discuss briefly, and as best as a non-meteorologist can, why real winter happens and why real winter is cold.

Real winter — the planetary fact rather than the enshrined season — comes to us for a simple reason: the planet tilts. The punishment that Milton's God gives to Adam and Eve, of placing the planet's axis at an angle, really is the reason we have winter. As the planet passes through its orbit, we get less sunlight. Less sunlight makes us a lot colder. It cools the air and brings us winter. What before was water freezes in ponds and lakes and rivers and becomes ice; what before was rain freezes in clouds and becomes snow. And that, very simply, is that.

Cold, of course, is in itself a variable, a relative concept. The world is always weather-tilted, but there have been warmer periods in earth's history, when the poles themselves were temperate and the temperature of the seawater around the South Pole practically tropical. And, of course, there have been colder periods, ice ages, when what we experience now as winter ran right through the year. In this way, what we mean by winter is, more narrowly, the experience of most northern climates as we feel it now, and have felt it for most of the past few thousand years.

Winter also arrives in long cycles, ice ages that come and go. We all know about the great ice age — which has been the subject of animated movies and elementary school classes — the vast one that swept over the planet fifty thousand years ago, but most climate scientists believe, and most historians second this belief, that for reasons still not well understood, a second and smaller and shorter ice age conquered our planet sometime between 1550 and 1850. Whether that cooling was limited to the northern hemisphere or was in fact earth-wide, it is certainly the case that Europe was much colder between 1550 and 1850 than it had been in the 2,000 years before or the 150 years since.

And as a consequence, the pre-modern winter scenes — those Bruegel pictures of hunters in the snow, the Dutch pictures of skaters on the ice, all of that world of Netherlandish recreation — are occasional art owed to the tiny period when people were first fully aware that the world had suddenly become very cold. There was, one might say, a kind of false spring of winter art right around the beginning of the seventeenth century. Much of the pre-modern winter material — Shakespeare's poem in *Love's Labour's Lost*, "When icicles hang" (the one with the great Greasy Joan who doth keel the pot) — comes from that period. And that little ice age persisted, if not at that same extreme of cold, right through the eighteenth century, and even well into the nineteenth, and in that little ice age people expected the world to be very, very cold in winter. (That's why you always have a white Christmas in eighteenth-century English literature; it's why, as no longer happens, the canals of Holland froze over.)

Yet, over time, one has the sense that what had been exciting in its first appearance became merely tiresome in its extension. So much so that as we approach the transition period between old and new, as we approach the birth of modern time — close to the moment when Vivaldi wrote his *Four Seasons* — we find the great Dr. Samuel Johnson sitting down in 1747 to write a poem called "The Winter's Walk." He writes:

Behold, my fair, where'er we rove,
What dreary prospects round us rise,
The naked hill, the leafless grove,
The hoary ground, the frowning skies,

Nor only through the wasted plane,
Stern Winter is thy force confess'd;
Still wider spread thy horrid reign,
I feel thy power usurp my breast.

That's a perfect sober statement of the neoclassical Augustan view of winter, as something impressive in its way but fundamentally negative, fundamentally unappealing, fundamentally off. Naked hills, frowning skies, horrid rain . . . Dating Dr. Johnson in December was no fun.

Perhaps the first unmistakable clear statement of an entirely new and modern attitude towards winter — neither the sporadic excitement of the little ice age nor the depression of the neoclassical attitude — is a poem written right towards the end of the eighteenth century by the modest and largely forgotten but gifted British poet William Cowper. Cowper was famous in his day as a writer of hymns and as a maker of popular verse. But in truth he had the most unique and undervalued of all poetic gifts, and that was the gift of chattiness. He was a wonderfully chatty poet. We tend to underrate chattiness in poets because we like sublime lyricism or melodramatic confession, but the ability to write a conversational poem (to give it a more dignified name), and to make it sound like conversation while still looking like a poem, is one of the rarest poetic gifts.

In 1783 Cowper wrote to a friend, "I see the winter approaching without much concern, though a passionate lover of fine weather, and the pleasant scenes of summer, but the long evenings have their comforts too, and there is hardly to be found upon earth, I suppose, so snug a creature as an Englishman by the fireside in the winter." And in a poem he wrote in 1785, "The Winter Evening," he turns that honest confessed pleasure into a beautifully chatty bit of poetry. He describes at length the arrival of the coachman at his suburban cottage—that herald of modernity coming from London to his rather remote vicarage—bringing him the paper full of parliamentary news, and the poet sitting down by the fire to read it, a cup of hot tea at his side. It's an incredibly modern moment: a little caffeine in one hand, the newspaper in the other hand, a fire going, while you're taking in all the political news of the metropolis at a reassuring and comforting distance. And after reading his newspaper he writes,

> O winter, ruler of the inverted year,
> Thy scatter'd hair with sleet like ashes fill'd,
> Thy breath congeal'd upon thy lips, thy cheeks
> Fringed with a beard made white with other snows
> Than those of age, thy forehead wrapp'd in clouds,
> A leafless branch thy sceptre, and thy throne
> A sliding car, indebted to no wheels,
> But urg'd by storms along its slippery way,
> I love thee, all unlovely as thou seem'st,
> And dreaded as thou art! . . .
> I crown thee king of intimate delights,
> Fireside enjoyments, homeborn happiness,
> And all the comforts that the lowly roof
> Of undisturb'd retirement, and the hours
> Of long uninterrupted evening, know.

What an alteration in twenty-odd years! No longer winter as the grim overlord of Dr. Johnson's not very winning walk, but Winter, "king of intimate delights and fireside enjoyments,"

drawing the family near. Now the whole new world of the bourgeois family, sharing one common hearth, one common table, is
made more appealing in winter than it is at any other time of the
year. That's Cowper's new view. In his own simple, chatty, infor-
mal, middle-class way, Cowper announces a profound switch, a
change in sensibility. It is a change that we tend to coalesce
around a philosophical ideal that historians like to call "the picturesque" — turning to nature not as a thing to be feared or even
as a thing to seek religious comfort from, but as a thing simply to
enjoy, to take pleasure in. "I love thee, all unlovely as thou
seemst."

Now, all poems have their place in time, and there is a great
deal of dour economic history going on in the background here.
One of the things that beleaguered England throughout the eighteenth century was, in effect, a crisis of "peak wood." The entire
island was being deforested, and fuel-wood prices rose ten times
in the span of eighty years, so the problem of how you were going
to heat all those cottages was enormous. But by the time Cowper
is writing, that problem has largely been solved by the beginnings of a full-fledged coal industry, and though Cowper is
probably sitting by a wood-burning fire, the existence of cheap
and abundant coal has brought down the price of wood and helped
invent those modern pleasures — a newspaper delivered to your
door, warmth in the kitchen, and the family gathered round.

This is the first unambiguous declaration of the winter picturesque, winter as all the more lovely because it is so entirely
exterior. With Cowper we're not simply experiencing an emotion
that has never been registered before; in a sense we are experiencing an emotion that has never been *felt* before. For the first
time you can have a cheap fire and a family around it and winter

going on outside. A crucial zone of safety has been sought and found (or bought, at least, by a snug and lucky few). The boy at the window is born today.

BUT THERE'S ANOTHER feeling about winter that begins to appear for the first time in the same orbit of English poets. That's not a sense of the winter picturesque, of winter as soothing, comforting, or appealing — by its very forbidding nature forcing people closer together indoors. It's the opposite sense: of winter as a mysterious magnetic season that the wanderer is expelled into for his own good, for the purification and improvement of his soul. And you find that new emotion first, appropriately enough, right at the turn of the century — in 1799, when the poet Samuel Taylor Coleridge goes to Germany on a winter walking trip and writes home to his wife:

> But when first the ice fell on the lake, and the whole lake was frozen, one huge piece of thick transparent glass, O my God! what sublime scenery have I beheld. Of a morning when I have seen the little lake covered with Mist; when the Sun peeped over the Hill, the Mist broke in the middle, and at last stood as the waters of the Red Sea are said to have done when the Israelites passed — and between these two walls of Mist the Sunlight burnt upon the Ice in a strait road of golden Fire, all across the lake . . . About a month ago the vehemence of the wind had shattered the Ice — part of it, quite shattered, was driven to shore and had frozen anew; this was of a deep blue, and represented [resembled] an agitated sea — the water that ran up between the great islands of ice shone of a yellow green (it was at sunset) and all these scattered islands of smooth ice were blood; intensely bright blood.

"What sublime scenery I have beheld!" Coleridge's words are one of those rare passages of prose that truly mark the arrival of an epoch. It would be impossible to find anything like it in European literature only twenty-five years before. The intellectual machinery might have been in place, but not the immediate emotional pressure. This kind of love of the winter scene is not of the force outside pressing in on the window, bringing the family together. Instead it is for the ice-spirit pulling us *out*.

That new idea is, of course, most often associated with Edmund Burke's great essay on the sublime and beautiful, from the middle of the eighteenth century. Burke's was one of the three or four most powerful ideas in the history of thought, because he wrenched aesthetics away from an insipid idea of beauty towards recognition of the full span of human sympathy. Oceans and thunderstorms, precipices and abysses, towering volcanoes and, above all, snow-capped mountains — they rival and outdo the heritage of classical beauty exactly *because* they frighten us; they fill us with fear, with awe, with a sense of the inestimable mystery of the world. This winter window is wrenched open by the lever of the sublime.

And beyond that there is a sense, one that will fill the minds of the artists of winter throughout the nineteenth century, that what makes winter wonderful, what makes winter sublime, what makes winter essential is this sense that you can project onto its forms of ice and snow anything you want to see. To Coleridge the sun on the ice looks as it did when the Israelites crossed the Red Sea. Later he goes on to say that "the water that ran up between the great islands of ice shone of a yellow green . . . and all these scattered islands of smooth ice were blood; intensely bright blood." Snow and ice, the winter forms, are potentially lethal but also potently labile; they can be re-formed, re-imagined, projected in ways that allow you to see Israelites and the blood of the Lamb and golden fire-shattered seas of ice and scattered islands of bright blood where there is really only a German lake, frozen hard as an ice cube.

Now, these categories — pretty, cozy nature on the one hand, scary, awe-inspiring nature on the other — are usually covered by those terms *picturesque* and *sublime*, and it does no harm to use that convenient shorthand. But such simple ideas are too crude and schematic to capture the complicated responses of artists to winter, or anything else — such categories are for critics to think up and for artists and poets to keep out of. (In truth, in the nineteenth century, *sublime* came to be used as a one-size-fits-all word, just as *ironic* was used in the twentieth century to take in both the deadpan parody of pop culture of Duchamp's sort and sincere tributes to it, as in Warhol. *Everything*, sooner or later, was sublime.)

Simpler and more transparent, then, to call these types "sweet winter" and "scary winter" — in tribute to the now disbanded Spice Girls — with the understanding that what is scary can also be sweet, what is charming, divine. A snow-capped mountain in Switzerland, seen from the comfort of an *auberge*, can set off a profound chain of thought about ice and ancient history; a gentle snow in the Paris suburbs can create images that show the transience of beauty. The winter window has two sides, one for the watcher and one for the white drifts, and the experience of winter is often not one or the other but both at once.

OF THOSE TWO sensations, though, the one that first gets fully realized as art among the northern Romantic painters and musicians of the early decades of the nineteenth century is the scary and sad side of winter. Searching for the first true winter masters, rather than just winter visitors — major artists who made winter one of their central obsessive subjects — we find two Germans: the painter Caspar David Friedrich and, later but still better, the composer Franz Schubert.

Friedrich, who lived and worked in the first decades of the century, mostly painting in obscurity around Dresden, was born in 1774. His is in some ways closer to what we think of as a Scandinavian rather than German sensibility, basing most of his painting on the Baltic island of Rügen. Gloomy, guilt-ridden, mystical — sort of an oil-painting Ingmar Bergman. He's an artist who has become newly fashionable in the past thirty years, partly because some aspects of his art anticipate the sublime stretches and blank forms of abstract expressionism, partly because he is, at times, a peculiarly pedantic painter, and therefore appeals to the pedantic imagination. (Professors like painters who anticipated the art of our time and were obviously part of the thought of their time: then the lectures practically write themselves.)

Friedrich's fascination with winter has a personal core: the key emotional event in his life was the death of his favourite younger brother in a skating accident when they were thirteen and fourteen; in front of Friedrich's eyes he fell through the ice and drowned. So for Friedrich the experience of winter is loaded with the most powerful kind of emotional freight, with intimations of death and hopes for immortality. An important early painting, from around 1819, is called *Monastery Graveyard in the Snow*, and it shows exactly what the title suggests, that is, a cemetery ruin, in winter. Fallen leaves, naked black velvet trees silhouetted against a violent and orange-gilt evening sky, intimations of Gothic architecture — all his winter landscapes are designed to reveal by this kind of stripping away that the forms of the German forest eerily mimic and echo the forms of medieval Gothic. The dead season echoes the lost time. Very often he has hallucinatory Gothic churches rising up in the middle of a winter landscape. The act of stripping away, the act of accepting winter as it is — and Friedrich is one of the very few painters of his generation who never goes to Italy or wants to go to Italy — is, in its first appearance, an assertion of religious faith, an assertion of a remade kind of medievalism that allows him access through winter to the lost Romantic past. Winter is haunting, but it's also healing.

But there also quickly came to be a nationalist politics linked to Friedrich's painting of winter. When Napoleon invades Germany in 1806, images of winter, which first have essentially a spiritual resonance, suddenly mark the arrival of modern nationalism in art. For what Germany has that France does not have is winter, a real winter, and its assertion in art marks the assertion of the German national genius.

The metaphors of the Enlightenment are, as the name suggests, those of sunlight (the French is even simpler: *les Lumières*). Its metaphors are of warmth, light, the sun returning to warm the human mind. Yet one of the ironies of the Enlightenment is that it also gives birth to the counter-Enlightenment idea of distinct national cultures reflecting different national climates. "If it be true that the temper of the mind and the passions of the heart are extremely different in different climates, then laws ought to be in relation . . . to the variety of those tempers," Montesquieu writes in 1751. Southern peoples have southern moods and northern ones have a temper made for winter. One law for both the winter lion and the spring lamb is folly.

This tolerant imperative is made, in resistance to Napoleon, into a form of national self-assertion, and the embrace of winter is its engine: *we have our own season up here*. In a Germany still marked by a longing for the South — the dream of the twin sisterhood of Germania and Italia was a pet subject of Goethe's generation — the imagery of winter works both as a thing to give identity to the newly unifying (or just beginning to be unified) German nation and also as a symbol of the things that the French Enlightenment and French reason will never understand.

One of Friedrich's most important pictures, from 1812, is *The Chasseur in the Forest*; it shows a tiny French soldier who is just overwhelmed by the pine trees of the German winter woods. He is clearly going to get lost, going to be sucked up, snowed over — going to be overwhelmed by the northern forest that defies not only Napoleon's army but defies the larger intellectual army of French reason. It is a picture not only about nationalist resistance to the French; it's also about northern, German resistance, Romantic resistance, to the Enlightenment idea of reason. *The snows of the mystical past will cover you over, little man, and with it your pathetic faith in your encyclopedic organization of the world.* Summer and the Mediterranean are mere sweet reason; winter is sharp instinct and keen memory.

Winter, for Friedrich, is the place where the revolt against reason begins, a place of national convocation more profound than cosmopolitan conversation. In return it gives elbow room for the imagination. The sleep of reason brings forth monsters, Goya said, and the sleep of nature, in winter, brings forth . . . Well, it brings forth bringing forth — it creates a space for imagination where ice floes become ghost ships and snowdrifts become cathedrals and the red light of sunset becomes the Red Sea parting.

What will become the brutal hallucinations of the Arctic explorers begins as benign projections of the German painters. Winter becomes in this way, in Friedrich's work, not only a place where you can see your own past and hallucinate about the lost days of religious purity; winter also becomes a powerful symbol of rejection of the French empire of arms and the French empire of mind.

Of all Friedrich's images, the most resonant and perhaps the most famous — perhaps the most famous of all nineteenth-century winter images, still visible on CD cases and paperback covers — is from 1824. Called *The Sea of Ice*, it shows a sailing ship being crushed in the ice, as helpless as a mouse half-devoured by a boa constrictor. It used to be thought of as reportage, an account of an actual incident, but it seems now to have been entirely imaginary, the fascinated dream of a northern mind. It is evident that this kind of neat pressure of a vision — in this case the ice that crushes the ship — also creates ghostly inanimate forms: the ship is being eaten by a second ship, itself made of ice, a sort of scary, hallucinatory parody of constructed form produced by the lethality of the cold.

Winter forms, ice and snow, are once again potentially lethal and potently labile; ice is capable of making forms, by accident, that are Gothic in their intricate tracery — a typical hallucination of the era, when the bergs and glaciers were constantly seen as passing ships, castles, cathedrals. A nineteenth-century vein of feeling climaxed, perhaps, in the observation of one of the few sailors who saw the fatal iceberg from the deck of the *Titanic* and lived to say that it looked like a six-masted schooner, a ghost ship floating by. For Friedrich, winter is the red pill of an awakened northern consciousness. Summer is the Matrix, the lie; winter is the truth. It might be bitter, but at least it's real. At the same time, if sweet winter is the season of intimacy, scary winter is the season of the imagination. By, so to speak, stripping down nature to her underwear, it lets us project our fantasies upon her.

SO NORTHERN EUROPEANS in the first quarter of the nineteenth century were drawn to winter as the season of the counter-Enlightenment, as the poster scene of a national revival, and as a landscape of the real. But they also were drawn to winter as a kind of X-ray of nature that showed her as she really is. You could therefore see the hand of God — or its absence — more clearly in cold weather than at any other time. The argument over whether the architecture of ice and snow was really a sign of God's purpose or only looked that way was a real one at the beginning of the nineteenth century, and it reaches a slightly alarming — and, in its way, comic — climax in a fierce, peculiar debate over winter windows between Goethe and his friend Knebel. It was a debate that took as its object the seemingly unoffending, indeed unspectacular, presence of *eisblumen*, "ice flowers" — hoarfrost, as it's sometimes called — on winter windows.

We live in an age in which frost flowers on windows appear very rarely, even in cold countries. But in a time when there was still no central heating and windows were made of cast glass filled with impurities, frost patterns "grew" on small irregularities in the window's dappled surface. And these frost patterns really do have an uncanny resemblance to biological forms. They look like ferns, like flowers — they have a graceful bend and sweep, that look of subtle variation within repeated shapes, of structure swelling outwards from an inner nucleus, that marks our experience of biological form. In fact they are merely — well, not *merely*, but truly — crystal lattices, the striking facets and lines that grow according to simple rules of molecular chemistry, combined with chance seizing on chance flaws — not organic generation. They're fascinating but they're really not alive.

Yet the German Romantic poets and scientists — the two disciplines were not yet ghettoized — became fascinated by these forms, and troubled by the question of whether they were truly living forms, made by the hand of God, or merely mimicry, an accident, a random constellation of crystals that only seemed to be alive. It seems, as I said, a very peculiar argument to absorb intellectuals and poets, but so it did, and for more than a decade. (Perhaps we can grasp what they felt was at stake if we recall the passion with which theologians and physicists have argued in our own time that the indeterminacy of the subatomic quantum world gives some reassurance of the existence of free will. We seem always to seize on the smallest strange thing we can detect to prove that there are more things in heaven than our physics can entirely show.)

In the end, as Andrea Portman explains in her eye-opening study of the subject, Goethe intervened to make a very powerful neoclassical and scientific statement: that you could not have faith in the patterns of ice flowers on windows, that they were the signs of death and not of life, that they were simply shallow mineral mimicry of biological form, and that they should be dismissed from the repository, from the vocabulary of the Romantic imagination. Winter's forms for Goethe were not, as they were for his contemporary Novalis, signs of life but of the hollow mimicry of life by rocks — just as for Goethe the cult of winter was a morbid nationalism that turned its back on Italian light and lucidity. (Goethe's own taste in winter was more hygienic and high-minded: as we'll see, he loved to skate.)

The ice-flower business might have sunk into the archival depths of scholarship had it not been quietly planted as a root fable beneath two great works of art: the best and most mysterious of all Romantic winter fables, Hans Christian Andersen's "The Snow Queen," and the most beautiful of all Romantic plaints of the season, Franz Schubert's *Winterreise*. Everyone has read "The Snow Queen," I suspect; it is the most many-sided and cruel and memorable of all Andersen's invented folk fables. Published in 1845, the crucial moment comes when Kay, the hero, gets a chip of glass in his eye — glass from an evil goblin's mirror that distorts his vision. Then, for the first time, Kay looks at a snowflake and sees its intricate internal form — and thinks it's more beautiful than a flower.

This isn't an accidental or spontaneous invention of Andersen's; it is a summation of the larger argument about the relation of crystal form, mineral form, to biological form. It's all about snowflakes and flowers. The notion that Andersen takes up is that only someone who has been paralyzed by reason — the Snow Queen sits in the centre of a cracked and broken "Mirror of Reason" — will confuse the cold form of death with the burgeoning warmth of life. What makes the Snow Queen so alluring is that she sits — reigns — between two traditions: the classical Christian idea of the North as bad, dangerous, to be escaped, and the Romantic idea of the wintry North as alluring, seductive, to be followed. The mirror of reason was always broken. Winter is a trap for the Romantic imagination, because it makes dead forms look as nice as living ones. The Snow Queen looks terrific, but she'll freeze your soul.

You find the same pattern, the same notion, in Schubert's great song cycle of the 1820s, perhaps the first true masterpiece of

modern times devoted to the new idea of winter. *Winterreise* —
the winter journey — is sung by a tenor to piano accompaniment.
Adapted from poems by Wilhelm Müller, the songs tell the story
of a lover, a traveller, a pilgrim who has been expelled from his
home and is forced to wander through that German winter that
Friedrich's painting describes in such unsparing and alluring
detail. It's the tale of a man forced to live in Friedrich's paintings,
and singing his pain at being lost there.

In the eleventh song, "Frühlingstraum," you hear the singer,
the voice of the wanderer in the white wilderness, looking at the
frost patterns, the ice blooms, on the window — which he sees,
significantly, from outside rather than from inside — and wondering who placed them there, who is their author. Is it God? Is it
man? Are they merely accident? It's unanswered and unanswer-
able, and presents again the essential question that winter raises
for the Romantic mind, the Romantic imagination: who made
winter, and why was it made? Do we project form and meaning
onto something that is just an absence, a non-happening of the
natural order of warmth and sunshine, or does winter offer some
mysterious residual sign of divinity — perhaps in a piercing and
haunting musical form or, for that matter, etched on a window? If
winter is ours, who are we?

All these visions and versions of winter take place at the pressure point where indoor warmth meets the frozen window. The
joy of winter is to see in imagination Gothic cathedrals and fleeing Israelites and passing ships and blood-red fields where there
are really only accidents of ice. The terror of winter is to recognize that these visions are just hallucinations, that mindless
crystals have no meaning, that snowflakes can't stand for souls,
that ice comes not from God's hand but from the broken mirror of

the mind — from our will to invest the world with meanings of our own. The joy is in projecting our imaginations; the fear is of getting locked inside our own heads. In Schubert, as in Hans Christian Andersen, winter's brutality to the wanderer in the wilderness is compensated for by its opening up of winter's mystery to the witness at the window. The special beauty of Schubert's song is that he imagines that the most soulful role is to be both wanderer and witness, and at the same time.

THIS ROMANTIC REASSERTION of the possibilities of winter, both as poetic material and as patriotic matter, is even more vehement at that early nineteenth-century moment in Russia. Russia is, with Canada, the other great winter nation, a place where snow is not a likely happenstance but a fixed certainty. In Germany the winter romance is always balanced by longing for Italy and the South — even Friedrich could not break the authority of Italy in the German mind. But in Russia the North–South dialogue was more narrowly centred on France, and so when the great Napoleonic invasion happened, a great reaction happened too.

Winter in Russia is an inescapable fact, an absolute force, and yet throughout the eighteenth century, Slavic scholars tell us, there is almost no literature, no poetry in Russian devoted to the praise of winter. But if winter became a potent symbol of German nationalism in the Napoleonic period, it became a still more powerful and potent symbol of Russian nationalism and Russian national identity. Napoleon could be symbolically "defeated" by the epic German snows; he was, in the campaign of 1812, actually defeated by the reality of the Russian winter. The French came, the winter arrived, the French fled. So there is a whole line of political cartoons around 1812 that show Napoleon being swamped by an avalanche of snow. It was so strong an idea that the tsarist government had to put out propaganda denying that Napoleon had been defeated by the Russian winter and had instead been defeated by the Russian generals.

This new patriotic appreciation of winter among Russian poets at the beginning of 1812 produces a great poetic literature. It produces it first in the work of Prince Pyotr Vyazemsky, who writes what is probably the first Romantic snow poem in Russia — for in Russia this new Romantic interest in winter takes an essentially poetic rather than pictorial or musical form, quite predictably, if you believe, as I do, in national genius. Vyazemsky's "First Snow," that first snow poem, becomes as central to Russian literature of the period as first love poems are elsewhere. It becomes a genre, something that every young Russian poet has to attempt: a description of the first snow as though it were a first love.

The poetry might not have come to maturity were it not for the reality that Vyazemsky was the best friend of Alexander Pushkin. Where the German embrace of winter was essentially melancholic, Pushkin makes his love of winter national and invigorating — even joyful — and always sexy. It is the super-abundance of energy, not a window onto death, that winter gives to Russia that fills Pushkin's heart and poems. In 1824 he writes a wonderful poem called "Winter Morning," singing to a girl with whom he has, it seems, just spent the night — a long way from Dr. Johnson's gloomy Augustan winter wooing — which celebrates the season both as post-coital paradise and as the haunt of memory:

Frost and sun, what a glorious day!
Yet still, sweet friend, you sleep away.
It's time, beloved, for you to stir:
Open wide your dreamy eyes
To catch the dawn glow in northern skies —
Rise up yourself, my love, like a northern star . . .

One of the things Pushkin emphasizes throughout all of his winter poetry is the essential paradox, known to Russians and Canadians alike, that while in the summer and fall roads can be impassable, in winter countries, especially before the days of paving, winter turns life in just the opposite direction. "A sliding car," as Cowper puts it a little coyly, is the sleigh Pushkin races around in. In the true North, winter becomes the season of speed, the season where you can put your loved one in a sleigh and whisk her off to an erotic rendezvous, and that theme — the eroticism of winter — is a peculiarly Russian one. It's all tied up in furs and snows and secrets, and it runs right through the Russian literature of the nineteenth century. It begins here with Pushkin. The Germans saw the enigmas of winter; the Russians see its eroticism. Where Dr. Johnson and his date had only a winter walk, Pushkin and his lover fly across the snow.

YET IF THE northern Europeans in the crucible of the Napoleonic Wars were the first to make a new winter art from the season's scary side, the real victor of the Napoleonic Wars was England, and it would be Britain and British culture that would set the tone and the key for a new, and on the whole sweeter, vision of winter in the 1830s and 1840s — those two decades of enormous prosperity and progress that marked the beginning of the Pax Angleterra.

Exactly the thing that haunted the Romantic imagination in Germany — that is to say, the permeable membrane between winter and the self, represented in the most literal way by the window — was no longer so strong a fact in England. Instead of pockets of warmth there was, increasingly, an envelope of warm air. Central heating was born in Britain.

Now, North Americans who have spent a winter in England and who, clutching teacups and shivering in shaggy sweaters, wonder if they will ever be warm again, may find it hard to believe that this was the first warm modern place. But in the 1830s and 1840s it was the first country with even a hint of central heating. Heating engineers from Poland and France actually emigrated to England because that's where the Silicon Valley — or, rather, the coal valley — of the time was. It's one of the oddities of cultural history that we tend to overlook the authors of our comforts, even though we are almost always perfectly knowledgeable about the poets of our distress. Everybody has heard of Caspar David Friedrich but nobody knows the names of the men who, in the first decades of the nineteenth century, invented central heating, and particularly steam heating by radiating pipes. Let us name them now: they included Thomas Tredgold and H. R. Robertson and an immigrant genius of central heating, the French engineer F. W. Chabannes (a Russian, Franz San Galli, would soon invent the radiator). For the most part they were, true to the *Star Trek* stereotype, from the north of England, the world of the Darwins, the Wedgwoods, the free thinkers and scientists who made industrial England.

The idea of centrally heating a large enclosed space had begun in hothouses and incubators as a solution to the problem of keeping vegetables and fruits warm in winter. But the British engineers soon realized — and it was no accident that among them was James Watt, inventor of the steam engine — that essentially the problem of central heating was more or less the problem of running a locomotive-like steam engine that wasn't meant to go anywhere. You had to build pipes that were simultaneously strong enough to withstand the press of steam heat but not so large that they made it impossible for people to live within them.

But the real triumph was intellectual. For the first time engineers and architects began to think of architecture explicitly in terms of interior air, of inner space. The Scottish engineer David Boswell Reid, put in charge of centrally heating the new Houses of Parliament after the great fire in the 1830s, wrote, "Though forgotten amidst the more obvious attractions of architectural art, still in a practical point of view, the visible structure is only the shell or body of that interior atmosphere without which existence could not be supported." The future of northern architecture might lie in making space mean more than structure. The mall and the underground city, with their interior atmospheres, incubate in those words. And central heating sweetened the view too. Once you were truly warm, winter was, more than ever, for watching. Winter became first of all a thing to *see*.

And nowhere could one see more winter from safer places than in the Alps. The same English prosperity (and Scottish ingenuity) that heated the Houses of Parliament gave even the upper-middle-class family the chance for instructive and improving travel, and those with no taste for the scary German forests found that their steps led to one destination on the other side of the Alps. Winter led the world to Switzerland.

Today, it's hard for us to feel very much of anything for Switzerland as a soulful destination. The Swiss themselves can't see it that way. We think of Switzerland as a bureaucratic place, we think of Switzerland as a wealthy place, we think of Switzerland — in the words of Orson Welles in *The Third Man* — as a place of chocolate and cuckoo clocks and of absolute bourgeois stolidity. In the middle of the nineteenth century, though, Switzerland was the ultimate Romantic destination, the place you travelled to witness scary winter and sweet winter together — the place where scary winter (snow-topped Alps) actually *became* sweet winter (comfortable ski *auberges*). Switzerland offered both mountain gloom and mountain glory, its mix of lowlands and heights — a powerfully emotional metaphor for man and nature — and of Protestant and Catholic faiths. (Protestant liberty established on the highlands, Catholic commonality by the lakes.) If Russia and northern Germany were the places where modern winter was made, Switzerland was the place where modern winter was *seen*, and seasoned, and made safe for an increasingly popular audience.

Two Englishmen lead us into Switzerland. The first is the great painter and watercolourist J. M. W. Turner. Turner "owned" Venice and Dieppe alike, but he makes Switzerland, the snows and glaciers of the Alps, his particular poetic subject. So much so that in Turner's watercolours of the 1830s and 1840s, it is hard to distinguish between what is snow and what is light. There is in his Swiss watercolours a merging of the picturesque light of the mountains with the sublime snows of winter, so that we no longer can tell, in effect, white from white.

And then the art critic John Ruskin, Turner's great advocate and analyst, follows his hero-painter to Switzerland, as John the Baptist might have followed Jesus, to articulate a whole kind of natural theology of the mountains and glaciers in Turner's honour and in light of what Ruskin imagined to be his practice (though Ruskin, as he later admitted, generally overrated Turner's piety and underrated his sensuality). Central to that new theology was a new equality of seasons: "Sunshine is delicious, rain is refreshing, wind braces us up, snow is exhilarating; there is really no such thing as bad weather, only different kinds of good weather," Ruskin wrote. He thought too that the stellate form of snowflakes and ice crystals — delicate spurred spokes radiating from a centre — was more beautiful even than the holy cruciform.

Ruskin's love of winter, form small, was reinforced by his love of winter, form large — by his exhilarated sense that, in their sweep and their capacity for catastrophe, the glaciers in Switzerland are in themselves proof of God's design, massive brushstrokes sweeping through time. This artistic and theological argument about glaciers would become a technical and scientific argument when Charles Darwin and Louis Agassiz, a great scientist and a Christian, fought over the real age of the glaciers, Agassiz insisting that they were signs of the kinds of ancient catastrophes one found in the Bible, Darwin countering that they were instruments of incremental change.

You can hear this alteration, the piercing Romantic questioning turning into more pious Victorian doubt, in the music of the era. Do you recall Virginia Woolf's question about what Shakespeare's sister might have written had she had the chance to write at all? Well, Fanny Hensel *was* Shakespeare's sister, or Mendelssohn's at least, and though her work didn't get the publicity of her brother's, it's consistently wonderful, partly for its enforced smallness. She wrote a sequence of seasonal piano pieces in 1841, *The Year*, and her "December" announces a new era of winter feeling. It doesn't have the bite and exhilaration of Vivaldi, nor the deep melancholy of Schubert; her winter music is rich and Romantic in a different sense — lulling and enclosing and bourgeois. Written on a long sabbatical holiday in Italy, her music signals the arrival of a different and evolving and more cosmopolitan Romantic sense of winter. It's music written in a hotel for the first generations of hotel-and-*auberge* people. Even her January storm is broken by a bright light of lyricism, and her February is positively gay.

For its first half-century, then, the Romantic rediscovery of winter as a site of splendour and significance took too many turns, from a scary one in Denmark to a more comfortable one in the Alps. But the romance of winter always kept a complex relationship with the central nineteenth-century question: Is God still up there? *Hello, God, it's me, Franz* — or John, or Joseph. Winter was the significant season, the X-ray time, when the green veil of warmth and verdure was stripped away and we saw the world bare, as it really was. But was it a place of order or a place of accident, made to look orderly only by our imaginations? Winter showed both, and you stood by the window to watch and choose.

OR TOOK A boat across the Atlantic to be instructed. That fascination with the problem of the meaning of glaciers, with the predicament of the meaning of frost, and even with the question of a winter God all naturally coalesces in Canada.

There is an old tradition in Canadian criticism and aesthetics, derived from the great critic Northrop Frye, that the first Canadian artists and poets didn't know what to make of the experience of winter. They cringed in fear, they withdrew into their houses, and they wished that they were back in the mother country. It was only much later that a genuine aesthetic of winter began to emerge in Canada. Before that, we all just suffered. The Canadian poet Susan Glickman has argued, quite rightly, that this misunderstands history, removes Canada unduly from the history of European responses to winter. Her point, I think the right one, is that all of the first generation of Canadian artists and poets responded to winter in Canada in exactly the same pretty or potent terms that European artists and composers and poets had responded to theirs. They were scared, sure, by glaciers and blizzards and mountains and vast whiteness — but hey, you were *supposed* to be scared. It was the trendy emotion of the time. They did what we all do: they took the conventional emotions of their age and refined them in the light of their own experience. That we sense the conventions along with the new landscape is only to say that we recognize the taste of real life.

But I do think there is a significant difference. The experience of the *mysterium tremendum,* the encounter with holy otherness that was at the heart of Friedrich's experience with winter — and of Schubert's and of Turner's — was one that, like a battle plan, could not survive too much contact with the enemy of real experience. Canadian poets and painters certainly felt what their European cousins felt, but it was a feeling that was always checked or chastened by another kind of awareness. Winter in Canada is an inescapable fact rather than a part-time recreational possibility. Quebec was not Switzerland. You couldn't go back to the green temperate climate on the morning train. You couldn't get away from winter even if you wanted to. You might tremble in wonder, but eventually you were going to have to go get the milk and break the ice in the pail.

And so a quixotic cultural historian might torment himself with the question of what might have happened if a highly cultivated person imbued in German Romanticism, *in love* with German Romanticism — someone fully aware of the responses to winter that had become part of the common coin of European civilization in the first half of the nineteenth century, from Goethe to Andersen — what if someone like that had come to Canada in the middle of the nineteenth century? What might that person have written and thought? Too much to hope for, surely ...

But there was such a person! He *does* exist, or rather, *she* does exist, and her name is Anna Brownell Jameson. In 1836 Anna Brownell Jameson was an Irish governess in an English household. She married a prim, dull English lawyer who was then sent to Canada to become the chief justice of Upper Canada, and she followed him to Toronto. It was a very unhappy marriage, for complicated reasons — or rather, for the uncomplicated reason that she was smarter than he was and he was richer than she was — but she kept a diary of that year, which was later published as *Winter Studies and Summer Rambles in Canada*.

She had a first-rate mind; Jameson's notes on Eckermann's *Conversations with Goethe* remain profound and original, and her comparisons between Eckermann's treatment of Goethe and Boswell's treatment of Dr. Johnson are, so far as I know, still unique. She runs with shocking ease from one reference to another and from one language to the next. ("The accusation which has been made frequently against Goethe, that notwithstanding his passionate admiration for women, he has throughout his works wilfully and systematically depreciated womanhood, is not just, in my opinion. No doubt he is not so universal as Shakespeare, nor so ideal as Schiller; but ... his portraits of individual women are as true as truth itself. His idea of women generally was like that entertained by Lord Byron, rather oriental and *sultanish.*" That's a completely typical February-in-Toronto entry from her journal.)

And so she began to write about a Canadian winter through the eyes of a European Romantic. She saw Canada through the prism of this kind of European sensibility — but she saw Canada. Niagara Falls was her first goal, as it was every Romantic's, and arriving there on a January day, she couldn't help but be disappointed.

> Well! I have seen these cataracts of Niagara, which have thundered in my mind's ear ever since I can remember — which have been my "childhood's thought, my youth's desire," since first my imagination was awakened to wonder and to wish. I have beheld them, and shall I whisper to you! — but, O tell it not among the Philistines! — I wish I had not! I wish they were still a thing unbeheld — a thing to be imagined, hoped, and anticipated — something to live for: — the reality has displaced from my mind an illusion far more magnificent than itself — I have no words for my utter disappointment: . . . Terni, and some of the Swiss[!] cataracts leaping from their mountains, have affected me a thousand times more than all the immensity of Niagara.

What went wrong? She had gone with a benediction of winter, sure that was the best and truest time to see the wonder — "where Nature is wholly independent of art, she does not die, nor yet mourn; she lies down to rest on the bosom of Winter, and the aged one folds her in his robe of ermine and jewels, and rocks her with his hurricanes, and hushes her to sleep." But on arriving she saw at one glance a flat extensive plain; the sun having withdrawn its beams for the moment, there was neither light, nor shade, nor color. In the midst were seen the two great cataracts, but merely as a feature in the wide landscape. The sound was by no means overpowering, and the clouds of spray, which Fanny Butler called so beautifully the "everlasting incense of the waters," now condensed ere they rose by the excessive cold . . . All the associations which in imagination I had gathered round the scene, its appalling terrors, its soul-subduing beauty, power and height, and velocity and immensity, were all diminished in effect, or wholly lost.

"All the associations which in imagination I had gathered round the scene . . ." Robbed of those associations by the hard, mineral truth of January, Niagara the everlasting incense vanishes and is replaced by Niagara the world's biggest cold-water faucet. Taken out of the safe Swiss sphere of imaginative projections, it's not sublime; it's just one big spigot. The ultimate destination of the Romantic imagination is, in reality and in the dead of a Canadian winter, big—too big to quite take in, and at the same time set against not the diminutive wilderness of Alpine scenery but the expansive reach of the true North: too *small*, too easily dwarfed by its surroundings to be quite impressive.

And then it turns out to be bordered by small, shivering hotels: "We held on our way to the Clifton hotel, at the foot of the hill; most desolate it looked with its summer verandahs and open balconies cumbered up with snow . . . its forlorn, empty rooms, broken windows, and dusty dinner tables. The poor people who kept the house in winter had gathered themselves for warmth and comfort into a little kitchen, and when we made our appearance, stared at us with a blank amazement, which showed what a rare thing was the sight of a visitor at this season."

She senses the two things at once — the wonder of winter scenes, the absurdity of idealizing them — and she senses them again and again. But there was more there than just the comedy of disillusion. She also gave herself an education in the real romance of a Canadian winter, the things that really did shine. She recognized, for instance, the thing that Pushkin had sensed in Russia — that where in other places winter was a time of stasis, in Canada it was paradoxically a time of freedom and movement. She writes: "It should seem that this wintry season, which appears to me so dismal, is for the Canadians the season of festivity . . . Now is the time for visiting, for sleighing excursions, for all intercourse of business and friendship . . ." Rushing off in the dead of a January winter to see Niagara. Winter sets us free.

Or else she sees that the evergreen forests, which in Germany, as we saw at the very beginning of this story, stand for the enveloping primeval forest, stand in Canada only for the occluded way. Trees in Canada are things that block your access to the next town, and so the denigration of trees and the denuding of the landscape are, in Canada, a primary and good thing — it is the thing everyone strives to make happen all the time. This is, of course, for someone raised on the paintings of Friedrich and attuned to the poetry of Pushkin, very strange — this notion of trees as the enemy of civilization, the enemy of a cultivated mind. But she likes it, and she learns from it.

Above all, Jameson is knocked out by the way, in a true winter, a Canadian winter, the slow sequencing of seasons from one to the other no longer takes place. She writes that the ice seems so thick and the snow so steep that you lose hope — it is eternal winter here. And then a month later everything is green and verdant, as though winter had never arrived. The lesson for someone experiencing a Canadian winter isn't just that Demeter has gone away, it's that when she gets back she'll have a kind of Alzheimer's; she won't be able to remember that she was ever gone. Anna Jameson sees sublimity but she reinforces it with sense.

What we see in Canadian winter imagery then, in the middle of the nineteenth century, is not some sad repetition of a template borrowed from abroad, nor mere journalism, but a significant variation on the Romantic sensibilities that are in place right around the Western world — similar, yet more subtly teased out and adjusted for a bracingly new and different place. Even if you look at such an easy, often patronized painter as Cornelius Krieghoff, that seemingly naive émigré painter in Quebec throughout the 1840s, '50s, and '60s — a kind of Christmas card painter who is always depicting sleighing scenes and pieces of merriment — we always see, somewhere in the background, a deep, cold whistle into an unknown North. What looks enormously naive and cosmetic is disciplined by the real observation that all this pleasure-taking activity, all this fun-seeking, takes place in the very shallow foreground of a white scene that reaches off into the distant snow and into eternity. That sense of pleasure-seeking in the near distance and of eternal snow far off — the sweet foreground, the scary background — is one that is the particularly Canadian articulation of the sublime vision. In Europe, sweet and scary mix pleasantly in a Swiss day; in Canada the sweet is won and the scary stays.

My favourite story about the Canadian winter, of this double experience of winter that is in some ways unique to Canada, comes when Jameson goes back to Niagara Falls during her second year in Canada, feeling hopeful again, fully poetic. An Irishman behind her, she tells us, "suddenly exclaimed, in a most cordial brogue, and an accent of genuine admiration — 'Faith, then, that's a pretty dacent dhrop o' water that's coming over there!'" The sublime hand of God and "a dacent dhrop o' water." Poetical feelings and emergent realisms — seeing them both was the hard work of a new country.

YET IF IN Canada at mid-century the Romantic vision of winter was receiving a bracing charge of realism, in Europe another winter mood was falling. In 1866 the young Russian musician Pyotr Tchaikovsky composed his very first symphony and called it *Winter Daydreams*. Composed under the influence of Mendelssohn (and thus conceivably connected to the older man's sister and her snow pieces), the symphony suggests a wholly new sense of winter. A new poignancy, a new serenity, a new turn to folk music's bejewelled instrumentation — winter tamed, surely, as it had been before. But also winter made exquisite. It is the first signal of a new winter feeling that will blossom best in French Impressionist painting in the 1870s and '80s, when for the first time *"effets de neige,"* effects of snow, appear in the paintings of Alfred Sisley and Pissarro and, above all, Claude Monet.

In the Romantic vision of winter I'm sure that Anna Jameson would have recognized many elements familiar to the Romantic movement in all its faces and phases: the fascination with the extreme, the love of the frightening, the prizing of passion for its own sake, watching water falling for the noise alone. But there is one key element in the Romantic mind, one crucial element, that is missing from the Romantic imagination of winter as we've described it so far, and that's a dream of the exotic — not of the unshaped other, the wilderness, but of a remote-seeming civilization where ideas and experiences take different forms.

The usual romantic sources lie in Egypt or North Africa — no good at all for our wintry purposes. The one distant, exotic culture that was known to have a fully articulated poetry of winter was Japan. And it was the Japanese idea of winter as it entered French culture in the 1870s and '80s, through the spread of *japonisme*, particularly woodblock prints, that marked the final transformation of winter, and the idea of winter, in Europe in the nineteenth century. Not the sublime snows of the Romantics, not the wilderness of Turner, not the peasant picturesque of the Swiss Alps and Quebec, but a winter of furs and finery and graces, of falling snowflakes and passing pleasures. This comes from Japan, and particularly from the Japanese woodprints of *ukiyo-e*, the floating world.

In the Japanese vision of winter, in Japanese poetry, and above all in Japanese prints — particularly those of Utamaro, Hiroshige, and Hokusai — in the imagery of the "floating world," there's no notion that winter has in any way fallen from the hand of God, or is in any way evidence of cosmic organization. The Japanese idea of winter simply speaks of winter as simultaneously empty and full; the emptying out of nature by cold, it's also the filling up of the world by wind and snow. Winter in the Japanese aesthetic is above all modish, it's above all an occasion for sensibility, it's a season that, in every sense, suggests not the enduring mysteries of "natural" meaning but the beautiful transience of creation — snow arrives, and then snow passes, just as a fashion does, or a love affair. This is not the peasant picturesque of the Swiss Alps and Quebec but stylish winter and stylish snow, more like the triangle-and-harp winter we also hear in Tchaikovsky.

That's the spirit of winter that the Impressionists found in the Japanese prints that began to fill their eyes and studios in the 1870s and '80s. When Sisley and Pissarro and especially Monet began to paint snow scenes in the 1870s and '80s, they were full of spiritual content, yes, but spiritual content of another kind, very different from Friedrich's stern sublime or Turner's rhapsodic snow peaks. The spiritual content of haiku, of the floating world, is all the more piercing because it disappears. *L'effet*, the effect, is all, and that is what the Impressionists sought when, fleeing to the suburbs of the Seine every February as the first frosts fell on the Île-de-France, they turned to winter as a subject.

The other element that is present, that we see so clearly in Monet's paintings of winter frost just outside Paris in the 1870s and '80s, is a sudden new love of white. Monet gets from the Japanese print a new infatuation with pure white — not a white that's laid down unvaryingly with single brushstrokes, but instead a white that is made up kaleidoscopically of tiny touches of prismatic colour. This is sweet winter at its sweetest, a winter so sweet that it loses the domestic tang of the picturesque and becomes entirely exquisite — not pretty but deeply, renewingly lovely. In the hands of Monet and Sisley and even the less gifted Pissarro, winter becomes another kind of spring, a spring for aes-thetes who find April's green too common, but providing the same emotional lift of hope, the same pleasure of serene, unfold-ing slowness: the slow weight of frost, the chromatic varnishing of snow on the boughs of the chestnut tree, the still dawn scene, the semi-frozen river.

It is the same idea of winter that we find in Debussy's beauti-ful late-century piano piece "The Snow Is Falling." Compare even Fanny Hensel's solid, hotel salon musical idea of winter with it, and we sense at once a newly lyrical, gentle, and even childlike tone. One finds it in French symbolist poetry too, as in Remy de Gourmont's likening of snow to a woman's throat. Winter is *whiteness* above all, and winter is a woman:

> Simone, la neige est blanche comme ton cou,
> Simone, la neige est blanche comme tes genoux.
>
> Simone, ta main est froide comme la neige,
> Simone, ton cœur est froid comme la neige.

* * *

> Simone, the snow is as white as your throat,
> Simone, the snow is as white as your knees.
>
> Simone, your hand is as cold as the snow,
> Simone, your heart is as cold as the snow.

Winter is no longer the sinister Snow Queen but her city relative, the *femme fatale* in furs, the icy society lady whom you take to the suburbs for a passing assignation when, if you're lucky, she (so to speak) falls. An irony that touches the edge of paradox is implicit. The first appearance of winter as a positive force in nineteenth-century European painting involved the rejection of the decadence and luxury of French culture. And yet by the end of the century the image of winter is reclaimed by just that French culture of luxury and reason and sophistication and sexuality, which takes you to your own neighbourhood, then ten miles outside Paris, to appreciate all the possible temporalities of the world.

The infatuation with winter that began with a rejection of French reason returns as a new kind of exquisitism, starring Reason's dancing stepdaughter, Sensibility.

I LOVE THOSE Impressionist pictures, and the irony of that circle closed. But it would be false not to see that the taste for extremes — for the exposure of the mysterious, the scrutiny of the hidden, the fascination with the huge and the little, the glacier and the *eisblumen* — is what gives the art of Romantic winter its charge and provides its richest legacy. We may love French lyrical winter, but the world's mind was remade by the more spectacular and mystical northern kind. To really fix the Romantic legacy of winter in art, and what it gave us, we have to look at the sweetest of the sweet and the scariest of the scary, at winter at its biggest and winter at its smallest — and that we find, I think, in the imagery of icebergs and the photography of snowflakes that push us out of the nineteenth century and into the twentieth.

The great pictorial poet of the iceberg is a Canadian, Lawren Harris. He is, of course, best known as one of the Group of Seven, a cell of Canadian painters that coalesces in the early years of the twentieth century. It is exactly one of the last Romantic movements in Western art — that is, it is the last time when painters try to coalesce around a vision of landscape in order to give themselves and their audience a national identity, and the identity of Canadian painters was naturally tied up with the idea of the North, and of winter. Harris and Caspar David Friedrich would have understood each other perfectly. (Harris studied in Germany, and what, and how much, he might have known of early German Romantic painting is unclear.)

If one exempts Tom Thomson as a maverick, Harris is the most gifted of his generation by far. He turns to theosophy in 1923, a familiar move in those days. But where, say, the Russian painter Kandinsky leapt from Madame Blavatsky's vague penumbra of mysticism immediately into abstraction, for a while at least the theosophical Harris remains doggedly aligned with the real world—only now the real world must be shown to pulsate and vibrate and glow with the presence of the higher spiritual force that lies beneath mere appearance. "Harris is rising into serene, uplifted planes, above the swirl into the holy places," an admirer wrote.

Just how seriously he took its doctrines is hard to know. Did he really believe, for instance, as Madame Blavatsky did, that an imperishable "root race" of man had once lived on an astral plane at the North Pole, and that the lost continent of Hyperborea had sunk there too? And that both might still be beaming occult energies into the world from their cold grave? His pictures suggest that he might have. Icebergs that glow like mystical monoliths, icebergs that rise like ancient dolmens, icebergs that float in sinister array, and icebergs that glare accusingly at the painter. They are the artistic fruition of what began with the science of glaciology, this sense of icebergs as living, moving, ominous things that seem to have formed themselves, and whose mystery—the nine-tenths just glimpsed beneath the icy water—is their truth.

If it takes an effort of patriotic will to love his later, slightly dopey and derivative abstractions, Harris's portraits of icebergs, which he painted after his one safe, touristic trip to the Arctic with A. Y. Jackson—not the world's most comfortable voyage, but still far more Swiss than Scott's—require no will at all to swoon over. If *Icebergs: Davis Strait*, of 1930, and *Arctic Sketch IX*, of the same year, have in their smooth, worked surface, without visible brushstrokes, a touch of mere scenery, they still have the weird, otherworldly light and strange, striated, layer-cake shapes that make all Harris's icebergs exist in some haunted land between Walt Disney and C. S. Lewis's White Witch. There is some schlock to them, but more that really is sublime. If his icebergs can sometimes have an unintentionally comic or cartoon-like effect — he paints them with movement lines and broken sunlight and spectres of eerie eeriness coming off them — and the occult Hyperborean energy can seem a bit hyper, if they sometimes seem to skate, so to speak, on the edge of kitsch . . . Well, all successful Romantic mystics skate on the edge of kitsch; kitsch is just our shorthand for failed Romantic mysticism. Most often, they are truly sublime.

In this period people talk about icebergs as calving, giving birth, breaking up, appearing out of nowhere, most famously when an iceberg seems to sneak up behind the *Titanic* and stab it in the back with a stiletto. And Harris's pictures exemplify the crucial psychological metaphor of the "animate iceberg," the notion that an iceberg — only one-tenth visible while its real, submerged depth is mostly out of sight — is a portrait of our mind.

It's in *Harper's* magazine in 1906 that some students of the great psychologist John Dewey seem first to suggest the by now clichéd notion that the iceberg is a good representation of the human mind, since one-tenth is visible and nine-tenths is submerged. But one finds the same idea in William James's statement in 1902 about religious mysticism, which rises from a "B-region" of the mind: "The B-region, then, is obviously the larger part of each of us, for it is the abode of everything that is latent and the reservoir of everything that passes unrecorded and unobserved." Freud and the Freudians employed the iceberg analogy all the time, though Freud credited its origins to his predecessor Fechner; only ten percent of an iceberg, he insisted, is visible (representing the conscious) whereas the other ninety percent is beneath the water (representing the preconscious and unconscious). Where Freud and Fechner's Germanic predecessors had looked for signs of the Designer's hand in hoarfrost, the new psychology looked for images of the psyche's shape in icebergs.

This move from theology to psychology is typical of the turn from the late nineteenth to the early twentieth century. Instead of thinking about God's hand extending down, you think of man's mind radiating out. Harris's iceberg is the perfect symbolic image of that idea of the psyche — Plan B from inner space. The long arc of Romantic winter takes us from a natural theology that was no longer credible to the "depth" psychology that replaced it. You can't believe that God made an iceberg but you can believe the iceberg looks like your mind. And acts like it too: shining, strange, sneaky, hidden, gleaming to the eye but cold to the touch.

IF THE VAST, scary iceberg becomes a sort of image of the über-soul, in the same period the tiny, sweet snowflake comes to represent the distinctiveness of the human personality. Looking at icebergs, we see a signal of a hidden dimension; looking at snowflakes, we see a principle of individuality. The snowflake comes to resonate in this way mostly through the work of a Yankee eccentric named Wilson "Snowflake" Bentley, the hero of the best movie Frank Capra never made.

Bentley was a Vermont semi-recluse who had an obsessive, beautiful, inexplicable devotion to snow and to snowflakes. In 1885, at the age of nineteen, he photographed his first snowflake, against a background made as dark as black velvet by long hours spent scraping emulsion from the negatives around the image of the snow crystal. His motives were artistic, like those of Audubon with his birds or Joseph Cornell with his boxes: on the one hand, an urge to document a hidden universe of form and feeling; on the other, some kind of fixation on a small and exquisite world that seemed blissfully different to the workaday world in which Bentley in Vermont, like Cornell in Queens, found himself. Both men were loners, perhaps not coincidentally, who cared for an ailing relative, Cornell for his brother and Bentley his mom. (There was also in both a slightly creepy, largely touching fascination with young girls and actresses. Along with his snowflakes, Bentley collected the smiles of silent-movie actresses, torn from fan magazines.)

Over his lifetime, Bentley took portraits of 5,381 snow crystals (to give them their proper scientific name; flakes are when the crystals clump together) and inserted into the world's imagination the image of the stellate flower as the typical, the "iconic" snowflake — and he inserted, as well, the idea of the snowflakes' quiddity, their uniqueness, their individuality. It is to Bentley that we owe the classic crystalline snowflake that we see in Christmas ornaments and cards, the kind that hangs above Fifth Avenue as well as the crossroads of a small Manitoba town: that beautiful symmetrical star shape, the flower of the snows.

But in truth, most snow crystals, it seems — as he knew and kept quiet about — are nothing like our hanging star-flower; they're asymmetrical, irregular, bluntly geometric: typed as solid columns and simple prisms and simple needles, plain and blunt and misshapen as, well, people. The Fifth Avenue snowflakes are the rare ones, the diamonds in the snowflake pile. The discarded snowflakes look more like Serras and Duchamps; they're as asymmetrical as Adolph Gottliebs and as jagged as Clyfford

Stills. The beautiful radiating stellate flowers are as exceptional as, well, movie actresses and supermodels. They're the Alessandra Ambrosios of snow crystals — long and lovely and rare.

Bentley was responding to an existing nineteenth-century aesthetic. Recall Ruskin in Switzerland and his laws of forms and you'll remember that he insisted that stellate forms are the most beautiful of all forms in nature. So much so that even cruciform shapes, Ruskin wrote — the cross itself, despite its divine associations — are meagre beside the star. Bentley was not just responding to his own idiosyncratic tastes; he was expressing a common taste of his culture.

But a taste is what he was expressing. He deliberately left out, in his published records, the countless cases that he photographed at various times in his life of all the non-symmetrical, all the modernist, all the awkward, all the eccentric snowflakes. It was on the basis of that smaller class of snowflakes that he made the great generalization complementary to the notion that the iceberg was a representation of the human psyche: that the snowflake was the representation of the human soul, because each one was microscopically distinct, different from every other snowflake that had ever fallen.

So at this moment at the end of the nineteenth century we see a kind of coalescing between the Romantic fascination with scary winter, immense and large, and sweet winter, tiny and near at hand. The iceberg becomes representative of the ultimate common mystery of the mind — what you don't see is what counts most — and the snowflake becomes a representation of the radical individualism of each person. We're all ineluctably different. (That's why the Starbucks chain keeps that sign up: "Friends Are Like Snowflakes: Beautiful and Different.")

A LONG JOURNEY. A very long journey—this Romantic winter, this *Winterreisse* of the Romantics—but it seems to me, ironically, a wonderfully enlightened one: from winter as the national season of the northern man to winter as the place where we can realize the sublimity of each single snowflake. At the beginning of the nineteenth century, winter was massed together into one chilly and indistinct thing, a desert we crossed to get to spring. By the end people could resonate to an iceberg newly calved from a glacier, or to this single snowflake. Bentley's snowflake, seen up close, is a homely sign of that sensitivity, that readiness to vibrate at improbable objects that is the essence of our experience of art.

Art is a way of expanding our resonances, civilization our way of resonating to those expansions. The Romantics transformed winter from a single, sharp sound heard out of doors to this bright, muffled chromatic keyboard of extended feeling, full of sharps and flat runs, diminished chords and pedal effects. It is certainly, as poets have said, a good thing to see the world in a grain of sand. But it's an even better one, and more to the purposes of art, to see a single grain of sand in the whole world. Or a single snowflake. The Romantics saw their snowflakes, embraced their glaciers, and, remaking our minds, remade our world. A fearful desert had become a new province of the imagination.

Oh yes, what about those two metaphors? Have they survived their century? The submerged nine-tenths of the iceberg and those singular snowflakes? Well, we know now that those final discoveries of the Romantic imagination of winter are both touched with more than a little myth. The mysterious, sinister, stiletto-bearing iceberg that can stab ships in the back turns out, in fact, to be largely imaginary. The nine-tenths of the iceberg sunk beneath the water simply follows a natural rule of physics and is not a peculiarity of glaciology. And far from having stuck a stiletto into the side of the *Titanic*, we now know that the iceberg in question merely crushed it, like an awkward adolescent boy at a dance, popping the rivets and stays of the great ship. The iceberg is neither the radio beacon of earth consciousness nor the white shark of the seas, but just a great big, overgrown ice cube, as innocent (and dumb) as ice cubes are. And, in parallel, we might say that though "iceberg psychology" and its notion of unconscious motives still haunt us, the coming of cognitive psychology has also taught us that the overt and explicit part of thought matters most. It's the part of the iceberg you *do* see that sinks your psychic ship.

And snowflakes? Are they all unlike? And does that difference give us some natural evidence for individuality? It turns out that, as recently as 1988, a cloud scientist named Nancy Knight took a plane up into the clouds above Madison, Wisconsin, and there found two simple but identical snow crystals — hexagonal prisms, each as like the other as one Olsen twin is like the other. Snowflakes, it seems, are not only alike, they usually start out more or less the same. But if this notion threatens to be depressing — it was only the happy eye of nineteenth-century optimism that saw radical individuality there — one can in the end put a brighter spin on things. It turns out that, while it's true that snowflakes often start out alike, it is their descent from the clouds into the world that makes them alter. ("As a snowflake falls, it tumbles through many different environments. So the snowflake that you see on the ground is deeply affected by the different temperatures, humidities, velocities, turbulences, etc., that it has experienced on the way," Australian science writer Karl Kruszelnicki writes.) Their different shapes are all owed to their different paths downwards. So snowflakes actually start off all alike; it is experience that makes each one just different enough to be noticed.

In a way, the passage from "Snowflake" Bentley to the new snowflake stories is typical of the way our vision of nature has changed over the past century: Bentley, like Harris, and the Romantics generally, believed in the one fixed and telling image. We later moderns believe in truths revealed over time — not what animals or snowflakes or icebergs really are, mystically fixed, but how they have altered to become what they are. Those ice flowers formed on that long-ago German window really are like life, in the end, if only because they are lucky to be here, and at the mercy of the elements, as we all are. The sign at Starbucks should read "Friends Are Like Snowflakes: More Different and Beautiful Each Time You Cross Their Path in Our Common Descent." For the final truth about snowflakes is that they become more individual as they fall; that, buffeted by wind and time, they are translated, as if by magic, into ever stranger and more complex patterns, until at last they touch earth. Then, like us, they melt.

TWO

RADICAL WINTER
The Season in Space

FEW OF US remember, if any of us ever knew, that the first great modern horror story, Mary Shelley's *Frankenstein: or, The Modern Prometheus* (as it's properly titled), of 1818, takes place not in Germany or Bavaria or, for that matter, Hollywood, but in the Canadian Arctic, very near the North Pole.

To be sure, it's mostly a long flashback set elsewhere, in which Doctor Frankenstein explains how it was he came to make the Monster. But the novel really begins on a ship when, after a preamble, the narrator explains that his ambition in life has always been to go north to explore the Arctic and find the North Pole: "This expedition has been the favourite dream of my early years. I have read with ardour the accounts of the various voyages which have been made in the prospect of arriving at the North Pacific Ocean through the seas which surround the pole." And it is in the Arctic that he sees the hallucinatory image of Doctor Frankenstein on his sled, in hot (or cold) pursuit of a creature as yet nameless, who is someplace out there on *his* sled. The flashback takes place as Doctor Frankenstein, after he is brought to the narrator's ship, relates his terrible tale.

Frankenstein, it turns out, made his monster where he lives, and that's in Switzerland: the early nineteenth-century abode of tamed winter; neutral winter; safe, domesticated, picturesque winter. It's almost too neat an image for our purposes. The sleep of Switzerland brings forth monsters; the creature breaks out of Chapter One, the Romantic winter of middle Europe, and heads to what he feels is his true and natural home, and that is right here in Chapter Two, the radical winter of the Far North.

He wants to leave the comfortable Romantic winter paradise because he believes, rather pathetically, that his monstrous traits will at least let him live in comfort and alone in the Arctic, maybe with a wife. And so he says to Frankenstein, his creator, rather prosily (that's the way Romantic monsters sounded): "My vices are the children of a forced solitude that I abhor; and my virtues will necessarily arise when I live in communion with an equal. I shall feel the affections of a sensitive being, and become linked to the chain of existence and events, from which I am now excluded." He goes on to say that he hopes to flee to "the everlasting ices of the north, where you will feel the misery of cold and frost, to which I am impassive."

The image, the idea, is quite straightforward. The Frankenstein story, which, after all, has that subtitle, *The Modern Prometheus*, is a story about man attempting too much, about man tempted by knowledge to do things that he shouldn't do, and the natural destination of that kind of story is the North Pole. Frankenstein's is a Promethean story in every sense: *don't go there, because if you go there you will lose your humanity in your search for knowledge*. It's an allegory of science — and of scientific exploration. Get too crazy in Geneva and you'll end up chasing a monster to the top of the world. And it's quite spooky and strange that Mary Shelley makes the climax of her story a sled race between Frankenstein and his Monster towards the Pole, a race that eerily and, with the prescience available only to the deepest kind of poetry and myth, directly anticipates the end of the century and the twin doomed and fatal races for both poles that will take place between Scott and Amundsen, Peary and Cook.

To race towards winter is different from ruminating on it. For the Romantic painters and musicians and poets, winter became a season of seductive charm, deep fascination, and profound meaning as intense and significant as any other season. But in looking through their window on winter we were looking mostly at winter as we experience it when we're staying in one place — the winter that *is* a season, bounded by fall and spring on either side, by the knowledge of a gradual decline and by the certainty of an eventual return. I want to look next at a different face of winter. It's the winter of the Far North and, eventually, the Far South — the winter of the Arctic and the Antarctic, the permanent winter of the globe's two poles, and the search for them. Radical winter, I'll call it, because its subject is extreme conditions, and their meaning. If the first window on winter was a winter largely of the eye, recorded in paintings and photographs, showing things *seen*, this is a winter of electric enterprise, recorded largely in journals and memoirs, registering things *suffered*.

The music to have in mind is by Harry Somers, the twentieth-century Canadian composer, and it's called, simply, *North Country*. It's meant to evoke the idea of the journey north, the journey towards the poles, the journey towards the extremes. Its biting strings and relentless tempo recall in some way Vivaldi's "Winter," that first memorable pre-modern winter theme, but Somers' music is different in the extremity of its torment and the certainty of its bite. (Although my good Canadian wife said instantly, as I played it for her, "Ah, the CBC on a Sunday afternoon in my childhood, and my mother making dinner!" Music makes many kinds of memories, indoor and out.) Northern winter isn't radical winter or temporal winter, it is *spatial* winter — the winter that you travel towards. To tell the tale of winter without the story of the Far North and the twin poles is not merely Hamlet without the prince but *War and Peace* set in the Bahamas.

For winter is a place as much as a time, a season that comes heaving into sight while we sit. We can, as I've said, experience winter temporally, as the ever-returning season, or experience it cyclically, as the product of a series of ice ages — the planet, after all, was once uniformly warm — or we can experience it spatially, as something up there that's trying to get here. After all, there is always winter far enough north — those everlasting ices — and then every fall that snowbelt begins to broaden, coming farther and farther south and bringing colder snow with it. By November it's arrived in the lower part of Canada; by December it has arrived in the northern United States; as December bleeds into January it works its way down to the top fringe of the southern United States, even into Texas — and year after year that charge is defeated, and then winter recedes, back to its permanent summer encampment in the North. That's one thing that winter is: this Far North thing that charges south and then goes back. And so if we want to experience winter in the fullness of its moral challenge — and in all its potential spiritual blessing — we can't wait for it to happen but have to go out and get it.

And so to find it, we go towards . . . the North! And, for that matter, the South. The search for that spatial winter, the search for the poles, has become an obsessive subject for modern people.

It's the model of all exploration for exploration's sake, exploration undertaken with a minimum of national advantage, a marginal economic purpose, and a maximal amount of adventure taken for adventure's sake. Even, if you like, suffering taken on for suffering's sake. Winter for most of us is a temporary space that comes and goes. The explorers turned winter into a permanent space, a place you went to endure and explore and, just possibly, get rich.

History comes in two flavours, the archival and the available — the past we have to dig out and the past that's always there in front of us. And the polar past is *available*; the big names are known to everybody. Franklin and Peary, Scott and Shackleton — we know of their exploits, in a way that we don't know the names of many of the men and women who brought us greater comforts. No one knows the name of that blessed nineteenth-century man who invented the steam-heating radiator (Franz San Galli, if you're making notes), but every schoolboy and schoolgirl knows the names of those who fled it. We all know the names of those who took up arms against the tide of central heating and went north and south in search of the True Cold. They continue to inspire literature, feature films, documentaries, even poetry — in the past twenty years alone, two collections by woman poets have been devoted to the metaphor of Arctic and Antarctic travel — in a way that no other adventure story of early modern times can do. The makers of our comforts, past and present, pass; those who fled them have become immortal so that we can read about them in the comfort that the forgotten ones made.

And this at a time when most other imperial and colonial expeditions have melted from glory into shame. We look now at the exploration of Africa, the search for the source of the Nile, the search for the heart of the Congo, with at best ambivalence and more often simple guilt. But the northern and southern searches still have an aura of significance, an aura of meaning — even, if you like, a halo of glory — that makes them different from all the other great imperial adventures of the nineteenth century. (With, of course, the permanent irony that, like the Sherpas who eventually schlepped Hillary to the top of Everest, the Inuit, the aboriginal people, had been there all along, had seen it all, and could have told them which way to go and how to get there, if they had only stopped to listen.)

"It is eternal winter there," William Blake once wrote about a place without love, and there in the North it really is eternal winter, though not always untouched by passion. The subject of this chapter is not winter the visitor, to be endured or enjoyed and then overcome, but winter the destination. Winter, if you like, as the woman to be won — at least, the men winning it would have seen it on those terms — the goal to be taken, the well at the end of the world, the pole on top of all else. Winter the prize — though, most often, in the end the most pyrrhic of all possible prizes.

THOUGH THE FAR North was in many ways a perfect blank to the nineteenth-century explorers, that blank was filled with words before it was ever filled in by first-hand experience. You could read all about what the North Pole was like before anyone went there. When Greek geographers first began considering what might lie at the top of the world, one idea was that the Arctic would not be, as one might expect, a forbidding white blankness but would instead be paradisiacal and welcoming and wonderful. It's an idea that in the eighteenth century, and even into the early nineteenth century, still holds strong. There's a partial justification for this: one of the things that whalers and explorers had already noticed in the seventeenth century is simple — the ice flowed south. Ice from the Arctic tended to flow south, which suggested to them that something hot was breaking it up farther north. And they turned that simple observation into the idea that there must be a kind of "open polar sea" up there heated by ocean currents. Perhaps the Pole was not merely warmer than you might expect but was itself a temperate region, a paradise of green that sat on the very top of the world.

And this idea in turn transmuted into the even more extravagant — yet in its time surprisingly credible — notion that the top of the world might be an open well and that the poles were giant caverns that went right through the earth. That idea *was* eccentric, and hardly accepted by anyone. But the larger idea, part of the common coin of the period and into the beginning of the nineteenth century, was that the poles, particularly the North Pole, were, despite their fearsome moat of ice, themselves paradisiacal. If you could ever break through the citadel, cross the moat of ice that surrounded them, you'd find not just a new colony but a place to luxuriate in, and one where you could in every sense dominate the world — the ultimate rich and warm high ground of the planet.

So Santa's workshop is not the first projected imagination that showed a happy commune at the top of the world. Some of this was false deduction from that partial evidence of warmer water. But some of it reflects a need to believe that the Far North is vibrant and alluring, along with a need locked deep in our nomadic hearts to believe that the next place we get to will be the good one. Incantation has its power to stir modern people. The "open polar sea" is an idea, but also a phrase to recite again and again, with its beautiful open vowels at the beginning and its long, sibilant endlessness to close ("circumnavigable Arctic Ocean," the alternative phrase, doesn't touch it, though it's the same idea).

Now this idea of a green, much less an open, Pole strikes us as just wrong — crazy speculation — and the search for it as a classic example of throwing good money after bad (or good men after bad voyages). But if you think about it, you'll see it's also the kind of unconscious and conscious salesmanship that goes on whenever powerful people are urging you to go someplace you might not normally think of going. Though it is true, for instance, that every planet beyond our own that we've encountered so far is airless, sunless, frigid, uninviting to life, still when someone says that beyond the belt of uninhabitable planets there must be another, better belt, with planets like our own that are inhabitable . . . Well, we don't have to imagine such talk. We hear that kind of talk going on all the time, about the discovery of earthlike planets in the distant galaxies. We don't often say, *That seems improbable. We'll trust our inductive logic and expect that all the other planets will be as uninhabitable as the ones we know now, as barren as Mars or the moon.* We say instead, *Oh, that sounds possible!* because we want to believe that it's so. The paradisiacal pole, though it seems a bizarrely counterintuitive idea to us now, was, in the context of exploration of the unknown, a rational notion, and so it became a resilient and robust one.

For the undiscovered country is always either very good or very bad, as the folks in the next valley are usually either elves or cannibals. If in the imagination of Western man at the beginning of the nineteenth century there was this notion of a paradisiacal Pole, there was at the same time a rich and urgent imagination of its direct opposite, what we might think of as that Promethean

Pole, Frankenstein's Pole — the poles as the ultimate testing place of man's hubris. As Prometheus in Greek myth was punished for stealing fire, we'd be punished for underestimating ice. We see a stark, indelible picture of the Promethean Pole in both of the writers who made the modern horror story, and, indeed, later on in the modern horror film. We've seen it already in Mary Shelley's *Frankenstein*, the perfect parable of the Promethean Pole. The right setting for a horror story about going too far was the everlasting ice of the Far North.

The same kind of voyage to the Promethean Pole, with the same terrible outcome, also occurs in Edgar Allan Poe's *The Narrative of Arthur Gordon Pym of Nantucket*, written in the 1830s. Instead of going north, Poe sends his hero in the opposite direction, to the South Pole. I don't know how many of you recall *Arthur Gordon Pym* — it's the longest single story that Edgar Allen Poe wrote — but it's extremely spooky and effective because it starts off as a more or less realistic, if gruesome, tale about shipwreck and abandonment, then slowly, step by step, turns into a tale about supernatural hallucination. The story is Pym's imaginary diary, and as we're reading it entry by entry and as Pym goes on, he finally approaches the South Pole and writes:

March 21. A sullen darkness now hovered above us — but from out the milky depths of the ocean luminous glare arose, and stole up along the bulwarks of the boat. We were nearly overwhelmed by the white ashy shower which settled upon us and upon the canoe, but melted into the water as it fell. The summit of the cataract was utterly lost in the dimness and the distance. Yet we were evidently approaching it with a hideous velocity. At intervals there were visible in it wide, yawning, but momentary

rents, and from out these rents, within which was a chaos of flit-
ting and indistinct images, there came rushing and mighty, but
soundless winds, tearing up the enkindled ocean in their course.

March 22. The darkness had materially increased, relieved only
by the glare of the water thrown back from the white curtain
and before us . . . And now we rushed into the embraces of the
cataract, where a chasm threw itself open to receive us. But there
arose in our pathway a shrouded human figure, very far larger
in proportions than any dweller among men. And the hue of the
skin of the figure was of the perfect whiteness of the snow.

And *boom!* — at that point the Pym "diary" ends, and then
there is pseudo-objective speculation of what it means. So there
you see, in the minds of the two great makers of modern horror,
the notion that at either extreme, actually getting to those poles
is a very bad idea. That what awaits you is monstrous self-
knowledge at one pole or the ultimate sinister spectre of snow at
the other. Counterbalancing the idea that to go all the way north
or south is to get to a lost Eden is the idea that to go all the way
north, or south, is to tempt fate. And fate, the Snow Queen herself, has a way of paying back those who tempt her.

It's not just the myths of the poles, paradisiacal or Promethean,
that tell us something. It's that the myths were so potent, the
words carried so far. For, though as a proportion of the popula-
tion, the number who went towards the poles was essentially zero
and, viewed in the broad commerce of the time, what they
brought back was essentially nothing, those who cared were
essentially everyone. In that way the polar journeys were word-
bound literary journeys — fuelled by fiction, supported by stories,

and ending in memoirs; the travellers wrote, got read, and caused others to write, and then they went to write again. These were expeditions in which words went in one end, experience passed through the middle, and words came out the other—a kind of vast digestive system of bitter cold and better writing.

But if in one sense people already had a word picture in mind of what they'd find in the eternal winter of the polar regions, in other ways they were intrigued because the path itself remained provocatively blank, unknown. You may recall that in Lewis Carroll's "The Hunting of the Snark," his dark comic allegory of imperial adventure, the Bellman's map, meant to guide the crew as they go in search of the Snark that might be a Boojum, is "a perfect and absolute blank"—and all the better for being one.

> Without the least vestige of land:
> And the crew were much pleased when they found it to be
> A map they could all understand.
> "What's the good of Mercator's North Poles and Equators,
> Tropics, Zones, and Meridian Lines?"
> So the Bellman would cry: and the crew would reply
> "They are merely conventional signs!"
>
> "Other maps are such shapes, with their islands and capes!
> But we've got our brave Captain to thank:"
> (So the crew would protest) "that he's bought us the best —
> A perfect and absolute blank!"

That was the radical winter map, as it was the map of much British imperial adventure (with the necessary addition that what looked blank was often heavily populated by those you did not want to see). Yet in this case there was some truth to the fantasy: if the polar goal was known, or imagined, the map that took you there *was* largely blank. Even well into the nineteenth century, the *there* there is shown, even on sophisticated maps, as a series of uncharted circles.

And that made it all the more intriguing. For every modern nation needs a nothing. Every nation needs a blank on which it can imprint its mark — its idea of itself, its fantasy of its history and of its meaning. Every modern country finds some vague, unsettled, ambiguous, and complicated area — either very short-lived or very broken up into bits — and makes of it an epic world. The first vast nothing for Europeans was the medieval past, and they populated it with fantasy forebears. The Americans found their blank map in a frontier neatly peopled with bad guys. And the Arctic, or the polar regions, and later on the Far South, for the British and Americans and Canadians, was certainly one such place. What *was* the good of Mercator's equators and North Poles? (Mercator was an important mapmaker.) They *are* merely conventional signs. The point of the voyage was not to follow the tracks but to find the unknown, the mystical whirlwind of Poe's imagination, the icy racetrack of Mary Shelley's.

This sounds exciting but it could often play out absurdly — comically, with a comedy often touched by a grim spectre of death. And of course it hardly needs saying again, I hope, that far from being any kind of blank, the Far North, at least, was a populated and civilized place — the Inuit dance in and out of these European adventures as onlookers, helpers, aides, and wondering audience.

For certainly there was much to laugh at. A grimace of black humour haloes the adventure, and as much as radical winter leads us towards images of nineteenth-century endurance, it also fuels the black comedy of the skeptical twentieth. Scott warming his colleagues becomes Chaplin eating his shoe. Given the technology the Europeans had on hand, given how little they knew, given how meagre were their resources, the heroism of this attempt is still striking. But just as striking is the absolute absurdity and foolishness of it. They went in the face of all reason, and they went in the face of all warning.

And yet they really did go. Beginning in the early 1800s, under the direction of an extraordinary British navel bureaucrat named John Barrow, the British navy began the search for the Pole. One of the first people whom Barrow, who was responsible for priming almost all the polar exploration between 1816 and 1845, spoke to about the idea was a whaler named Scorseby, one of the few sailors with wide experience in the Arctic — at least, as much as any man could have at that time. Now, the ostensible goal of the British exploration was, of course, the Northwest Passage — the much dreamed-of throughway that would lead from the Atlantic to the Pacific by way of a great circle route above Canada. A northwest passage to India in particular was the goal, which would obviously give the British Empire a kind of unity, a kind of geographic simplicity that at that moment — and indeed until much later, when Disraeli swindled the French out of the Suez Canal — it did not possess.

What Scoresby tried to remind Barrow was the simple truth, which was that finding the Northwest Passage and *not* finding the Northwest Passage would in the end be almost exactly the same thing. "Now it is evident to those who visit the Greenland seas that were such a passage once accomplished it might not again be practicable in ten or even twenty years . . . I do not mean to imply,"

Scoresby wrote in a letter, "that there is no such thing as a north-ern passage to India . . . yet I firmly believe that if such a passage does exist, it will only be open at intervals of some years." And then only after an insanely wasteful and interminable-seeming search. And that, among the first advice given and not taken, was in some ways the soundest advice anyone ever gave. Even if the Northwest Passage existed, which eventually it was shown to do, it would be of minimal or no value to actual navigation, because of the circumstances of the Arctic. Winter was stronger than water.

But Barrow did not listen; no one listened, and they pressed ahead. In 1818 Sir John Ross, a Scottish admiral, led the first offi-cial expedition to set out in search of the Northwest Passage. Now, imagine what this was like. Really try to picture it. There is still little central heating back home, no electricity, no ironclad ships. Canned food has been invented but the can opener has not, so all the canned food taken along on the first trip has to be opened with an axe and a mallet. That's the early modern nature — pre-technological in many respects, set in the very beginning of the Industrial Revolution — in which these Arctic voyages take place. And yet, very coolly — if that's the right word — they set out for the top of the world.

Now Ross, famously, screws up. He looks around at the foot of Lancaster Sound and insists that what he sees in front of him is not any kind of open passage but a wall of mountains that shuts him off from further exploration. He charts them, he names them, and then he turns around and goes home. He's usually thought now to have seized upon a common mirage of the northern waters, one in which the extreme refraction projects onto the horizon mountains and other forms that are not there — a winter illusion that would have delighted Coleridge or Friedrich. But it is certainly true that Ross did not wait too long or press too hard to see if he was right. And so those back in London redoubled their will and purpose to send more people out. Ross was court-martialled, and a whole new generation of Arctic explorers was sent out in the firm belief that Ross had only imagined his mountains.

And in this way the British polar program quickly becomes the original type of modern government-funded research — an anticipation of the space program and the particle collider, research for research's sake. The money comes from government funds, sometimes from philanthropists, rarely from any kind of speculative investment. It's mostly done, as splitting atoms and shooting men into orbit is done, to see if they can do it. It is rooted in some vague idea of national prestige, married to what Norman Mailer, in the context of the U.S. space program, once quite rightly called the WASP dream of doing things for their own sake, as a purely existential test of the national and personal will. "The Protestant Brit is," he wrote in *Of a Fire on the Moon*, "disciplined, stoical, able to become the instrument of his own will, has extraordinary boldness and daring together with a resolute lack of imagination. He's profoundly nihilistic. And this nihilism found its perfect expression in the odyssey to the moon — because we went there without knowing why we went." The polar voyage is also undertaken to show that those who go are capable of heroism because they can endure suffering. That's what makes the radical winter of polar explorations radical — in search of Paradise we end up tethered to an iceberg, where penguins or petrels, so to speak, gnaw our livers. There's a lot of pain in it, but some kind of glory too.

ONE BY ONE the expeditions go out, get wintered in, iced in; mountain ranges are charted, bays and rivers are named, but nobody gets closer to the Pole. Finally, in 1845, Sir John Franklin, already the captain of several expeditions, is sent in two ships, the *Terror* and the *Erebus*, with 133 men and a surprisingly casual plan to report back next year — and he is lost. He doesn't come out after wintering in.

From that moment on, that existential accent, the existential slant of the northern expeditions of polar searches becomes more and more pronounced. Because every expedition that goes, for almost another decade, is an expedition that threatens to become lost while searching for the lost expedition. One after another they are sent to search for Franklin, though Franklin is clearly lost, and surely dead. No one can rationally expect the man and his crew to have survived unaided for four or five winters in the Far North. Nonetheless, Lady Franklin, who in particular is wealthy and determined — Charles Dickens called her pig-headed at one point — has twenty thousand pounds sterling offered for his rescue, and one after another the expeditions go on. In 1850 fifteen separate ships are engaged in the search for Franklin. *We'll go out in search of Franklin because the previous expedition that went in search of Franklin got lost, so now we need to find them.*

You can begin to sense that between the lines — indeed, right within the lines — of the official literature of the polar period, they all knew that there was some deep pointlessness to this enterprise. It was almost like something out of a Samuel Beckett play. At one point E. K. Kane, a U.S. naval master, sets out on a search for Franklin, and one of his subordinates, Hayes, addresses him officially as "Doctor E. K. Kane, USN commanding Arctic expedition in search of etc. etc." *Etcetera, etcetera* — that was the wary motto. Everyone knows that the formula "in search of Franklin" has become at this point an empty set of words, and yet it's an empty set of words that continues to propel these expeditions. The goal had become a kind of weary permanent ellipsis in the imagination of the Far North.

And yet, absurd or not, they kept on going. Detailed accounts of the polar voyages have been written many times. I won't narrate all the stories of success and, mostly, failure again but ask instead that other, deeper question: Why do we still care? Fewer men died with Franklin than under the orders of the average dunderheaded British infantry officer. Why do we still care about their fate, so much so that well into our own time, one scientific expedition after another, one documentary after the previous documentary, is devoted to the story of their loss and recovery? What happened to Franklin is, in its way, a trivial question. He had a wooden ship in the Arctic and no idea what he was doing — what do you mean, what happened to him? But we still ask why. Why did they go then, and why do we care now?

Part of it is just our voyeur's fascination with hard times being had by other people. They went in search of absolute winter — and got it, good and hard. The title of Apsley Cherry-Garrard's account of Scott's last expedition to the Pole, *The Worst Journey in the World*, covers them all, and its first sentence — "Polar exploration is at once the cleanest and most isolated way of having a bad time which has yet been devised" — the moral all shared. These are the hardest journeys men have ever willingly undertaken. One expedition after another involves extreme suffering in extreme cold, chill and frost and hunger almost unimaginable for us to contemplate. Kane and his men, on their way to rescue four of their companions in the Arctic in 1854, suffer from hypothermia so severe that they would fall asleep for hours at a time standing up, then turn and wake, then turn and mutter, delirious, as a group: "[We] laughed immoderately, gibbered, uttered the most frightful imprecations . . . After the lapse of a few minutes . . . the raving maniacs were changed to sullen and moping idiots, weeping and blubbering like children; and in this condition all would move on mechanically for perhaps half a mile, when, as if all were actuated by one disorderly spirit, another outburst would take place, and the former scene of maniacal fury was reenacted." Then they would pause, fall asleep, or keep themselves awake by eating snow — not as a frozen liquid, not for water, but because it burned their faces so intensely that it would keep them from that hypothermic slumber. And stumble on, and hallucinate, and sleep for a few minutes, and burn their mouths awake, and stumble on again. On another voyage, rats sneak on board in New York, breed inside the ship, and then come out to ravage all the stores when the cold strikes in Frobisher Bay. And the rats ravage the stores so thoroughly that the men are then forced to eat rats as their regular diet! (The Inuit dance in and out of these stories in much better shape; an Inuit woman travels forty miles with a newborn baby just to see white men, and then she goes back while they shiver in wonder at her aplomb.)

What moves us and stirs us about all the polar expeditions, I think, as we read them, is the tension between the suffering they endured — what one can only call the existential daring of their actions — and their matched love of the bourgeois, quotidian manners of the nineteenth century, which they evidence every day in their daily lives and recreation. Upon that blank map of the way north, they imprinted, as we all do, the signs of their own experience. The bad times were real, but so was the "cleanness," the absence of sordid motives, and that isolation that threw them back upon each other for company and comfort. They brought the bourgeois, optimistic society they lived with into a land neither middle class nor hospitable, and so made a stylized image, both comic and courageous, of their time — a kind of polar refraction of its own, casting their own image upon the icebergs.

There's no better place to get the taste, the vibe, of high Victorian virtue and nonsense than in the loneliness of the Far North. The Arctic, and later the Antarctic, explorers are prepared to face the snows in exchange for the absolute experience. They are also sponsored by Nabisco and Cadbury and Harrods. They go out to show what men can endure, and on board ship, as they winter in, publish their own newspapers, one called the *Polar Times*. They put on pantomimes, they engage in burlesque cross-dressing, they perform puppet shows and Shakespearean plays. The intersection of Romantic and middle-class values that marks the entire century is never more comical and touching than it is on board the polar vessels. Henry Feilden, the naturalist on the *Alert*, near the Pole in 1875, writes with a lyrical joy about his surroundings that is typical of the era:

> The air was so exhilarating that we hurried over the crisp snow singing, shouting and laughing . . . And what a moon! Like a great mirror or shield of burnished steel, not as you see her in the tropics or the Mediterranean, pale, warm and soft, dimpling land and sea with shadows, but cold, bright and stern . . . And then we looked at the great frozen waste in front of us, smooth ice, crooked ice, hummocks, floes and packs all jumbled together in mystic confusion . . . We trotted back to the ship and as we

gathered round our own bright lighted social table, with many
luxuries on it, we laughed and talked and were as fully a party
as could be found in Christendom."

The cold, stern truths of natural theology, the warm, bright
social table of the middle classes — the two conditions were
their . . . well, two poles, and they oscillated happily between them.

Plays, masquerades, concerts, shipboard newspapers — they
even try to keep from despair by regularly overeating. Far from
the imaginary abstemious, purifying diet of hardtack and pem-
mican that they often ended up with when the ship went down,
they actually lived rather well. A birthday feast on one of Hayes'
voyages in 1860 "included a cheerful household soup, salmon,
duck, a huge plum pudding from Boston, blancmange, mince
pies, raisins, olives, cheese, and coffee." And always coffee,
because coffee was easy to carry and easily made. Though it's
true that eventually, at one point, Kane's men on board were
reduced to the diet of fashion models: two cups of coffee a day and
a bowl of soup.

The nineteenth-century diseases, the nineteenth-century
mental complaints, are evident as well in their life together. They
suffer from too much intimacy and overcrowding. Suffer from
those things, one sometimes feels, even more than from the cold
and dark. Every polar ship finally ends up with fifty Madame
Bovarys coming to hate the look of their lover's ears. Though the
notion of comradeship usually, briefly, zips up the discontent and
dislike on their return, when it gets censored, their journals and
diaries reveal the inevitable and perpetual grumble of men in too-
tight quarters who can't stand each other's habits. Kane's men, for
instance, came to dislike him, not because he flogged them, not

because he was tyrannical, not because he was cool, not because he was remote, but because, as Fergus Fleming writes, "He developed an irritating habit of dropping French and Latin quotes into the conversation." Madame Bovary's neurasthenia, that nineteenth-century sense of having to be too polite in too-tight clothing and too-tight quarters with people you can't quite stand, is never more palpable than in the diaries of the polar men.

In most accounts of European imperial adventures, the sexual appetite that ornaments — or sometimes underlies — the expedition is transparent: we need think only of Richard Burton and T. E. Lawrence during their different moments in Arabia to recognize this. Naturally so: adventure doesn't end appetite, and imperialism of other lands easily becomes imperialism of others' bodies. But one of the strangest things is that no matter how long you pore over the accounts and chronicles of the northern voyages, what you don't find are tales, or even intimations of tales, of buggery and sodomy of the kind you find elsewhere in stories of imperial conquest, and that are always part of the reality of men living with other men in close quarters for long periods of time. It seems almost as if the choice of polar exploration was, for many of the men, a kind of middle-class monasticism. After all, the allure of surrendering ordinary sexual pleasures in exchange for some notion of a purified existence is a very powerful urge in Western culture. The drive to escape the sexual urge that dominates men's lives, an urge that lived so edgily and uneasily with the official virtues of their time, was part of what marked the polar men. There was the allure of money and the allure of fame and the allure of accomplishment. But there was also the perpetual lure of escape — escape from the meaningless claustrophobia of ordinary life for the potent crowding of the winter boat.

Sometimes I think there must have been a man who put the sex in *sextant* and the pole in *polar* . . . And yet where the stories of African exploration always involve intimations — or outright explications — of sodomy or forced cohabitation, on the whole the polar stories emerge, however improbably, as chaste in tone and sound. A low-calorie diet and extreme cold and exposure seemed to be enough to suppress sexual appetite. The polar men were the monks and hermits of the middle classes, the Benedictines of the bourgeoisie. You have to come into our own time to find poetry of homoerotic engagement at the poles. Elizabeth Bradfield, the American poet, has a beautifully long poem in her Arctic sequence called "In Solitude," which begins

> Leave your reindeer bag, damp and moldering
> and slide it to mine. Two of us, I'm sure, could
> warm it, could warm. Let me help you from your traces,
> let me rub what's sore. Don't speak. Your hair has grown long
> on the march, soft as my wife's.

Something like that must have happened in the nineteenth century, but it takes the imagination of the early twenty-first century to give it form and words.

And yet there are other, louder kinds of joy among them too. They sing "Oh, Susanna" as they sledge from the ice to the perilous safety of a boat, or they make "Off to Charleston" the anthem of the trip. One expedition brings a French cook, whose name, you will be surprised to know, is Schubert, to be sure that they eat well. And they constantly engage with the enterprise, the creative act, of naming things. What I referred to as the Adamic act — the notion that we take control of the world by giving it a particular name — is never stronger than it is in the mid-century polar men. Kane calls one bay Rensselaer Harbor and another landmark Mary Minturn River, after the sister of the wife of the New York philanthropist who is paying the bills — a sort of slow crawl of strange names in places that, to European eyes, had until then been just *oh, that place there*. The names stick and change to suit the mood: in a dark moment on the same expedition, the explorers felt bound to change the name of their hut from Fort Desolation to Fort Starvation.

There may be moments when we feel there is play-acting hypocrisy among the polar men: they squabble, they manoeuvre, they try to make money. But this touching and immediately affecting core of familiar behaviour is one of the things that makes them appealing. They took themselves up to the remote regions — what else could they take? — and so in their accounts we see the shape of their time and the play of its manners with a silhouetted clarity, the clarity of shadow puppets playing against a bright white screen, in a way that we see it nowhere else.

THIS ELEMENT OF show, of performing for a remote but eventual audience, becomes more powerful as time goes on; the economic and military rationales fade and the search for absolute winter, both north and south, becomes openly a race for glory. By the later nineteenth century the polar explorers, mostly privately funded, become as famous as opera divas, and on the whole with an opera diva's temperament and generous attitude towards the competition. Peary and Cook, the two great American explorers, are like an Arctic Duse and Bernhardt: only their competitions end in screaming rage. Strong elements of comedy lie in the last race for the poles, a set of paired assaults in which Mary Shelley's early-century image of crazed competitive sledding by two doomed and driven protagonists actually takes place at either extreme of the earth.

It is, though, a new generation of gloomy Scandinavians who seem, in their fatalism and determination, much better cut out for the job than anyone else, and who possess winter survival skills they have acquired through long traditions of skiing and sledding and enduring. On the whole the Scandinavians are the most successful of all the men of the Far North; Nansen's expeditions, though they never quite make the Pole, never lose a single man. And eventually, of course, there is the matchless Amundsen, a true polar man, who goes north and then eventually conquers the south. (He proved, among other things, that there was in the eyes of the time just one great polar region, one big white blank, all open to the same kind of exploration. This may explain why the popular imagination still places penguins at the North Pole.) There is even a single, sparkling Italian expedition, which has the comfiest tents and the best food and actually gets remarkably near the Pole. It's a reminder of just how much national pride projected onto that seeming nothing becomes something. Much more than an imperial program of conquest, it is a kind of nationalist program of transferred pride that's at play.

In the North, in 1898, the final conquest of the poles begins. It's typical of the time that Jules Verne, the great French science fiction and fantasy writer, takes up the story of Arthur Gordon Pym that Edgar Allan Poe left unfinished and writes a two-volume sequel in 1897, *The Sphinx of the Ice Fields* (in English, *An Antarctic Mystery*), the story of Pym and his attempt on the South Pole. But instead of being about strange misty spectres and eerie fatality, it becomes one of Verne's very workmanlike, well-explained stories about how submarines and sledges manage to conquer the Pole.

A new note of mechanical ingenuity and rational self-confidence inserts itself into what was once the remote spectre or the Promethean Pole. At last, in 1909, after mad balloonists and grim, determined Scandinavians fail, two men, both Americans, claimed to have achieved the North Pole: Frederick Cook and Robert Peary. What's astonishing about it is that the debate about which of them got there first continues to this day. It's a long and complicated story, but essentially Cook got *somewhere* first, then came back and declared that where he had got to was the Pole. Peary went second and, having far greater access to the machinery of publicity, managed to drown out Cook's announcement, notably with the help of the National Geographic Society, which had sponsored his journey. The real fight turned out not to be to get to the Pole but to get credit in New York for getting to the Pole. Even as Peary was approaching ultimate north, by his own account he kept his spirits up by counting the dollars he imagined he would win with the syndication of his story.

The fight continues to this day. Cook later got into legal trouble and was imprisoned for an unrelated fraud, and so the notion that he had always been a fraudster became widespread. Yet his claim to have been the first man to the Pole is taken seriously by some. You can go online and find websites devoted to the "Alfred Dreyfus of the North" — that is, the man who was cheated and disgraced unfairly by the forces of hate. Expert opinion now suggests that neither of them actually got to the North Pole. Peary probably was about a hundred miles short, and Cook was two or three hundred miles short. In any case, it seems that wherever Peary ended up, the people who ended up there first — very much like Hillary and the Sherpas — were his African-American assistant, Matthew Henson, and the troop of Inuit who accompanied them. It was they who actually made the final expedition, wherever it was that it really ended.

So Cook had no proof that he had arrived at the Pole, and Peary very little. Cook was sloppy but Peary was a jerk; he never got to enjoy his success, dogged as it was by dislike for his arrogance, which he did not try very hard to cover up. (Peary would surely have done better if he had acted more like an American hero, noble and restrained — his best play in the circumstances would have been to say something like, "I say nothing of Dr. Cook's claims. He must speak to his own conscience and evidence. I know only of my own experience," or the like — and leave it to fate.) He couldn't do it. Perhaps you or I couldn't do it either.

Peary couldn't act like a hero, or rather, he was so concerned about acting like a hero that everything he did made him look like a schmuck. The Greenland Inuit — the "Eskimo Highlanders," as the British called them, with reference to their own remote peoples — had for centuries used as their super-valuable source of iron three lumps of extraterrestrial meteorite, fallen out of the sky long ago; the Dog, the Woman, and the Tent, the Inuit called them (the Tent weighed one hundred tons). The meteorites had been their Fort Knox, their Stonehenge, their particle accelerator, their nuclear reactor — the inexplicable source of their technological supremacy as they chipped away tools to skin walruses and disembowel whales.

In one of the worst acts of cultural vandalism in the not-very-auspicious nineteenth-century record, Peary, in 1894, carted away the three meteorites — and sold them to the Museum of Natural History in New York for forty thousand dollars. It was like the theft of the Elgin Marbles, with the worse consequence that where the Greek marbles were loved and cherished when they landed in London, the Inuit iron hauled away looked, in its Upper West Side dwelling, as it does to this day: like nothing but puzzling inarticulate lumps, to be rushed past by schoolchildren on their way to the totem poles and war canoe. It is true that once Europeans and other, easier and cheaper sources of iron became available to the Inuit, they hardly needed their three magic stones again. But the callousness and condescension with which Peary did this made him look terrible. (Curiously, though he is superficially still cast as a hero, publicity is an oddly transparent thing; people see through it, and Peary's reputation was always as more of a manipulator than a mensch.)

The search for the North Pole ended, not in the arid purification of heroic adventuring but in a slightly seamy squabble of national chauvinism, greed, fortune hunting, and publicity—all the elements of the modernity that had been born then and of which the Pole was supposed to be the, well, polar opposite. There is something comic in the figure of the Italian explorer Nobile, who, in 1926, on an expedition with Amundsen, dropped a hundred pounds' worth of Italian flags from a plane onto the spot that he decided was the Pole. Small green, red, and white pennants plummeting down towards what he imagined was the exact spot. So the first of flags *dropped* on the Pole was the flag of a warm southern country—Vivaldi's country, the country where a generation of angst-ridden Germans had gone to escape from the palace of Teutonic snows in the Gothic North to the sunny south. Italy's flag was not only *on* the Pole, it was all over the Pole. The absurdity of the enterprise was ensured by the necessity of the gesture.

BUT WHAT OF it? That's one of the questions we have to ask ourselves. There was, after all, nothing there except an abstract point on a chart. There was, as Julius Payer, a German explorer in one of Weyprecht's expeditions, struggled to explain, no real reason to try to find the Pole. Payer, wintering over during that 1872 trip, attempted to teach the men the geography of the poles. He faltered. "After many painful disillusions," he wrote, "the pole was ascertained to be the intersection of lines in a point, of which nothing was to be seen in reality." The big blank at the top of the world — no glamorous monsters or doctors on sledges, no spectres sucking you in upon your arrival — was just imaginary lines, a fictive point, a geographic concept. The blank map that Lewis Carroll imagined was the real map. Is it any wonder that Payer fled the North for Paris, where he made a living painting ever larger and more theatrical melodramatic images of imaginary Arctic horror? Hideously unreal images of men struggling with whales and storms — what matter that it had nothing to do with the auroral beauty or bitter austerity of the real place? The North was better imagined than actually seen, for you could imagine it as theatre and experience it only as endurance and abstraction.

Yet the fight that went on between Cook and Peary still excites arguments and Internet pages. Fifty miles short, a hundred miles short, three miles short, right on top of it — the question is, in a sense, absurd. But the whole enterprise had been absurd from the beginning — *no point to it but the point of doing it* — so that to doubt the achievement, in a sense, was to doubt the purpose. If it had been an adventure or an imperial conquest, then the geography would have been seconded to the reality of the goods that would have flowed from it. But nothing could flow from this action, nothing could flow from this discovery. The abstract point was the absurd point precisely in the totality of its abstraction. It was not merely that the journey was not worth the pain, the game not worth the candle. It was that there was no game, and no candle either, just darkness and an abstract notion made by mapping. There was a point *at* the Pole, but there was no point *to* the Pole. The Nile has its source, Everest has its summit, but though the poles exist as points on maps, they have no existence apart from that, no special quality or quiddity that exists outside an abstract model of the earth. The great destination turned out to be . . . nowhere in particular, indistinguishable from all the other places you suffered through for the sake of arrival. *For the Snark was a Boojum, you see.*

THIS NOTE OF absurd existential quest, touched and humanized by the sheer endurance of the questers, is even stronger in the still more famous 1911 conquest of the South Pole. Everyone by now, I think, knows the stories of Sir Robert Scott and Roald Amundsen: how Scott set out first for the final conquest of the Pole after a series of expeditions he had taken over the previous five years; how he was, in his view, cheated by Amundsen, the great Norwegian explorer who was infinitely more skilled on the ice, and was also prepared to eat his expedition's dogs on his way there and then on his way back. We know how Amundsen skied in, skied out, devoured his dogs, and planted his flags — an accomplishment without, oddly, much of an aura, much of a legend attached to it, even now. And we all know of the site of legend, Scott's last camp, after their by now doubly pointless attainment of the Pole, and of how Scott's polar party died, a short, unobtainable distance from a food depot.

And we know too of those heroic and moving final moments of Scott's expedition when Lawrence "Titus" Oates, a man whose frostbitten foot leaves him unable to walk anymore, turns to his companions and says, "I am just going outside and may be some time." Words that sum up centuries of British understatement and British upper-class stolidity. It is, in effect, a kind of South Pole, frigid version of Mr. Kurtz's cry — "the horror, the horror" — at the heart of darkness. But in this case the heart of whiteness is not the dim, dark guilt of imperial adventuring but is instead the bright, glowing heart and heartbreakingly understated sound of British gallantry.

To mock Scott is easy, and many people do. When we read through his diary with its firm stiff-upper-lip-ness, when we look through his claims, we see something that seems very remote from us, something that can even seem to us, well, *spoiled* — tainted by the eternal condescension of the European to everything outside himself. We can't accuse Scott in this case of being an imperialist, a colonizer; there was no one there to imperialize or colonize except those penguins — whose eggs did indeed get stolen and taken back by one of the youngest members of his final expedition south, Apsley Cherry-Garrard, who wrote that great book about it afterwards. That subsidiary expedition, sometimes called "the winter journey," in which Cherry-Garrard and two companions set out from Scott's camp to bring home the egg of the emperor penguin, was truly the worst journey ever made of all those bad journeys. So horrible that the sweat of the men on the expedition froze inside their clothes, making it impossible for them to move more than several feet every day (it took them forty-five minutes simply to light a match, because their hands had become so stiffened by their own frozen perspiration, there in the South Pole winter).

But besides those emperor penguin eggs, there was very little colonial damage done to the South Pole. And yet there is a whole literature today in which poststructuralist and postmodern critics go after Scott's scalp for his stiff-upper-lip-ness, for his condescension, and see that final, doomed expedition as summing up all the ills of imperialism. It's true that Scott was an English gentleman, with the vices and virtues of his kind. He was incompetent, he was condescending, and he was locked into the clichés of his class, though no more than you and I or the average college professor is locked into the clichés of ours. He was also courageous and gallant right to the end, and those two things — the condescension and the courage — run together. Only someone who starts with an unduly high opinion of himself will be forced to keep his own opinion high till the end. The words that Mary Shelley gives Dr. Frankenstein near that far-off North Pole haunt our reading of Scott's pitiful and pathetic diaries of the last days of his expedition: "I trod heaven in my thoughts, now exulting in my powers, now burning with the idea of their effects. From my infancy I was imbued with high hopes and a lofty ambition; but how am I sunk! O my friend, if you had known me as I once was, you would not recognize me in this state of degradation."

And then Scott's last expedition, in 1911 and 1912, on the eve of war, is soon followed by Ernest Shackleton's attempt in the *Endurance* to find the South Pole, with England already in the midst of the First World War. Allowing his ship to get crushed by the ice pack, Shackleton then takes his crew on their famous harrowing cross-ice and -ocean voyage to safety — safety achieved, but no more than safety accomplished. Another story of near-complete incompetence and failure, basically Shackleton's expedition gives nothing to science, goes nowhere, spends other people's money; its only real virtue is that, in the end, somehow he manages to get only three men killed.

Why, then, do we admire them? Why do they continue to haunt our imagination? Part of the answer, as I said, is that, even in their extremity, we recognize them as like ourselves. They are our civilization, or ours as it was: greedy, wordy, racist, sentimental. But a deeper answer, I think, is a simpler one, summed up in three blunt monosyllables: *they were brave.* They did less good, created less comfort, clothed fewer naked, and fed fewer hungry than countless others. But they were brave. Brave in ways that are hard for us to imagine, brave in ways that still in some sense overwhelm our imagination.

We read about Shackleton dividing his boatless party into two camps: one had to stay on desolate Elephant Island waiting for friends who might never return, for a rescue that would likely never come, while the other group had to share the tiny lifeboat that would make the trip to South Georgia Island, searching for help. And we ask ourselves, *Which would have been harder, which would have been worse, to stay behind or to go across the Antarctic Ocean in a tiny boat?* And we recognize that either choice would be heart-wrenching, and either choice would demand all the courage we possess.

We care because they were courageous, and as C. S. Lewis once said, anticipated by Dr. Johnson, "Courage is not simply one of the virtues, but the form of every virtue." And though we know that moral courage is not the same as physical courage — many people who have great physical courage have no moral courage at all — we also know that those two things, moral courage and physical courage, are not as different as those of us who have little enough of either might desire them to be. That the courage to endure physical hardship is linked in deep and mysterious ways to the courage to be bold, to take risks, to act nobly, to act *properly,*

In Caspar David Friedrich's 1819 *Monastery Graveyard in the Snow* (*Cloister Cemetery in the Snow*), winter scenes recall ancient ones — snow opens the door unto a lost, mystical, medieval past. (Winter is haunting, but it's also healing.)

The Romantic image of the small French soldier lost in the vast northern winter, shown in Friedrich's 1812 painting *The Chasseur in the Forest*, is a reproach to all the encyclopedic certainties of the Enlightenment.

In the Romantic imagination, ice crushes and destroys, but it also liberates the mind to project new, surrealist landscapes, as seen in Friedrich's famous 1824 painting *The Sea of Ice*.

The simple hoarfrost, or *eisblumen*, on winter windows, became the locus of a raging debate between Goethe and his contemporary Knebel about nature, crystals, and God's designing hand.

J. M. W. Turner took the world to Switzerland and made the snow-capped mountain the icon of the sublime, as shown here in *The Blue Rigi* (1842).

Within even the most Christmas card–like of Krieghoff's Quebec sleighing scenes, as seen in his 1860 painting *Bilking the Toll,* the long perspective whistles us back towards a forbidding winter wasteland.

The nineteenth-century Japanese aesthetic of winter was more stylish than sublime, and devoted to the cult of the transient: fashions fall on women like snow on wooden temples in Utagawa Hiroshige's *One Hundred Famous Views of Edo #99, "Kinryūzan Temple, Asakusa"* (1856–58).

The iceberg was Lawren Harris's great subject: his arctic scenes are animate, alive, and became images of the hidden mysteries of the human psyche. Above, Harris's *Icebergs, Davis Strait*; below, *Arctic Sketch IX*, both completed in 1930.

Wilson "Snowflake" Bentley made almost two thousand images of snow crystals: some, like this one, titled *Dendrite Star* (c. 1885–1931), are exquisitely symmetrical; others, more rarely seen, are tellingly off-centre and askew.

is a thing we know from all of history and biography. We don't know what the exact path is between the two, but we know it exists. It's why we watch war movies and follow winter sports and, sometimes, admire even brutal and dim-witted boxers or the enforcers on hockey teams.

And in a society like ours that increasingly reduces obvious displays of physical courage to stylized entertainment, an expedition in which courage is not merely the product but the whole point — not just what you need to get there but the reason why you go, the *raison d'être* — that kind of expedition is bound to hold us rapt. Never, I think, in the long history of human adventure has there been courage so pure, so distilled down — courage like vodka, courage as absolute, hundred-proof liquor, pure and clear and cold — as we find in the polar expeditions of the nineteenth and early twentieth centuries.

And this leads us to an irony. The bourgeois-comfort society they so eerily, at times so cartoonishly, exemplified often made men act more bravely than the aristocratic society it replaced, with its occasional, buffoonish displays of courage and prudent withdrawals from giving battle. Bourgeois-comfort societies turn out to fight the bitterest wars and take the most daunting routes — whether in the American Civil War or the British First World War, on trips to the South Pole or to the dark side of the moon. The question we ask of the explorer — *What made you go there?* — is like the question we ask of the soldier: *What made you stay there?* And we know some of the answer: the good opinion of their fellows — they fought and died and fled for each other — and the unspoken principles of their lives. Ours is a society capable of much greater acts of mad bravery than one might imagine, and at the same time, and for the same reasons, curiously unresistant to organized stupidity—to the Scotts or, much worse, the Frenches and Haigs of the world, the Great War generals who sent millions needlessly to their certain deaths. The regimentation and industrialization of life seem to have produced, as emotional self-defence, new rites of courage—and, of course, suicidal impulses of self-destruction. The same desire to submit that makes us face front in Grade One, and accept other unnatural acts of self-denial, made Titus Oates go out into the storm. God knows it's dumb, but God knows there's grace in doing it.

THE STORY OF radical winter, of eternal winter, and the search for the poles began at the start of the nineteenth century in literary fantasies with either paradisiacal or Promethean flavour. Its real rationale was to create *exempla virtutis*, virtuous instances, to impress and inspire. You didn't have to report what had happened if you went to darkest Africa (though many did), because you had the scars or jewels to show for it. But being able to say what it was like in the permanent winter of the Far North or South was the reason you went there. You took the path to tell the tale.

But writing has a way, like the ice pack, of taking its own course and crushing our best intentions. Scott's polar diaries, which are discovered by Cherry-Garrard, the man who finds Scott and his polar party dead, are taken back to England in the midst of the First World War and published. Scott's life had long been intertwined with the imagination of J. M. Barrie, the great Scottish playwright—and, ironically, fable-maker of "Englishness"—the author of *Peter Pan*, as essential a myth of Scott's era as "The Snow Queen" had been for an earlier one. At least one of Barrie's biographers has insisted that it was Barrie's influence alone that had first turned Scott from a nervous military man into one "possessed of a sense of the significance of the explorer as the custodian of British heroic vision." And it is in Scott's last letter from the hut, written to Barrie, that the myth of Scott as heroic stoic, the man who suffered and transcended without succumbing to anything as vulgar as mere expertise, gets fixed. Barrie, in turn, wrote the myth-making introduction to the first collection of the explorer's diaries, *Scott's Last Expedition*, and, rumour long has it, was among those who did some neat, bowdlerizing editorial work on Scott's last journals as well. (It has often also been rumoured, probably falsely, that Oates, who disliked Scott, far from wanting to "go outside," was more or less pushed.) So in that sense Scott's last diaries are an ongoing collaboration of a kind between Barrie's touching schoolboy heroic imagination and Scott's actual experience.

A little later on, the other great final record of this story, of the 1913 polar expedition, Cherry-Garrard's book, *The Worst Journey in the World*, is written at the behest — and I think quite possibly with the active help — of his close friend, the Irish playwright and wit George Bernard Shaw, who is quoted throughout the book and supplies an epigraph for one of its chapters and, if you like, its attitude. And so, as much as Shelley and Poe are present at the birth of the polar adventure, Barrie and Shaw are present at its burial. Barrie's version of Scott presents Scott and his men as a missing troop of Peter Pan's tribe: boys who never grew up, boys who continue to have the essential adolescent masculine virtues of comradeship and courage and pluck in the face of danger — taken to the ultimate and final extreme. Through Barrie's presentation and, indeed, through his prior influence on Scott himself, Scott became the last of the Lost Boys.

Cherry-Garrard and Shaw have a very different story to tell. Instead of locating the heroism in the final voyage, they locate it in the return to London, when Cherry-Garrard takes to the British Museum the emperor penguin egg that he suffered so much to obtain. He waits patiently for a bureaucrat in the museum to come and take it, and is simply given a receipt to show that it's been entered into the collection. It's that — the piece of paper, the bureaucrat's slip — that becomes the seal not so much of the expedition's success as of its *existence*, of its having accomplished anything at all. The receipt does come at last, but too late for comfort. No one will stamp the penguin egg's passport.

So the deepest Shavian irony, which Cherry-Garrard understands and represents, is that the whole brave journey was, in the new world of mass war and mass casualties, pointless. Against the overwhelming force of the modern state, the little match-light of individual courage is meaningless. There is no point in being Peter Pan in a world of machine guns and the Western Front. Scott had sought a "good death," but there is no good death in a world where everybody dies. The grim Shavian joke is that the journey really ends not with the discovery of Scott's last resting place but with the saga of the penguin's egg. *This* journey — the journey of heroic man to meet the indifferent official — really is the worst journey in the world. And as much as the words of Poe and Shelley anticipate the adventures of the nineteenth century, Cherry-Garrard's egg moment anticipates the Kafkaesque tragedies of the twentieth century: the doomed search for the one right stamp on your visa that would shape the tragic arc of life for so many in the decades to follow.

And so we have two highly self-conscious, artificially constructed literary ways to understand the story: as the last efflorescence of the true courage of Victorian and Edwardian England and as a final demonstration of the falsity and hypocrisy of the civilization that sent those men south. The other side of bravery is absurdity; the other side of courage is the extreme complacency that shuts down the imagination long enough to let you be courageous. It is an ambiguity so deep that we perceive it to this day. Should we see Scott's expedition and its extraordinary display of both incompetence and courage as a premonition of what would happen to Britain in the First World War, when countless lives would be lost for no good reason? Or should we see it as another premonition, of Britain in the Second World War, when men and women would hold on in the face of extreme odds just as Scott and his men tried to do, through sheer will and heart and last-ditch morale? Was it the act of bravery that marked that English resistance or the act of foolhardy self-destruction posing as amateurism that marked the first war? Both at once, of course, which is why the voyages are both exasperating and admirable, maddeningly inept and shimmeringly courageous as we remember them.

I ASKED YOU at the start to think of Harry Somers' beautiful Canadian music about the pure Romantic call of the North. The voices, the fugal voices that I'd like you to imagine now, behind my own, are from the great Glenn Gould's *The Idea of North*, the aural collage of many voices that he made in the 1960s, of people telling stories of the North, one laid on top of another in a kind of Bach-like fugue.

What Gould was after was that the idea of the North, however seductive it might seem to us in Somers' clarion call to the world beyond, is in fact finally this overlay of voices, this tapestry, this fabric of different experience — that the true sound of the North is not the sound of one courageous individual but the sound of all these many stories coming together, laid out one on top of the other. Gould, apart from one quick trip, never went north, but he always went back to Bach for wisdom, and to Bach's sense that the best human sound is one theme laid on top of others. There's a humane truth in this, in its invocation of the made-up and contradictory North — the North of many stories told together — as the real North.

It is fashionable now in historical writing about the Arctic to mock and scorn Scott and Shackleton and Ross and all the others as men who were turned into icons by a cynical nineteenth-century myth-making machinery. But surely this perpetuates, unwittingly, exactly the note of smug condescension towards the Other — those with values and traditions unlike our own — that the worst of those nineteenth-century people exhibited in their day, only in this case the Other being patronized and sneered at are the inhabitants of that uncomfortable and exotic place, our own past. To imagine Franklin and Scott as mere pitiful puppets dancing on the end of a myth-making apparatus, moved by some impersonal force of history, is to cheat them of their suffering and of their bravery — and for all our absurdities, we suffer and are brave too, from time to time, and surely will not want anyone to cheat us of ours. The tone of insufferable bored condescension to all those who walked the past — the filmmaker Robert Flaherty, who saved the forms of Inuit culture in his documentary *Nanook of the North*, was a lecher; the explorers were really colonizers; the Inuit themselves were greedy and far from noble — is unearned not because such behaviour was often not so, but because it was *always* so. We all share our time's absurdities, we are ourselves enumerated in that always; if we knew what our descendants would think of us, there'd been no living.

Adventures always become absurdities when we look back at them, and that is why there is always a close relationship between courage and comedy. There *is* something ridiculous in the polar tales, something implicitly comic in all that self-regarding display of bravery. Indeed, the possibility of radical winter, the winter of the Far North, as the natural setting for burlesque and comedy of the absurd, has been seen and seized on by great comic imaginations again and again. In Charlie Chaplin's 1925 *The Gold Rush*, for instance, Chaplin builds up, in effect, a little encyclopedia of all the risks and horrors of radical winter, of the extreme North of the previous century. But he puts humour in place of heroism. The tramp doesn't endure misfortune and cold and hunger passively or stoically; he acts against it. Unintoxicated by the romance of endurance, he recognizes its unreason. And the only way he can act, given his circumstances (trapped in a cabin with a large and hungry companion; ignored by the dance-hall girls), is by constructing a kind of parallel imaginative world in which he chooses to live, rejecting the blizzards and insults of the cold outdoors. He's never going outside; he's living inside. The greatest of eating scenes in movies — the tramp eating his own shoe — comes right out of the reality of polar exploration. Franklin was already famous in the 1830s for having eaten his own shoe and having reported on it after one of his polar expeditions. Chaplin saw an opportunity for comedy in the tales of the Yukon because he saw in the northern world what comedy demands: a big, white straight man on a massive scale. The only way to oppose the existential trap of the Far North — nature's noose around your neck — was by eating your shoelaces as elegantly as you could.

The burlesque of the idea of North, as much as its epic realization — the idea of an entrepreneurial comic North marked by
energy and mischief and the triumph of the trickster over the
virtuous gentleman — still resonates today, in Mordecai Richler's
Solomon Gursky Was Here, as close to a Great Canadian Novel as
we have, whose essential theme is basically that only Jews and
Inuit are worthy of the Far North, have the ingenuity and wit to
survive and flourish while the Brits die nobly and the French
shiver wearily. The cunning trickster lives and triumphs while
the noble explorer dies. The trickster triumphs just by living,
even if he lives on only shoe leather and imagination.

Yet if the poles offered a theatre of the absurd — and they
did — what the theatre of the absurd always insists on, and
Chaplin is as wise about this as Beckett, is that existence itself is
courage enough: simply living demands all the courage that we
have. Every nation, as I said in the beginning, needs a nothing,
and every nothing, perhaps, needs a nation. When the two col-
lide, what we get is the usual mongrel of real life, exactly because
there is in fact no nothing on earth.

We seem to have travelled a long way from the Romantic
exquisitism of Debussy and Monet, which brought to a climax
the nineteenth-century story of the Romantic vision of winter in
art. And yet we circle around, I think, to the same themes of
inside and outside, and their intermingling — the bourgeois civilization that the polar men try to counter always comes back to
haunt them. We can expel nature with a pitchfork, the antique
poet says, but she will always return. We can flee civilization on
snowshoes but she will always entrap us in the end. Search the
Romantic winter you see for meaning and you will find your soul
in a snowflake. Jump out of the window into the winter you

search for and the last thing you will find at the end of the earth is another kind of window, showing your own reflection. The doctor and his monster race each other across the ice in the everlasting snows, but Mary Shelley's point is that whoever wins, there's no real difference: the man's the monster, the monster's the man. What we end up with when we journey to absolute winter is nothing absolute at all, just the usual mixed-up muddle, half brave and half batty, that persists in the world as it is. It's a moving *métissage* that, over history, stretches from the African equator in both directions, and finally towards the extremes of the two poles. Because that line is the track, the ever larger web spun by the endless flight of man, who goes out in search of meaning to find . . . only more man. The Bellman's blank map has one line upon it, and it's ours.

THREE

RECUPERATIVE WINTER
The Season in Spirit

IN 1869 AN expedition to the North Pole, this one German, was wintering over in the Arctic. Their ship had sunk and been crushed by the ice and the explorers had been forced to live in tiny shelters on the moving ice floes, which brooded and growled and broke apart with terrifying regularity as icebergs higher than any tower yet built by man glided close by.

One late December night, this little expedition opened a leaden box that they had carefully salvaged from their sunken ship. As the wind blew, in their absolute desolation, the men broke it open and to their joy saw that the box contained (as they had hoped it would) mouth harps and bright crackers, toys and tiny playthings. The German explorers had brought the toys along so they would be sure to celebrate Christmas in the Arctic—and that they did, even now.

If that first Romantic winter of the eye made what had been a mere blank season into a subtly differentiated field of meaning, if the radical winter of enterprise found in that blank a theatre of the heroic (and the absurd), could another winter become the setting for our hopes for recuperation and rebirth? It seemed that way on that winter morning on the ice. A winter celebration had become central not just to the idea of the holy but also to their idea of home.

The making of the modern Christmas — winter's holiday — is this chapter's subject, so let's begin with a Christmas carol. It's called "In the Bleak Midwinter" and, though evergreen, it bears a date. It comes from the middle of the nineteenth century, first as a poem by Christina Rossetti and then, while there are a couple of different musical settings, the most famous (sung beautifully by the great Loreena McKennitt) is by no less a composer than Gustav Holst — the *Planets* man, a fact I hadn't known until I went to find out (I had always assumed it was a folk, or hand-made, melody).

It's always been my favourite carol — one of them, anyway — and I was pleased to see that it was voted best carol in 2008 by a kind of international jury of such things. The music feels timeless while still rising from a particular time, and folk-like despite having specific and highly celebrated authors. It is not nineteenth-century music, or even Victorian music. It is *Christmas* music. Christmas music is one place in the highly self-conscious history of modern music where the neat distinction between old and new, medieval and Victorian, contemporary and archaic, is very poorly marked, so we generally don't know which of our Christmas carols are very old and which are in fact very new, which were touched by the hands of eminent poets and composers and which just happened in an anonymous past. A medieval carol such as "Verbum caro" can be sung side by side with a bit of Pre-Raphaelite Victoriana like "In the Bleak Midwinter."

Whatever the music's origin, the carol's seasonal setting is clear, and essential. It is a song about the remaking of the world, and it also is a song about, well, the bleak mid-winter. Our subject now is what I call recuperative winter: the invention and uses of Christmas — the holiday of Christmas — in modern times. A holiday that is eclectic, banged together, yet remains the central winter ritual, the central mystery, the central rite of our year's end celebration. It extends its spiritual reign from the true North down to the strange South, where fake icicles, plastic snow, fibreglass evergreens, and false fireplaces all testify to its spell.

That composite quality of Christmas has been part of the holiday since the very beginning. Christmas, December 25, is the winter holiday and always has been, almost certainly long before there was a Christ owed a mass. There has been a mid-December holiday to celebrate the winter solstice by appeasing the sun god and assuring the return of spring since people first noticed the sun's retreat. For as long as there have been winters, people have had solstice festivals celebrating the low point of warmth and the high point of winter — the shortest day of the year. And that festival is almost always a festival of supplementary light. The light's going out in the heavens, so we light one here. (The Jewish holiday of Hanukkah, though modern Jews have made far more of it to compete with the modern Christmas for their kids' favour, is in fact an *older* celebratory feast of lights.)

The one thing we can say for certain about Christmas is that whatever it is we're celebrating, it's not the birth of Jesus of Nazareth. Or not his birthday, anyway: Jesus is thought by some to have been born in September (for complicated reasons having to do with dating in the Gospel of Mark), and we know that some time during the fourth century the Catholic Church, or possibly the Roman bishop Liberius, decided more or less arbitrarily that December 25 would be the date when the birth of the Christ would be celebrated. (It's a *very* complicated story, because until then the standard festival of the birth of Jesus had been January 6 — Twelfth Night, Epiphany, the day of Jesus' baptism — and it's made even more complicated because you have a change of calendar in the middle of the story, so that the holiday we celebrate on December 25 was, by the older Julian reckoning, actually . . . January 6.)

Though Hanukkah looms as the Jewish festival of lights somewhere in the background, far more important in the making of modern Christmas is the pre-existence of two Roman solstice festivals, both also celebrated in late December: Saturnalia, the festival of Saturn, which took place every year in mid-December, and a festival on the Kalends (as in *calendar*), or first day, of January, which came right after. The meaning of Saturnalia is still apparent in the way we use the word today. A saturnalia is a festival of overcharge. It's an upside-down feast. Originally it was one where slaves literally became masters for a day, children were allowed to boss adults, a lord of misrule was crowned, and all the normal rules of order were not just relaxed but reversed. Saturn is the centrepiece of the holiday, the patriarch of Saturnalia, and he's no Jupiter. He is Jupiter's banished father, the same figure as Kronos in Greek mythology — an old man who is so full of robust fertility that he has to be sent away from civilization, and allowed back into the cautious circles of normal life only once a year. He's a familiar figure — a kind of space-granddad fertility figure — in all of mythology. Tolkien calls his Middle Earth version Tom Bombadil, and you don't have to be a Jungian to see a direct line between Saturn and the figure of Santa, the white-bearded old man who is welcomed home, though only once a year, to turn the world upside down again.

After Saturnalia comes the Roman Kalends festival of early January, which seems to have been much like Saturnalia but apparently less jumped up and festive, more domestic and serene — a festival of light and greenery and gift-giving. Both were recycled by the early Christians, who absorbed their mythology and also their symbolism: the act of lighting candles, the practice of giving gifts, even the use of holly and ivy. In the anthropologist J. G. Frazer's late-nineteenth-century classic *The Golden Bough: A Study in Magic and Religion*, he finds in these rites even traces of pagan human sacrifice — remaking, re-fertilizing the fields exactly at the moment of maximum winter.

A series of northern festivals also gets fed into the Christian Christmas; Yule, which is a northern European festival, takes place at exactly the same time of year and involves a blazing log, the lighting of bushes, the display of lights in the darkest time of year. Throughout, pagan feasts got turned opportunistically into Christian ritual. (In 245 the Christian polemicist Origen complains about people celebrating birthdays at all, citing pagan kings as the only "sinners" who did so! Not long after, this seemed like a good idea — if you can't beat 'em, join 'em, and the best way to beat 'em is to join 'em and then beat 'em.) So Christmas from its very beginning has the quality of being a composite feast, understood to be such by the people in authority: one religious feast made up from a palimpsest of older, pagan religious feasts.

All faiths are compound and syncretism is the world's one true religion — fundamentalist sects tend to be the most unconsciously syncretic of all; insisting that Christmas is either truly pagan or not pagan at all is equally fatuous. But you can understand the persistence of Christmas more deeply if you see that it is, in effect, a *profoundly* compound festival, marrying not just many different pagan holidays but also the two chief kinds of festivals that exist in the world: the reversal festival and the renewal festival. Our feasts most often celebrate either the world turned upside down, the reversal of our normal expectations, or else the table set for all, the renewal of our regular order. Halloween is the perfect example of a modern reversal feast: the things you are never allowed to do over the course of a year — going door to door ringing strangers' doorbells, demanding treats, wearing masks — are for one night not only allowed but encouraged. Thanksgiving, and the Fourth of July in the United States, is an ideal example of a renewal feast. You are supposed to feel a powerful reborn sense of common purpose. Renewal feasts are meant to reassure everyone that the social basis of the community is secure; reversal feasts are meant to recognize that there are moments when it is healthy to overturn the social order for one escapist night. The point of a renewal feast is to enforce the illusion of community where it doesn't always exist (as among disparate relatives at a Thanksgiving table); the point of a reversal feast is to bestow the illusion of power where it doesn't really exist (among children allowed to impersonate fiends at Halloween, or among grown-ups free to get drunk and act like libertine sophisticates on New Year's Eve). We celebrate continuity and want to renew it; we recognize that continuity has its discontents, and want to reverse it.

The funny thing about Christmas is that its pagan origins all lie in reversal feasts, in Saturnalia and the Kalends festival, and, secularized today, it continues to have some of that character as we do things we do but once a year: buy too many presents, dress up as Santa, love our siblings. Yet it's also a renewal feast, a feast that restores and reiterates and italicizes and underlines the existing order. While most of its rites are obviously derived from or, at the minimum, echo the pagan Saturnalia and Kalends — lighting candles, staying up late, giving gifts, all that one-night-only stuff — it also has at its core the imagery of mother and child, the idea of the essential rite of fertile renewal, all that *ongoing* stuff. That isn't original to Christianity — the imagery of the Madonna and Child, of Mary and Jesus, has parallels in Egyptian art's divine mother-and-son pair of Isis and Horus — but Christmas is more strongly marked by this tension between renewal and reversal, between the two basic kinds of human feasts, than any other holiday I know, and that tension gives it shape, character, and resilience throughout its history. Christmas drives us crazy because it asks us to be just the same and yet completely different, and all on one day. No wonder it is the best day of the year — and, for many, the worst.

ONE OF THE most striking things about the modern winter feast, *our* Christmas, is that it is in origin and accent more Protestant and northern than Catholic and southern. That's partly because the solstice is felt much more intensely in northern countries and climates where winter is real and threatening — where December 21 and December 25 mark a genuine change in the calendar, in the climate, and in the temper of the world — but it's also in part because the Roman Catholic calendar, like the Orthodox calendar, is extremely expansive. There are something like seventy saint's days in the Catholic calendar, which is dense with holidays and festivals and observances. Though those of us who have inherited a piece of the Protestant calendar think of it as being marked by many festivals, in fact it isn't, and therefore each festival that occurs matters. (North Americans like to think of themselves as being a peculiarly festive people, despite the reality that we celebrate relatively few holidays by European standards. Anyone who has lived in France and gone through one three-day weekend after another knows that even though we're the ones with a cult of summer, with its own songs and lore, we generally have only ten days of vacation.)

No accident, then, that modern Christmas would turn out to be largely northern and Protestant in its evolution and its flavour. The tragic side of Christmas would be almost unbearable if we could take it seriously: the baby doomed to be tortured to death in the most public possible way in order to save us all *in potentia* in an unknowable future. This tragic side of Christmas is audible in the great Bach Christmas masses, in the arias of the Mother with the Baby at her breast, and is unlike what we expect. And yet, at the same time, Christmas has a natural northern Protestant enemy: the Puritan. Part of the mythology of the modern Christmas involves the idea that the Puritans once banished Christmas and we're trying to bring it back. Now, there is an element of truth in that. In the seventeenth century it was indeed the case that the Puritan parliament in London did (briefly) banish Christmas. And there is a famous passage from the memoirs of the American Puritan governor William Bradford, in which he talks about trying to banish Christmas in the early Plymouth settlement and being unable to do it. He announced that everyone had to work on Christmas — *our sort doesn't celebrate this popish holiday!* — but when they came home at noon, all the Puritan kids went out on the streets celebrating, along with most of their parents. He writes (speaking of himself in the third person): "He went to them and took away their implements and told them that was against his conscience, that they should play and others work. If they made the keeping of it [a] matter of devotion, let them keep [to] their houses; but there should be no gaming or reveling in the streets. Since which time nothing hath been attempted that way, at least openly."

On the whole, though, the Puritan suppression was sporadic and mostly unsuccessful. The myth that it happened matters more than if it did. The odd thing is that the anti-Christmas moment is exactly when you find the most beautiful and elegant of all Christmas poetry. The seventeenth-century Christmas poetry of Richard Crashaw and Henry Vaughan, George Herbert and Robert Herrick — Christians of various kinds — finds in the constant dialogue of opposites that mark the Christmas holiday its collision of reversal and renewal, the basic paradox that the theology presents: God, the omniscient, omnipotent creator, is instantiated and embodied as a tiny, mewling baby. That kind of paradox is one that Crashaw in particular makes beautiful much of:

> Poor world, said I, what wilt thou do
> To entertain this starry stranger?
> Is this the best thou canst bestow —
> A cold and not too cleanly manger?
> Contend, the powers of heaven and earth,
> To fit a bed for this huge birth.
>
> Proud world, said I, cease your contest,
> And let the mighty babe alone,
> The phoenix builds the phoenix' nest,
> Love's architecture is His own.

The babe, whose birth embraves this morn,
Made His own bed ere He was born.

The metaphysical poets of the British seventeenth century write best about Christmas because no season or event so answers their hunger for the paradoxical and sublime. Tiny babe . . . cosmic event that reshapes all history . . . wee, mewling baby in a poor manger — a manger! — the omnipotent and omniscient ruler of the universe. Though the seventeenth century may be a dim time for Christmas cheer, it is the high time of Christmas art. For once, genuine religious passion and fidelity joins easily with sophisticated taste and scientific elegance.

And the metaphysical poets create the deep grammar of the holiday as a series of antitheses: a renewal feast that's also a reversal feast, a child-centred holiday that's really about the cosmos, and a winter feast of light that is also marked by the intimation of darkness: a starry stranger in a cold bed. Against the much larger and longer pagan and classical background, it is this unapologetic wonder at opposites that modern people inherit at Christmas.

BUT OUR SPECIAL concern is not with Christmas through all its history but with Christmas of the modern period — the Romantic period in which northern landscapes of snow and glaciers can find their own true forms, and in which the fur-bedecked traveller to the Pole becomes a kind of ecstatic monk of nature. That is our time. And it *is* a modern festival, first of all, set apart and secularized — or, if you prefer, restored to its early pagan truths — by the will of a few modern men and women.

Everyone knows, or thinks they know, that it was in the Victorian era in England that our modern winter holiday got made, with its meanings having carried over ever since. It's the time of what historians now call the first Industrial Revolution, when agricultural labourers were forced into cities and kids were forced down mines and into factories, and the whole created a lowered standard of living for most people — the first time of mass urban poverty.

And with that mass urban poverty came, in the 1830s and '40s, a series of urgent responses and calls for reform whose political programs still echo today: the liberal reformist response of John Stuart Mill calling for both more personal and economic liberty, the radical response of Karl Marx and Friedrich Engels calling for revolution and an end to the oppressive order. And conservative responses, calling, often idiosyncratically, for restoration and renewal of the old order of paternalistic aristocratic rule. In 1843 the Scottish historian and oracle Thomas Carlyle wrote his *Past and Present*, decrying poverty and calling for a return to Romantic heroic leadership. All of these responses, and a hundred others, crowded in with an urgency that makes the period feel and read more like contemporary South America than contemporary Europe: the social question seemed so grave as to be essentially insoluble. Thinking people sought ways not just to grasp what was happening and reform it, they also sought hard for new ways even to symbolize it. *What's going on?* New times demanded new fables.

And new fables most often demand old occasions. Christmas, the old holiday remade, became the central fable in dispute. And the real author of the modern Christmas, as everyone says in popular books and popular recollection, was that great, mixed-up reformer and fable-maker, Charles Dickens. Now, it is not true, as is sometimes said, that Dickens's *A Christmas Carol* is the entry to a new ideal of Christmas. It is the now forgotten Thomas

K. Hervey, whose *The Book of Christmas* appears in 1837, who deserves to be known as the real father of the modern Christmas, if anyone should be. Hervey writes about all the ways of celebrating the holiday since medieval days, and the myth of the cancellation of Christmas is terribly important to him. Hervey believes there was once a time when we celebrated Christmas as it really ought to be celebrated, and then Christmas got cancelled, so now what we're doing is trying to renew it, not invent it. Even though this myth of rediscovery has a very fragile and only partial relationship to the historical truth, it's central to the reintroduction of Christmas as a holiday in the nineteenth century. "There has always been in England another older England . . . you feel the nostalgia for it in Chaucer, and you feel it all through Shakespeare. Camelot is the great English legend," Orson Welles once perceptively observed. In Victorian times this Camelot is Christmas. The English idea, wholly mythical though it is, of a better lost and festive past annexes a whole season. The Victorians thought of what we call a Victorian Christmas as a medieval-revival Christmas. Not only is the idea of a renewed or revived Christmas already in place in the 1830s, through the quasi-historical work of people such as Hervey, but the joy of a secularized Christmas has long been present in Dickens's work. It's there in his very first book, 1836's *Sketches by Boz*, where there is a wonderful description of a Christmas dinner, and in *The Pickwick Papers*, his first novel, there's the winter pastoral ideal of Dingley Dell, where they celebrate Christmas with ice-skating and eating and general cheer.

But it's true that Dickens doesn't give permanent form to his instincts and beliefs about Christmas until he writes *A Christmas Carol* in 1843. *A Christmas Carol* is one of the great allegories of the complicated relationship between capitalism and charity — *caritas*, in the Christian sense of universal love — ever written, but that subject is itself part of the history of its making. In 1843–44 Dickens is writing and publishing as a serial *Martin Chuzzlewit*, his most ambitious and in some ways his most interesting novel to that date. But it also becomes his first failure. He has already written *The Pickwick Papers, Oliver Twist, Nicholas Nickleby,* and *The Old Curiosity Shop,* all hits, but with this one, the sales — the week-to-week sales of the serial — plummet, *whoosh!* Using his earlier travels to America as inspiration, he tries to revive *Martin Chuzzlewit* by giving him American adventures — anti-American adventures, as it happens — and that doesn't work. So he finds himself up against it in every sense; he has that panicky feeling that young people who find too much success too soon often have: that he is going to fall off the world, that one failure marks the end of all success. He's the Justin Bieber of the novel and suddenly his hair has fallen out. What's he going to do? One thing he thinks of is the idea of writing a Christmas story.

He thinks not just about writing a Christmas story but particularly about the idea that he will become an entrepreneur of Christmas. Through a complicated series of moves, including disentangling himself from Chapman and Hall, who have been his publishers since *Pickwick*, he sets out to finance the publication of *A Christmas Carol* by himself, for himself, believing that this is the way he'll solve his economic difficulties. (It's the classic doomed move of a cornered creative man — Francis Ford Coppola starting his own movie studio, Mark Twain setting up his own publishing house. It's the kind of thing that appeals to energetic artists coming off a few big hits, and it's the kind of thing that never works.)

So Dickens goes about writing *A Christmas Carol* not simply because he has this tale of renewal and reform to tell but also because he sees this as the one way of reconciling his own enterprise and altruism: restoring his pocketbook by saving his readers' souls. *A Christmas Carol* is published to great success, but for complicated reasons — mostly having to do with the lavish way Dickens goes about publishing it — it makes much less money than he hoped.

We know *A Christmas Carol* so well, it's such a familiar story, such a central fable of modernity, that we probably don't reflect adequately on how odd its structure is and how peculiar its politics are. We all know what happens: Scrooge, the model of a wicked, grasping, money-obsessed self-made miser, the perfect capitalist merchant, believes in the free market in its most brutal and grasping form. Scrooge isn't a reactionary; he's on the side of the free-market reformers. Remember when the two charitable gentlemen visit him at the beginning and say this is the time of year when the poor need special provision, and Scrooge mocks them and asks if there are no workhouses, no prisons? Well, those workhouses, those prisons embodied reform, a kind of hard-headed, utilitarian reform that was meant to cure the mass poverty of the Industrial Revolution. (One of the things that is appealing about Scrooge is that he is personally witty and rather intelligent throughout the book. He's not dumb, just mean. Intelligence is never a problem for Dickens's characters; his bad people are always more than smart enough.)

Dickens's point is that Christmas is a season of charity and compassion and companionship, that capitalism has left Scrooge dead to all three, and it's through his experience of the three matched healing spirits — the ghosts of Christmas past, of

Christmas present, and of Christmas yet to come — that he gets recalled to life. What these three spirits do is remind him not so much of his abstract responsibilities to other people but of the reality that he was once a man among men (and a boy among boys) — that earlier in his life he participated in a circle of commonality, and that when he did he was happy. He is saved by being reconnected to the feelings of his youth.

Scrooge's illness isn't just indifference to the poor; it's that he suffers from amnesia about his own history. By restoring his memory, the three spirits restore his virtue. And that sense — that the necessary cure for the capitalist lies not simply in seeing the evil of his system but rather in being reminded that there is a larger humanity outside the narrow world of the counting house — is exactly what Dickens's Christmas is all about. Scrooge falls asleep and is awakened to a realm of responsibility where he is once again "bound on that common journey" with the rest of us. Being connected makes us naturally charitable; the alienation of capitalism is worst of all for the capitalist.

The arc of the story is in that way simple, cleansing, and reformative, but it's also unusual. It's not Dickens's point that moneymaking materialism is empty compared to the spiritual life. It's that the spiritual life ought to be the spur and solace of moneymaking materialism, and then that moneymaking materialism ought to spur on the spiritual life, in an endless virtuous spiral. What Scrooge does the next morning, after all, is not to bring spiritual solace to the Cratchit family — he gives them a big turkey. The reason we should be engaged with material life is that our abundance can lead us to acts of altruism.

Dickens's Christmas fable is completely secularized; there is just a single, sideways reference to Jesus buried in the middle of the book. (This secularization of the holiday was so complete that Dickens's protégé and successor in Christmas storytelling, the novelist Benjamin Farjeon, himself born a Jew, called his holiday family the Silvers and gave them two daughters named Ruth and Rachel.) But the novel is fiercely reformist. In Penne L. Restad's otherwise admirable *Christmas in America*, his claim that *A Christmas Carol* "underlined the conservative, patriarchal, individualistic qualities" of Dickens's philosophy is the direct reverse of a rather easily ascertained truth. A familiar conservative, patriarchal society was the last thing Dickens wanted. Only by eliminating the general evil can Scrooge be made to see the specific truth. Change is what Christmas insists on.

Dickens was an individualist, though. He thought that good arrives one heart at a time, and spontaneously, not through inculcated abstract ideas of virtue — the utilitarian reformers who set up workhouses have those. Buying one particular turkey for one particular family is not the end of Scrooge's good deeds or of his duties, but it is the necessary beginning of them.

IN ALL OF these ways *A Christmas Carol* would seem to be a perfect document for the great movements of liberal reform that were part of the texture of this time. You would expect *A Christmas Carol* to be the ideal fable for Dickens's great contemporary and sometime friend John Stuart Mill. For it seems that this is Mill's vision of the world — a vision of gradual, indeed sometimes radical reform, but set within the structures of capitalism as it was already understood, a vision in which faith in the free market and faith in human freedom are intimately joined. For Mill, as for the reformed Scrooge, emancipation and enterprise are one.

But Mill and his followers don't care at all for the phenomenon — and it is a phenomenon — of *A Christmas Carol*. Pretty much the only bad review that *A Christmas Carol* gets in its own time is in Mill's own journal, the *Westminster Review*, where the reviewer says — it reads rather comically now like something right out of Dickens's later attack on utilitarianism, *Hard Times* — that the real question is: What hard-working family didn't get that turkey because Scrooge bought it for the Cratchits? There are only so many turkeys in the world, and if people like Scrooge are going to pass them out haphazardly it's going to destroy the whole structure of the free market, which allows turkeys to be an earned reward for the people who actually earn them through their work throughout the year — rather than getting them through unreliable acts of *noblesse oblige* in which turkeys are stubbornly bestowed upon the unworthy. The *Westminster* notice might be considered a reactionary review of *A Christmas Carol*; not at all, it's a radical review — a review from Mill's circle saying that this returns us to an old, feudal order in which we expect people to be saved through acts of individual charity rather than through the increasing prosperity of a liberal society. Getting a "free" turkey from the boss is a way of always remaining a peasant.

Mill throughout his life had a very complicated attitude towards Dickens, whom he found personally sympathetic but politically unreliable, good on poverty but terrible, for instance, on women's suffrage. The Victorian prophet who embraced *A Christmas Carol*, who loved it and saw it as the embodiment of all his dreams of social salvation, was Thomas Carlyle, the great *reactionary* intellectual of the era. Carlyle's *Past and Present* is a plaint against the hideous poverty of the early Industrial

Revolution and also a call for some kind of half-defined radical overthrow of the existing order, particularly the existing free-market order. And when Carlyle read *A Christmas Carol*, his formidable wife, Jane Welsh Carlyle, reported that, for the first time in his life, "he was seized with a perfect convulsion of hospitality and actually insisted on improvising two dinner parties with only a day in between." Temperamentally, Carlyle could be pretty much a scowling Scrooge himself, and so he is a perfect instance of the power of the imaginative transformation Dickens made seem so real. Christmas dinner with the Carlyles would have been a pretty grim business without the Dickensian epiphany (and probably still was, even with it).

What is it in *A Christmas Carol* that appealed to Carlyle? It's the notion that the only way a commercial man can be remade is through a nightmare, through an epiphany, by being totally remade through the course of a single night. He has to be cured — *we* have to be cured — not by education and improvement but by vision and rhapsody. The missing term between *enterprise* and *self-emancipation* is *epiphany*. Mill and his circle mistrust Scrooge's charity because it is so impulsive. That's what Carlyle loves about it — this sense that the whole world needs to be turned upside down. There needs to be a total, radical remaking of man's consciousness in order for Christmas to mean anything.

For Carlyle, as for Dickens, the concepts of reformist liberalism — the gradual, the incremental, the evolutionary, the empirical — all seem inadequate to cure what's wrong with Scrooge. He needs an epiphany, not a bill of reform. In *Past and Present*, certainly, Carlyle argues from injustice and interrelation. We are all fellow passengers; to neglect the poor is to neglect our own welfare, not just prudentially but psychologically as well:

typhoid in a poor neighbourhood will infect the whole West End. But just because our problems are so interrelated, programs of gradual reform are inadequate in their measure.

The Carlyle of *Past and Present* is a little frightening to read today, because his hope for social salvation is so absolute and apocalyptic. Having passed through the apocalypses that Carlyle — who was, it must be said, Hitler's favourite historian — helped to make, we are still more wary of it. The impatience with the material of everyday life, the desire for a total change, the urge towards the remaking of man in devotion to the greater cause of the nation — having seen these utopian dreams too firmly realized in Stalinist Russia and Nazi Germany, in the Cultural Revolution and the Khmer Rouge, we fear their maker. We know exactly what it would be like to dismiss the tawdry compromises of mass democracy and begin again with pure virtue and absolute unity. Year Zero is not the first of new years but the worst of all years.

Yet if we have doubts about his Romantic absolutism, Carlyle's vision still seems essential to Dickens's Christmas parable. Marley's great cry, "Mankind was my business!" echoes Carlyle's prophetic impulse and inspires Dickens. But in Dickens's fable we sense something more delicately ambivalent. Scrooge is both remade entirely and merely woken from his dream; he rejoins his old life as a better man but knows too what the machinery of the story cannot quite announce: there is another world beyond the material one. To be woken from a dream and to be born again are not quite the same thing, or anywhere near. The man, or child, woken from a dream is changed but can rejoin his life whole; Alice comes back to the meadow or to the warm fire of the living room. The man truly born again becomes . . . another man. Does

Scrooge become a better Scrooge or another Scrooge? Is he a better materialist or no longer a materialist at all? Certainly all the evidence points to his being a better Scrooge: he keeps Scrooge & Marley's going but does it with more heart and soul, and he now knows how to keep Christmas. But he is also, or might be, another Scrooge entirely: a man transformed and no longer caring for his old life, a Christian who has thrown it all away — a convert, in that sense. Scrooge wakes up, but as a reconciled capitalist or a secret revolutionary? Dickens never quite says and we never quite know.

Dickens thinks that what Christmas offers us, properly understood, is a kind of tiny revolutionary moment in the year when everything can be remade, not just our hopes but our hearts too. *A Christmas Carol* is a reassuring book. Yet it's that insistence on epiphany — that only Spirit can save us, that what society needs is not improvement but a total remaking of its regimen — that gives the book its inner tension. It's what made it so potent in its time and, indeed, in ours. Dickens oscillated throughout his adult life between a belief in reform, restoration, and piecemeal change and an impulse — Romantic and not very well worked out — for sweeping semi-religious radicalism. (The not-very-well-worked-out bit was why Mill mistrusted him; consistency may be the hobgoblin of little minds but it is the archangel of political philosophers.)

But however complex (or just confused) Dickens's ideas of reform were, he never thought that the alternative to Christmas ambivalence was clear authority. As Dickens's later Christmas stories appeared, Carlyle seems to have been appalled that Dickens never "advanced" beyond his original "sentimental" view, saying that Dickens "thought men ought to be buttered up, and the world made soft and accommodating for them, and all sorts of fellows have turkey for their Christmas dinner. Commanding and controlling and punishing them he would give up without any misgivings in order to coax and soothe and delude them into doing right." Carlyle was right. Dickens did think it was better morals, and better politics, to coax and soothe than to command and control. Carlyle couldn't understand how you could believe in the overthrow of the capitalist order without having some idea of an absolutist heroic authority to put in its place. Christmas matters so much to Dickens exactly because it is a celebration of reversal that is also a celebration of renewal. He revels in the contradiction rather than attempting to reconcile it and this was in a deep sense outside Carlyle's understanding, as it lies outside those of modern critics who think of Dickens's Christmas as *merely* sentimental. Dickens thought that if all sorts of fellows had turkeys for their Christmas dinner, then there would be no need to control and punish them. Men buttered up *were* men made better. It's at the heart of his view of the world.

In this way, the Dickensian Christmas, far from being a minor sentimental construct or a mere affirmation of smug bourgeois values, is a complicated and tellingly ambiguous festival, instinctively seizing on the ambivalence between reversal and renewal deeply imprinted in the holiday's past. In part it's a dream reversal festival in which Tiny Tim and the afflicted many are brought out of the corner and made central to Scrooge's consciousness, and in part it's a renewal festival in which the order of the family is reaffirmed. (Remember, the Cratchits are a very happy family; although they suffer externally they don't suffer internally — they don't feel themselves to be oppressed or miserable.) In this way this most familiar of all modern fables of recuperation is morally double and sends a double message: reform — *and* be reborn! Let Christmas be a time of taking stock; let Christmas be a time of spending pleasure. Be buttered and be bettered. Both at once, and God bless us all, or everyone. Visions at midnight are a morning reformer's best ally and Dickens knew it. His are not the failed dream politics of a Victorian fable-maker. They are the successful real politics of the liberal imagination in power — when it allows itself the liberty, and the power, to imagine.

We can see the special qualities of Dickens's imagination, and its power, if we compare his Christmas stories to that of his single greatest contemporary, Anthony Trollope — yes, he did write them. In Trollope's Christmas stories, the Dickensian apparatus is spoofed and treated sardonically: a woman in a Paris hotel on Christmas Eve is suddenly filled with the Dickensian Christmas spirit and goes, in the middle of the night, to make a healing mustard plaster for her husband's sore throat, only to enter, farcically, into the wrong room and plaster the sleeping throat of a shocked bachelor. Nighttime's altruistic impulses, the sensible Trollope implies, shouldn't be trusted, even at Christmas. In those stories by Dickens's disciple, Benjamin Farjeon, the ones with the obviously Jewish family at the heart of an entirely secularized holiday, the empathy for the poor is even greater than it is in Dickens, but the imaginative fantasy is replaced by mere melodrama: poor people die in the bitter December. (Though Farjeon's tragedies of the frozen poor may at least remind us that the politics of Christmas still have winter at their heart. It's cold outside.)

SO THE WINTER holiday as it emerges in British fable-making beginning in the 1840s isn't just "secularized" — a sacred holiday made into a commercial occasion. It has an idea of the sacred of

its own, and the thing made sacred is the idea of political transformation through family solidarity. You find in the next decades
a very similar kind of transformation taking place in the politics
of Christmas in the United States. There, though, it takes place
through popular imagery, and particularly through the work of
an artist who is the other great maker of the popular Christmas:
the New York cartoonist Thomas Nast.

Nast was the single greatest image-maker who ever lived in
the U.S. More of the American canon of imagery is owed to Nast
than to any other creator. He invented the Republican elephant
and the Democratic donkey. He popularized the image of the
capitalist as a hugely corpulent man and the image of the corrupt
politician as a capitalist in a shining vest. And he was the man
who single-handedly created the image of Santa Claus.

There are, of course, old Dutch legends of a Middle Eastern
saint, Saint Nicholas, who lived in the fourth century BCE. His
feast day was celebrated on December 6, and he got established in
northern Europe in time for the Reformation. He's essentially a
Protestant symbol and saint. In Germany he assisted Jesus — the
name Kris Kringle, a synonym for Saint Nicholas, was originally
Christkindl, the Christ Child. And so the same process of syncretism that generally characterizes Christmas characterized its
patron, although it was now Protestants adapting a Catholic figure rather than Catholics adapting pagan ones, but with the same
purpose: to drain the figure of its original content so that it could
be, so to speak, repurposed and preside over a new kind of feast.

It is this secularized figure, brought to New York by the first
Dutch settlers and made literary by Washington Irving, that
Nast transforms. Nast takes the Dutch Saint Nicholas, a tiny,
benevolent but imp-like elf, and turns him into our vast, corpu-

lent, white-bearded figure. And just as Dickens has a particular politics attached to his Christmas inventions, Nast has a very particular politics attached to his. The first time that Santa Claus appears as a figure unto himself is in 1862. It's the very height of the Civil War; in fact, it's at the low point of Union fortunes. It's in a picture called *Christmas Eve*, published in *Harper's Weekly*: a young mother prays as her two children sleep on Christmas Eve, while her pensive bearded husband is in uniform on the Potomac, far away. Above are two tiny Santas, one leaving toys for the children, the other throwing gifts to the soldiers. Santa becomes a kind of benevolent Union spirit who will eventually unite them all.

It's a hit, and it's followed up that same year by a second image, *Santa Claus in Camp*, which shows Santa at greater length as a chubby, rotund elf dressed in the Stars and Stripes and passing out presents in a Union army camp. That's the thing about Nast's Santa: he never evolves. He is always Santa — fur-trimmed suit, white beard, pink cheeks. And at that very moment Santa Claus becomes not only the embodiment of a spirit of American abundance, he also becomes a specifically Union local deity. He becomes the positive spirit of northern plenty and domesticity to set alongside and against the southern myths of chivalry and tradition and indigenous culture. *The South has chivalry, but we have Santa.*

Santa as Nast drew him over the years is benevolent, but he is also, above all, *busy*. He rushes from rooftop to rooftop, practises the piano, visits soldiers at camps, consults with bad children, wipes the sweat from his brow. Nast gave the American Christmas its patron saint and its particular tone of abundance distributed rather than virtue rewarded. Santa brings good

Americans stuff because they deserve to have it. Nast's American Christmas is entirely child centred. Dickens's Christmas is essentially family oriented. In Nast's drawings it's Santa and the kids and no one else.

Nast's great theme, as for Dickens, was reform, but his great subject was the triumph of materialism, a triumph that had become so vast in America after the Civil War that it could absorb the national myth entirely. It was a triumph that could be imagined benevolently, but it was also a gilded age, an age of corruption and bad faith, and Nast immortalized that age too. He was the great cartoon enemy of Boss Tweed and the Tammany Hall ring in New York — "It's them damn pictures," Tweed said in exasperation — yet the eerie thing is that Nast's caricature of the Boss throughout the 1870s is a perfect twin of his Santa. The embodiment of everything corrupt and wrong in American civic capitalism and the figure of Santa Claus look like identical twins, one evil and one benevolent but both entirely material incarnations of American life. For Dickens, Christmas poses the problem of reconciling charity and capitalist ethics, but he is still working within the relatively parched terms of the first Industrial Revolution — one turkey for one family is still a big deal. There's not a lot of butter to go round. For Nast the problem is different because the issue is different; Nast sees the Christmas struggle as one between ever-growing prosperity and ever more corrupted politics. For Nast in America, life is one endless cycle of Christmases and corruption, two brother deities that can't quite be separated.

BUT IT'S ONLY in the 1870s, after the Civil War in America and the Reform Bill in England and the establishment of the Third

Republic in France, that the transition from the Dickensian–Nast Christmas, which is still essentially domestic, to our contemporary commercial, urban Christmas takes place. It's in the 1870s when we move from the domestic Christmas, the Christmas of the heart and the hearth, to the department-store Christmas, the Christmas of the city street. In one way it's another move from an indoor Christmas to an outdoor Christmas — the back-and-forth between indoor Christmas and outdoor Christmas has always been fundamental to the way people imagine the holiday. Is it a reversal festival, where everybody rushes into the street at midnight, or is it a renewal festival, where they've withdrawn into their homes? That tension, that doubleness or ambiguity, still goes on today.

Though marked by economic recession, in many ways the 1870s are one of the most pivotal decades of modern times. It's the moment when what historians call the second Industrial Revolution begins, and while the first Industrial Revolution, of the 1820s and '30s, sees a drop in general living standards in which great masses of people become impoverished — that's what leads to *The Communist Manifesto* and Marx and Engels in the 1840s — the second Industrial Revolution is the one in which living standards suddenly start to shoot up. You begin to get for the first time a broad urban middle class. And this festival becomes their festival.

Though the intellectual and moral premises of the modern Christmas are set in the 1840s and '50s, and most of the rites and characters are formed then, most of the rest of what we think belongs to our Christmas begins in the seventies. Christmas carols are first introduced in that decade as a distinct form. The practice of poor children singing in the streets has been going on for centuries, but it's only in the 1870s that people self-consciously become aware that you have a body of musical literature worth conserving and expanding. So not only do you have traditional carols such as "God Rest Ye Merry, Gentlemen" and "I Saw Three Ships" being transcribed and published for the first time, but you also have newly written carols like "Hark! The Herald Angels Sing" and "In the Bleak Midwinter" entering the Christmas canon on equal terms, as though they've always been sung. From the very beginning, these two bodies of music — the very old and the very new — are completely mingled. The first important publication of carols, in 1871, is called, significantly, *Christmas Carols: Old and New* — the barriers between present and past come down musically, as they do on the feast.

Goose and turkey clubs spring up all over the Western world. In every capital people put aside money so they'll have a Cratchit-sized turkey for Christmas. Gift giving, which, dinner aside, played a very minor role in Dickens's Christmas, becomes customary and even *de rigueur*. So do Christmas cards. And it's in 1871, in both Britain and the United States, that Christmas becomes an official holiday; it becomes a bank holiday in Britain and a national holiday in America as well. *The Times* of London writes that "Christmas as their feast is secured to our people now by an act of Parliament." Scrooge's epiphany and Santa's feast have become the revived neo-pagan Saturnalia of the Western world.

And something else is going on too. It's now that Christmas becomes the winter holiday of city people, with its special public hearth — the department store, with a dress-up Santa inside and animated Christmas windows filled with puppet figures outside. (It is not for nothing that the second Industrial Revolution is often called the Technological Revolution; its sign is not the factory but the mechanical marvel.) The Christmas windows of department stores become the new hearth of the public holiday, stretching from Paris to San Francisco. (My wife and I cherish a Christmas window of this legacy at Ogilvy's in Montreal, famous in our childhood — "The Enchanted Mill / *Le Moulin Enchanté*," with a thousand clockwork dolls — intricately intact until very recently. We eagerly took our children there when they were ten and five, and watched their video-trained faces go slack with bemusement.)

Now, there's a fascinating line of sociological research showing that city winter is a time of two transformations in what the Canadian-born sociologist Erving Goffman calls the micro-order of behaviour — the largely unconscious order of small manners that shape our lives and express our feelings. First, winter creates a suspension of normal rules; next, it enforces a dramatization of normal events. We act out in winter cities. When we're cold, we stamp our feet, we shiver — we *show* that we're cold. In temperate weather we behave temperately, but in cold weather we aren't just cold, we're theatrical. We show each other that we're cold even if we all already know it. (People do this in steam rooms too, in the opposite direction. You're expected to groan and shake your torso to show you're hot. Kids not initiated into this social rite find a visit to a steam bath with their fathers deeply embarrassing.)

And at the same time it seems that the small laws of urban life — parking regulations, rules about drinking in public, jay-walking — are discreetly suspended. It is in some way normal or expected to ritualize our condition in winter and to suspend the micro-order. In this sense we might say that winter in cities is an inherently festive time, pregnant with a festival's two impulses: to suspend the rules and to heighten the actions. Cities in winter are natural stages for holiday theatrics. The city street in winter is intrinsically made for a show.

As the urbanization of the world gathers speed in the 1870s, what has been a solstice holiday in origin becomes a harvest holiday in realization. The new fields to be reaped are the streets and stores of the new winter city. It's in 1867 that Macy's in New York stays open till midnight for the first time, in a kind of unconscious commercial parody of the ancient Catholic rite of the midnight Mass. By 1875 steam-powered animated figurines are acting out imaginary medieval scenes and Christmas tableaux in Macy's windows. L. Frank Baum, author of *The Wonderful Wizard of Oz*, begins his career as a Christmas-window designer, making miniature cities of mechanical marvels that anticipate the Emerald one. (Ogilvy's in Montreal begins in the 1860s, though its windows come later.)

Christmas becomes a business. It's around this time that Frank Winfield Woolworth, the creator of Woolworth's, says bluntly to his employees: "This" — meaning December — "is our harvest time. Make it pay." By 1888 Macy's is promising that anything bought as late as Christmas Eve will be delivered within New York City on Christmas Day. And the next year 162,624 Christmas presents are delivered by the store in New York alone! Thanksgiving, the invented harvest holiday, is becoming the renewal feast of family life; Christmas, a once sacred holiday, has become the national harvest festival of commercial culture. (It's in these years that Dickens makes his last tour of the United States reading *A Christmas Carol*. By the end of the century the *New York Tribune* actually has the nerve to say that Dickens didn't care about Christmas at all until he came to America the year before *Martin Chuzzlewit*.)

To realize just how widespread, just how universal this largely new and largely made-up holiday has become, perhaps the best way is to go to the New York Public Library's menu collection and look at Christmas menus from Europe and North America in the century's closing year, 1900. If you look at Christmas menus from 1900 and compare them with menus from 1850, fifty years before, you realize that you have a kind of Christmas culinary empire that stretches across the seas. On the SS *China*, for Christmas of 1900 they are serving mallard duck with currant jelly and turkey with cranberry sauce. At the Russell House Hotel in Ottawa they serve roast turkey with Christmas plum pudding and brandy sauce. At the Griswold Hotel in Detroit there is roasted possum, but there is also turkey with cranberry sauce and a plum pudding with brandy and hard sauce. At the Arlington, in Hot Springs, Arkansas — in Arkansas! — they serve turkey with chestnuts and cranberry sauce and Christmas plum pudding with hard and brandy sauces. On and on . . . at the Pabst Hotel on Broadway and 42nd, right in the heart of New York City, you get stuffed turkey with chestnuts and truffles for eighty cents, with forty cents more for plum pudding with hard and rum sauces to follow.

The old winter holiday has conquered the world. In 1912 you have the first scholarly history of Christmas, with all its syncretic intertwining, its pagan sources, frankly acknowledged. Its author, Clement Miles, concludes: "At no time has so much been made of children as today, and because Christmas is their feast its luster continues unabated in an age upon which dogmatic Christianity has largely lost its hold, which laughs at the pagan superstitions of its forefathers. Christmas is the feast of the beginnings, of instinctive happy childhood." And Miles goes on — this in 1912, right on the brink of the First World War—to survey all the people who have taken up celebration of this secularized, non-Christian festival: the robust English and the unsentimental French, and indeed the Germans, whom he calls "the sentimental children of Europe."

Well, we all know what happened in the following two years between the robust English and the sentimental German children, and we all know how that vision of a kind of bourgeois commercial compact came apart amid the fires of nationalism and militarism. But there is no more telling or touching incident in all the stories of modern times than the story of the "Christmas truce" of 1914, a mere two years after Miles writes his too-complacent history.

The Christmas truce has a life in movies and music videos and popular memory—and it's astonishing to discover that this is a case where the myth is absolutely true. On the first Christmas of the war, in 1914, on impulse and in a totally self-organized way, the German and British troops along the Western Front chose to celebrate Christmas by ceasing to fight, trading family photographs, playing games, and sharing what good cheer they could find. It was a kind of quiet mutiny rising out of what had become a common Christmas culture throughout Europe—a popular movement on the part of the men, and greatly discouraged by the officers. It was completely out of order, it was completely illegitimate—and it was nearly universal on the Western Front.

It wasn't in any sense a religious impulse; the soldiers didn't want to pray or sing hymns. They talked, they traded mementos, and they played a little football. Two photographs survive of the Christmas truce in 1914—only two, hazy and hard to read—which show the two sides mingling together in this heartbreaking way: the pointed kaiser helmets of the German soldiers alongside the caps of the British soldiers, standing side by side, unable to understand why they would shortly have to return to slaughtering each other. In every subsequent year of the war the generals of both sides made certain that there would never be a renewal of the Christmas truce. They knew all too well what the truce meant. However silly or even sordid the commercial rites of the ever-more-secular Christmas had been in the soldiers' early lives, it still represented values — of community, family, renewal — that were directly opposed to the murderous practice of mass warfare and to the mad nationalism that had driven Western civilization to suicide. Intellectuals thought that life had become too easy and toy-like in the soft and material years of the 1890s; the men fighting on the Western Front longed for that softness and for those toys, as the men lost on the polar ice had longed for them half a century before.

AFTER THE FIRST World War, the pre-war Christmas becomes a source of nostalgia. That is, people look back to the Victorian Christmas, which in its heyday no one thought of as being a "Victorian Christmas" — if anything, they thought of it as a medieval Christmas — as the ideal kind. And so the iconography, the imagery of Christmas, becomes, and remains to this day, frozen as largely nineteenth-century Victorian, an inspiration in feeling. The Dickensian Christmas is in some ways a product of the Somme.

But something else rather strange begins to happen, particularly in the 1920s and '30s, as the world recovers from the First World War, and then even more strongly in the late 1940s, accompanying the exuberant abundance of the post–Second

World War period. And it is that the study of Christmas, the description of Christmas, the analysis of Christmas passes from the hands of storytellers to sociologists, from poets to psychoanalysts, and from animated-puppet makers to anthropologists.

In the 1940s, for instance, an enormous psychoanalytic and psychological literature about Christmas begins to appear, all keyed to one new sense about Christmas — that the very pleasure one is supposed to be taking from Christmas creates impossible stress and pain and misery. This feeling isn't entirely new. Already, back in the 1880s, the stress and strain of present-giving and, more generally, of abundance have been felt. The liberal magazine *The Nation* noted in 1883 that Christmas mixed "so much hope and dread — hopefulness at the thought of what we might get, and dread at the thought of all we have to give," and the more conservative *New York Tribune* complained that "the modern expansion of the custom of giving Christmas presents has done more than anything else to rob Christmas of its traditional joyousness . . . the season of Christmas needs to be dematerialized."

In the 1940s and '50s this huge new literature rises up that asks us to explain why it is that Christmas, which is supposed to be the happiest time of year for people, is almost always the time of maximum suicides, maximum depression, maximum family misery. It's a plain truth, and another kind of doubleness — a modern, neurotic kind to put alongside the ancient paradox of the Incarnation and the optimistic ambiguity of Victorian reform. We experience the happiest time of year as a time of maximum stress, with feelings of sadness, disappointment, confusion, depression — even suicidal impulses — more often than feelings of elation.

Much of the analytic literature is, or now reads as, unintentionally funny — like a kind of parody of, a cartoon version of psychoanalytic ideas. One analyst proposes that the reason people feel sad at Christmas, though they are supposed to feel wonderful, is that Jesus is the ultimate sibling, and sibling rivalry between you and Jesus can never end happily; no one can ever compete with the Christ child, so everyone feels terrible. Another suggests that the real reason Christmas is experienced as pure misery, although it ought be experienced as pure joy, is because Santa is actually a personification of labour pains, of birth and its painful process: he comes down the chimney with great difficulty in the middle of the night, there is hushed difficulty surrounding his entrance, and so on. (We don't take psychoanalysis as seriously as we once did, and it's easy to mock its tenets and falsify its theories but the gift of openness about the permanent ambivalence of our emotional lives is still one of the valuable legacies of the Freudian tradition.)

Sociologists take up the study of Christmas as well, scrutinizing the new customs of gift and card exchange — after all, almost twice as many Christmas cards are sold and delivered in the 1950s as there are people in the United States: five hundred million during one Christmas. There's an insistence in the literature that Christmas has become essentially a competition of prestige, of status, of compulsive gift giving and compulsive card sending. The counting house has triumphed in another way. Capitalism once worked against the Cratchits' cheer; now it turns the Cratchits' cheer into a commodity. So we inherit a double reality: Christmas as a feast of abundance, secularized and even Judaized, made part of the cosmopolitan individualist whole, and Christmas as a stress point of anxiety about the space between our wants and our needs. Not capitalism and charity, as with the Victorians, but abundance and anxiety become the twin pillars of our feast. How much can a life of materialism give you? What good are goods?

And certainly all the Christmas myths and Christmas literature of the post–World War Two period, and stretching into our own, are remarkable for being highly anxiety-ridden. The imagery of cheer and the counter-imagery of poverty and suffering, which gave a kind of gravity to nineteenth-century Christmas literature, are largely gone. What's been put in its place is the suffering, anxious protagonist who is (terrible sin!) *not having a good time*.

The most obvious instance of this is the twentieth-century fable that is most often seen as our twentieth-century equivalent of *A Christmas Carol*: Frank Capra's 1946 classic *It's a Wonderful Life*. Though ostensibly a Christmas-card movie, it really comes alive when George Bailey rages at the situation he's in, at the trap that "normalcy" and domestic compromise have set for him. He's sick of all that Christmas crap. In the end, Clarence the angel doesn't awaken him, as Scrooge was awakened, to compassion for the poor. George is awakened to embrace his own complacency. And though his reintegration into Bedford Falls is real and not meant to be taken ironically, it is his anger at his own circumstances, his *anxiety*, that's likely to remain with us from the movie. He isn't lonely — his problem is that he isn't lonely enough. He can't escape the octopus of obligation. Morality tells him to settle down and enjoy the strangulation. Loudon Wainwright Jr. (the singer's dad) in 1965 called Christmas the annual crisis of love. The Cratchits have no crisis of love because the duties of necessity overwhelm them. More abundance means more doubt.

A festival of pagan lights becomes a festival of progress and poverty — and ends as a festival of overabundance and anxiety.

THAT'S THE COMPLEX inheritance of modern Christmas. Our recuperative winter is one in which renewal and reversal, anxiety and abundance, epiphany and uneasiness are knotted together. The questions it asks remain: Are abundance and altruism linked? Are capitalism and *caritas* a part of the same burden, the same carol or song? Is gift giving itself inherently good?

Part of me would like to bow and head back up the chimney at this point, simply appealing, as lecturers like to do, to the complexity of the history as if it were its own explanation: *Christmas has many mansions, the Nativity many meanings.* But if patriotism is the last refuge of the scoundrel, the appeal to complexity is the last refuge of the intellectual coward. *Of course it's complicated*, you hiss. *We knew that sitting down. You're the one with the pulpit. Uncomplicate it for us, now!* Okay, let me try.

A credible Christian idea of Christmas remains in our era, and it reaffirms the space between the commercial, secular reversal feast and the ancient renewal feast; it does this with affection and understanding, but it still says they're not the same. One sees this in the work of both the best Christian poet and the best Christian prose writer of the second half of the twentieth century.

W. H. Auden's wonderful *For the Time Being: A Christmas Oratorio*, published in 1944, retells the entire Christmas story in modern terms, in the form of contemporary musical comedy. Auden's idea is that it's the space, the eternal space between our desires for Christmas — not just our desires for Christmas in a grand religious sense but our immediate desires for Christmas as a festival at the end of the year — and our capacity to realize those desires that is the actual engine of our spiritual appetites. The yearly Christmas we celebrate reminds us how a hope too large to be realized will be perpetually disappointed, and then eternally renewed, put off till next year. The poem ends beautifully with a long passage called "After Christmas."

Well, so that is that.
Now we must dismantle the tree,
Putting the decorations back into their cardboard boxes —
Some have got broken — and carrying them up to the attic.
The holly and the mistletoe must be taken down and burnt,
And the children got ready for school
. . . Once again
As in previous years we have seen the actual Vision and failed
To do more than entertain it as an agreeable
Possibility, once again we have sent Him away,
Begging though to remain His disobedient servant,
The promising child who cannot keep His word for long.
. . . But, for the time being, here we all are,
Back in the moderate Aristotelian city
Of darning and the Eight-Fifteen, where Euclid's geometry
And Newton's mechanics would account for our experience,
And the kitchen table exists because I scrub it.
It seems to have shrunk during the holidays. The streets
Are much narrower than we remembered; we had forgotten
The office was as depressing as this. To those who have seen
The Child, however dimly, however incredulously,
The Time Being is, in a sense, the most trying time of all. . . .

Christmas as the prism of our anxieties. That's Auden's point: the ambivalence we feel about the modern Christmas is the ambivalence of all modern life, which once knew instinctive simple joy but now must repress it out of guilt. In a sense you might say that Auden sees, as Frank Capra does in a more popular form, that what we might call the order of convertibility has altered. The classic sequence was that the inside-out Christmas, the Christmas of remade souls, led to an upside-down Christmas, a Christmas of remade social order. Scrooge's dream ends with a turkey, not a potlatch. By the middle of the twentieth century that sequence has changed. The upside-down Christmas, the Christmas of the material festival, is being asked to do the work of an inside-out Christmas — the work of remaking our souls — and it seems always inadequate to the task.

The same space between material Christmas and spiritual Christmas, and, more important, the growing reversal of their order, is something that is also beautifully dramatized in John Updike's four *Rabbit* novels. There is a Christmas scene in each of the books, beginning in 1959, until, nearly forty years later, the series ends with *Rabbit at Rest*. Rabbit is Harry Angstrom, Updike's hero, who gradually becomes disillusioned until, at the end, at the climax of this very ambitious cycle of American novels, Rabbit realizes that the department-store Christmas of his childhood in Brewer (a town based partly on Reading, Pennsylvania, near where Updike grew up) was a fraud. All of that world of light and abundance, of animated figures in windows, was simply a scam designed to get you to spend as much money as you could, and the moment they couldn't make a profit on it, it ended. The department store has shut. It's all a scam, and so faith itself is a scam. If God chooses to manifest himself in

Christmas windows, they'll close him down, just as they closed down everything else. Rabbit dies soon after this final grim epiphany about the true — that is to say, the false — nature of the relationship between abundance and faith. For Auden and Updike, who were committed, if eccentric, Christian believers, the line that we try to draw tight between the lights and the Light will never be enough. The material festival is, finally, a fake: an imitation rather than an intimation of the Epiphany, a glimpse but not the glory.

Well, all faiths are a series of practices designed to achieve some social end. An ambivalent holiday is a holiday made for ambivalent people. If believers are disillusioned by our Christmas, skeptics may yet dance. There are, after all, rich rituals that replenish our imagination and impoverished ones that only dictate our responses. Perhaps by pulling back to some kind of safer, quasi-anthropological distance we can spy some meaning that our eyes might miss when our noses are pressed against that Christmas window at Ogilvy's. What we have in modern times, after all, is really a *season* of festivals — fall into winter, pointing towards spring, one following the next — and all involving the world's one permanent religion: the dream cult of rejuvenation. The earth does renew itself; we don't. And so we want to connect our human cycle of mere growth and decay, where winter holds no spring, to the natural cycle of renewal. We can't do it, of course, but we can't stop trying.

And so perhaps it is the *cycle* of the modern autumn-to-winter season of festivals that matters most. On Halloween the young are given authority to the point of seeming anarchy; at Thanksgiving a concord is played out — the children's table sits beside the grownups'. At Christmas the young become the specially privileged: it is their season, with a sacred child at its centre. And then at New Year's the adults become children themselves in one of the ways we can: by getting drunk and playful, to the children's great alarm. The cycle is played out against the entry of winter, and each of the roles is, so to speak, held up and considered as a possible masquerade. Then, as Auden says, the normal Euclidean city, where "the kitchen table exists because I scrub it," reasserts itself in January.

And in that way the secular holiday, in its secular sequence, rhymes most powerfully with the sacred holiday. The secular holiday *is* the sacred holiday. I find myself moved by the specificities of this holiday, as we celebrate it now, and if I were pressed to say why, it is because what we celebrate is an idea, though not a simple one. The truth is not that modern people have domesticated and democratized a spiritual impulse, but instead that we have made material an idea that is material at its very core. That is the idea of the Nativity: that the infinite idea, the permanent Presence, the Thing Beyond All Things, might become the finite fact, the impermanent infant, the Thing that Wets Itself at Night, that kid in the corner. We all recognize that human renewal through the newborn child, whether its mother be virginal or merely young, is a glimpse of something amazing and miraculous in itself. Love's architecture, as Crashaw wrote, is its own. The manger is inside us, and the mystery of birth and renewal, imagined as sacred or simply experienced as life, remains miraculous. It can never be parsed by critics, only praised by carols. The bleak midwinter passes as we sing the beauty of the baby. These feelings are tied so deeply to the rhythm of the seasons, and to the rhythms of human existence that we make within them, that to render them as mere ornament seems inadequate to their measure, just as taking them on entirely as dogma seems insulting to their universality. The force of the holiday is that oppression can produce new births, and that a light can go on in the middle of darkness. (Even "I Saw Mommy Kissing Santa Claus" testifies to this fact, an Oedipal triangle in a red suit.)

One thing we can say for certain: the symbolism of the modern, ambivalent, anxiety-ridden, double-faced Christmas is *winter* symbolism. We need the warmth in order to enter the cold, and at Christmas we need the cold in order to reassert the warmth, need the imagery of the bleak midwinter in order to invoke the star above the stable. If the world has globalized Christmas, Christmas has winterized the world. And so the empire of the winter holiday extends from one end of this continent to another: fake snow, phony icicles, that romantic hoarfrost beloved by Goethe now sprayed on California windows in honour of a Germanic deity Goethe could not have imagined—Santa. It is necessary to assert snow in order to evoke sunshine, to make a theatre of winter in order to promise spring, to chill the Baby in order to let him do his thing, to submit to helplessness and winter in order to evoke power and new light. The simplest description of Christmas, which stretches from Scrooge's social dream to the last chorus of the last bad song sung on Christmas Eve, is perhaps the deepest: it's a winter holiday meant for kids.

"Behold, I will tell you a mystery!" Handel's bass sings in the most beautiful of all Christmas pieces. Let me tell you finally a little puzzle. Years and years ago in England, in Oxford, when I was celebrating one more secularized Christmas with one of my many sisters, I heard a carol with a haunting tune and then kept in my head words from another carol. The tune of first the carol I found at last: it's a recent one by the fine English composer John

Rutter, "Born in a Cradle So Bare." The lines from the lyrics of
that other carol I have still never found: "The father sleeps and
can't imagine / The mother smiles and looks away / And in the
room where love is rocking / The baby knows but doesn't say, /
The baby knows but doesn't say."

FOUR

RECREATIONAL WINTER
The Season at Speed

I KEEP IN my wallet a five-dollar bill, a Canadian five-dollar bill, all blue on blue. It shows boys playing improvised hockey, skating on a frozen pond someplace in Ontario or Quebec or the Maritimes, an idealized Canadian lake, without adult supervision. It's one of my three wallet-talismans. (The others are two French fifty-franc notes from the years of my children's births.)

Like all nostalgic images of national spirit, the picture works best in the absence of evidence and experience. I've never been to that pond and the odds are overwhelming that you haven't either. But the belief in that pre-lapsarian pond is a crucial part of the mystique of hockey. Part of the mystique of hockey is to see it as something that grew up "naturally," beginning as a country game and coming to the city only to be first regimented and then commercialized until it eventually migrated to the United States, where — what else? — it got prostituted. It's a familiar story: country girl goes to city places, begins in wonder and ends as a whore. It's a tale told of a thousand things from folk tales to jazz and blues, and so no surprise that it is also told about the winter sport.

Our subject now is recreational winter, winter as a season of speed and play. Some by now familiar ideas, familiar people, familiar thoughts, even familiar patterns of explanation may appear. But my subject is also, more narrowly, ice-skating plain and simple, and you'd be right to see past the high-minded connections and allusions to a cruder motive. I see that picture and I ask a question: Is there a story about skating, about hockey, deeper than the myth, a truth beneath the tangle of stories that lie at the foundation of our fascination with it? Well, let's begin the search with a waltz — a skater's waltz, not the familiar one by Strauss, which is a bit oom-pah-pah, but a much later one by John Lewis for the Modern Jazz Quartet. It's a beautiful thing called "Skating in Central Park," taking as its subject just that activity. It surprises us, perhaps, by its languor and piquant charm, by its poignant slowness. We might even stop to think that this is one of the few titles to have created two wonderful works of art, a century apart: Winslow Homer's engraving from the 1860s and this jazz waltz. What do they have in common and how are they different; what do they, and ice-skating, so beautifully *mean*?

When I was working up these essays, knowing they would necessarily be stuffed tight with names and allusions, I made a little note for myself on each one, stating its central thematic premise, so that even if I went a bit off-centre I would never go too far off-theme. The first note, about Romantic winter, reminded me that the subject is the growth of resonances that winter began to evoke in the nineteenth century, how something went from being seen as bleak and bitter to sweet and sublime. The second one, on radical winter, was about how words get woven around Arctic expeditions. The third thematic note, about recuperative winter, was that its subject is the secularization of

Christmas and how that act of secularization invented a new idea of the sacred. For this fourth chapter, my thematic note to myself read in full: *Chance to talk at length about ice hockey.* So while I shall look sideways at sledding and sleighing and skiing, I shall concentrate most on the history and meanings of ice-skating—in part because it's the most varied and social of all the winter sports, in part because it points us towards the holy spot (or sport) and to the larger mystery of sports and national culture, and why watching people skate with sticks is for some of us as satisfactory an experience of theatre as any we know.

ONE OF THE things that struck the Romantics when they discovered winter was that while on the one hand it impeded comfort, it strangely accelerated *movement*. On skis and skates, on sleds and sleighs—and later, of course, on snowmobiles—you could actually move more quickly in winter in the cold countries than you could in the other seasons (a truth that would turn out to have momentous effects on history, when ski-mounted Russian soldiers, reposted to the Moscow front from Siberia, counterattacked the German invaders and their tanks in December 1941). It was a truth of pleasure too, one that Pushkin, for instance, celebrates with his poetry of sleighing—an imagery that moves on to Gogol's famous portrait near the end of *Dead Souls*, of Russia itself as a troika, racing through the snowy wastes while the rest of Europe watches:

And what Russian is there who doesn't love fast driving? How should his soul that yearns to go off into a whirl, to go off on a fling, to say on occasion, "Devil take it all!" How should his soul fail to love it? Is it not a thing to be loved, when one can sense in it something exaltedly wondrous? Some unseen power has caught you up on its wing and you are flying yourself, and all things are flying; some merchants are flying towards you, perched on the front seats of their covered carts. The forest flies on both sides of the road with its dark rows of firs and pines, echoing with the ring of axes and the cawing of crows. The whole road is flying, no one knows where into the unseen distance . . . The troika tears along, inspired by God! Where art thou soaring away to, Russia? Give me the answer! But Russia gives none. With a wondrous ring does the jingle bell trill; the air rent to shreds thunders and turns to the wind. All things on earth fly past, eyeing the troika and all the other peoples and nations stand aside giving it the right of way.

An image that is, to be sure, rather at odds with the stasis and corruption of the world that the novel details, filled with drunken landowners with absurd rosters of deceased slaves waiting to be sold for a tax advantage. (But then, surely, that play of stasis and sudden hysterical excitement is part of the national Russian style and national temperament.) The reality of troika riding in Russia in that period is probably better caught by the composer Hector Berlioz's account of an overnight sleigh ride during his concert tour in Russia in 1847:

The common assumption made in our temperate climes that Russian sledges, drawn by swift horses, skim smoothly over the snow as though crossing a frozen lake, has given us a rather agreeable idea of sledging as a method of travel. The truth is very different . . . Imagine a metal box, hermetically sealed yet subtly penetrable by the fine snow, which seeps in, powdering your face white. Imagine yourself shaken about in it, violently and almost without pause, rather as shot is shaken in a bottle to clean it. Imagine the resultant sharp contact with the casing of the sled. Imagine, on top of all that, a general sensation of malaise plus a powerful desire to vomit, which can fairly be called snow-sickness, from its strong resemblance to the state known to travelers by sea.

The same discovery takes place in Canada. Anna Brownell Jameson, if you recall, was the amazingly well-educated Anglo-Irish proto-feminist who came to Toronto in 1836 and in the course of a very unhappy marriage stayed for a momentous few years. Anna was also struck by the paradox that in December the social life of Upper Canada, as she knew it, instead of being confined and narrowed, village to village, suddenly opened up; the ice and snow allowed people to move rapidly from town to town, from place to place.

That winter could be complex and deep was news, but that it could be *fun* was news as well. You'll recall that one of the most important engines of the discovery of winter in the nineteenth century was the sense among the northern Romantics, in England and Germany and Russia alike, that they could identify the season with an escape from French rationalism. Winter was the pet season of the counter-Enlightenment. They saw winter as the opposite of spring, the place of instinct, the place of purity; the winter evening is a place of emotion and memory while spring and summer are seasons of reason and hope. And so the first Romantics didn't at first see sport, they didn't see movement, and they particularly didn't see ice-skating as social activity. They saw it as a soulful one, an escape into solitude: a kind of meditational aid, a way of escaping the social lies for the truth of Man Alone in Nature.

Now, ice-skating has been part of European culture for a remarkably brief time. Once again there's a kind of false spring of winter lore in the late seventeenth century that anticipates a more lasting one in our own time. Recall that at the beginning of that century the world, certainly the European world and probably the entire planet, becomes much, much colder for a brief time. Throughout Europe, rivers and ponds and canals all freeze up. There's a great frost in England in 1689, for instance, in which the entire Thames freezes for the winter. And by one of those strange coincidences in history, that's exactly the moment of the Glorious Revolution and the entrance of the Dutch as the English royal family.

One of the things the Dutch bring with them are their skates. Samuel Pepys writes in his diary for 1662: "to my Lord Sandwich's, to Mr. Moore . . . and then over the Parke (where I first in my life, it being a great frost, did see people sliding with their skeates, which is very pretty art)." And John Evelyn, that same year, notes "the strange and wonderful dexterity of the sliders on the new canal in St. James's Park . . . after the manner of the Hollanders, with what swiftness they pass, how suddenly they stop in full career upon the ice."

But ice-skating, like so many other aspects of winter, took hold of the European imagination only around the end of the eighteenth century. William Wordsworth's skill as an ice-skater was legendary among his friends — he was the Toller Cranston of the Lake District — and he offers a long passage on ice-skating in 1799, in his great *Prelude*, so far as I know the first extended description, much less poetic evocation, of a winter sport in all of

English literature. It's wonderful Wordsworthian poetry, and it describes his ice-skating in the evenings as a boy.

> . . . All shod with steel,
> We hissed along the polished ice in games
> Confederate, imitative of the chase
> And woodland pleasures — the resounding horn,
> The pack loud chiming, and the hunted hare.
> So through the darkness and the cold we flew,
> And not a voice was idle; with the din
> Smitten, the precipices rang aloud;
> The leafless trees and every icy crag
> Tinkled like iron; while the far distant hills
> Into the tumult sent an alien sound
> Of melancholy not unnoticed, while the stars
> Eastward were sparkling clear, and in the west
> The orange sky of evening died away.
> Not seldom from the uproar I retired
> Into a silent bay, or sportively
> Glanced sideway, leaving the tumultuous throng,
> To cut across the reflex of a star
> That fled, and, flying still before me, gleamed
> Upon the glassy plain; and oftentimes,
> When we had given our bodies to the wind,
> And all the shadowy banks on either side
> Came sweeping through the darkness, spinning still
> The rapid line of motion . . .

Wordsworth sums up the skaters' dilemma. On the one hand, he recognizes, in a way that might delight the current generation of evolutionary psychologists, that the thrill of skating is partly an atavistic, tribal thrill, recalling primitive pleasures: "games / Confederate, imitative of the chase / And woodland pleasures, — the resounding horn, / The pack loud chiming, and the hunted hare." The boys on the ice in Wordsworth's poem aren't, I think, consciously pretending to hunt; it's just that the act of ice-skating echoes all those other "games Confederate" in which people come together to lose themselves in a common purpose. It's the group action, the loss of self in the thrill of common action, that stirs him; but in the end, skating in winter allows him to escape the group — he finally finds a form of personal movement all by himself, spinning in the starlight. Ice-skating is for Wordsworth both a way to make yourself a captive of the wind and a way to escape from the world. "Behind me did they stretch in solemn chain, / Feebler and feebler, and I stood and watched / Till all was tranquil as a dreamless sleep."

And that idea is central to what winter sport gives us: a carved-out social space in which we find ourselves alone. On skates, we combine the pleasure of solitude with the virtue of energy. It's a common experience as much as a poetic idea: we arrive on the ice in company and find on the ice our selves. I know of no experiences quite like skating or sledding, in which one starts by feeling all together and ends by feeling all alone. There is, after all, no alone so *alone* as the alone of the downhill skier or the luger or even than the ordinary pond skater. The long-distance runner may be lonely but he is not alone: someone over his shoulder all the time, and crowds watching from the walkways. It takes an impulse to make a summer sport: you run or throw or catch in a meadow made by God that's just there. It takes *work* to make a winter one: you and your gang clear off the ice or ice up the track, build a ski lift or grab a blanket. (Even cross-country skiing, my own favourite, takes an elaborate preparation of winter woollens and careful waxing. Yet once you've prepared in common, you're soon isolated, alone.) This doubleness makes ice-skating something like a sacrament in the recreational winter of the nineteenth century. Its lesson is the double lesson of so much Romantic art: we dream of a tribe and end in a spotlight, search for community and end in solitude.

So when the early Romantic painters took up ice-skating, they took it up in Wordsworth's spirit, as a solitary meditational, ruminative act, focused above all on the single nighttime skater. And in the north — for Scots and Germans and even New Englanders — this led to a very peculiar and lovely and unintentionally comic genre of imagery: the painting or etching or engraving of a serious philosophical skater. You find that kind of imagery throughout Europe in the early Romantic period. In 1782 the American painter Gilbert Stuart portrayed the British MP Sir William Grant on skates, and we can actually see in the distance the (social) party the fine philosophical skater has fled in order to get in touch with his deeper nature.

You don't know which is more delightful, the dignity or the absurdity. Stuart, it seems, had agreed during his time in London to do a portrait of Grant, who announced on arriving at Stuart's studio that it was a better day for skating. He cajoled the young American out to the not-exactly-wilderness of St. James's Park, where he dazzled the ladies and the painter with his skill — until the ice began to crack and the painter had to help him escape. Stuart used the occasion for the portrait, elaborating his memories and perhaps his sketches of the occasion, and in *The Skater* produced his first real hit.

Yet it's not an image of winter energy, but more one of evening elegance, an image of what one art historian rightly called "Romantic melancholy." Skating, for Stuart's Grant, is a test of masculine dignity. The preacher or patriarch on skates shows his mettle exactly by testing his balance. Keep your dignity on skates and you can keep it anywhere.

In another wonderful portrait, painted around 1795, the Scottish artist Henry Raeburn, apparently influenced by Stuart's great success, shows a man of the cloth who is actually out on skates on a Scottish lake in the middle of this cold period. And though it looks to us as if he is skating very normally, untheatrically, this kind of assured skating — executed on a single stiff left leg and a confident leftward lean, brought off with the gaze firmly fixed outwards and seemingly indifferent — was unusual, highly prized, something worth painting. And yet he remains a Scottish minister, stern and severe and self-possessed. Stuart's Grant kept merely his dignity intact on skates; Raeburn's Presbyterian preacher actually keeps his divinity.

The most touching and funny of all these philosophical skating scenes involves what blossoms into a whole kind of subgenre of German Romantic art, showing the greatest poet of the period smugly demonstrating his mastery on winter ponds and river: Goethe on ice! There's a wonderful one, actually called *Goethe on Ice in Frankfurt, Germany*, from the 1860s, though obviously showing a scene from an earlier decade, where in the midst of a crowd of skaters Goethe takes a bow to them all, as the great poet he was, and his countrymen raise their winter hats to his grace.

An even better one — it may be my favourite of all modern winter images — dates from even earlier, from the hand of the painter Raab — *Johann Goethe Ice-skating in Frankfurt, Germany* — where you see Goethe not only on skates and on the ice but surrounded by admiring women, agog with admiration for the perfection of this poet who skates away in smug certainty, demonstrating his superiority to the things of the world, especially sex. He's lost, above it all, gliding in a Wordsworth-like reverie on ice — to the appropriate annoyance, one feels, of the women skaters watching, one of whom seems ready to throw a snowball at him.

So the first artistic use of ice-skating, and indeed winter sport, in the nineteenth century is not about social life. It's about solitary life. It's about the way in which skating can lead you into yourself, can lead you into a separate space — solitary and childlike in Wordsworth, rather smugly superior for Goethe, at least as Raab depicts him. You gain three inches and you glide and you're above it all. You have to do it well in order to get the new emotion, but getting the new emotion allows you to forget that you're doing it well. The subject of skating is balance, and achieving it on ice is a symbol of having achieved it in your soul. It's about the rejection of fear and falling — and even of femininity — in a sublime moment of exhibitionist equilibrium. It's the first image of the rock-concert kind. Poets and preachers throw their bodies to the wind, seemingly remote, and find their inner compass, while crowds of girls watch and wonder.

BUT IF ICE-SKATING begins as a solitary and poetic enterprise, by the middle of the century it transforms into something that is essentially social and overtly sexual. That wonderful engraving of Goethe on skates holds intimations of that transformation — though Goethe is in his own world, he is surrounded by girls who are desperate for him to pay attention to them, and they are ready to throw snowballs at him to make that happen. And when you begin to have urban and metropolitan skating in the middle of the century, that's what happens: skating becomes a form of sex, or at least of the social foreplay we call flirtation.

Technological advances helped make skating social and sexual. With the introduction of the one-piece skate — where the boot and blade are sewn together — in the 1860s, skating became less laborious than it had ever been: more people skated. But it is also a social change, and to trace its origins once again we find ourselves in Switzerland. As with winter landscapes, so with winter sports: the Alps are the hinge point.

Time spent in Switzerland was a product of the trains. You have to remember that by the time the railroads are in place in the 1840s, it was possible to leave London by 7.40am one day and find yourself comfortably in Switzerland by 7.00am the next. It was a twenty-four hour trip – or, put another way, it was only a twenty-four hour trip. A long day's journey but only a day, and in many ways more comfortable than the trips you would take now. And so, between the 1840s and the First World War, the Swiss resorts were, as John Houseman writes beautifully.

> A garden through which the moneyed middle-class journeyed incessantly in search of health and amusement . . . beneath racks that strained under loads of label covered cowhide luggage, leaning back on lace doilies pinned to seats of varicoloured dusty plush which at night were miraculously converted into beds by men in brown uniforms. They moved in well-ordered comfort between the resorts of Continental Europe . . . coming out of the early

table d'hote dinner while it was still light, Fraulein and I would pause to admire the translucent meringue castles topped with Swiss flags and the fabulous ice sculptures that rose glistening from long crowded buffets.

The Swiss resorts, Chamonix, St. Moritz, Lake Lucerne, were as central to this journey as those in Thailand and Amsterdam would be to their more uncomfortable but more far-ranging great-great grandchildren. (They went in search of health and release from intoxication; we, being healthier, go in search of it.) Switzerland was a winter place.

But though winter-themed, the travelling class still went to Switzerland mostly in the spring, when that basic rhythm of warm interior and sublime exterior was in balance. The shaping relationship, for Turner and Ruskin and the child all alike, was between the auberge where you spend the night and the Alps where you spent the day. Winter sports, skiing and outdoor skating and sledding called luge and the bobsled, remained quaint preoccupations of the locals in the off-season.

It was not till the winter of 1864 that a small, nameable quartet of Englishman were persuaded by their host that a winter holiday in Switzerland could be as fine as the usual spring alpine holiday – that you don't just have to go to Switzerland for those distant snow-cap't mountains, but that you could go in December or January and have a sporting experience, too, skiing and sledding and luging and skating. In early September of that year a St. Moritz hotelier named Johannes Badrutt made a bet with four British summer guests; Badrutt would pay for them to come all the way back to Switzerland from London that winter. If they liked a St. Moritz winter, as Badrutt thought they would, they could stay as long as they liked; if not, he would pay their way back. Since they would win either way, the four Englishmen took him up on the bet, arrived for Christmas – and stayed right through to Easter. Winter tourism was born through Badrutt's Bet. The four Englishmen stayed for the winter, and invented a new form of fashionable fun. (And though this story has the perfectly hollow ring of counterfeit history, it does seem to be true. Fashions have to start somewhere.)

Two things derive from this truth. One is that winter sports took on, despite the gray grizzle that passes for winter as the little ice age passed in Britain, a British character. Skiing, luging, bobsledding, and of course Alpine mountaineering – indeed, even the eccentric Canadian favourite of curling – all had British origins or were dominated by British athletes. Winter sports were British As late as the 1920s, the young Ernest Hemingway in Switzerland still sees luging and skiing as primarily English activities. "It is easy to understand," Hemingway wrote in the *Toronto Star* in 1922, "how the British have such a great Empire after you have seen them luge. "A great deal of the growth of winter sport in the nineteenth century involved questions of absorbing and then at times decisively rejecting a British model.

And, where the imagery and aura of skating in the early Romantic period were meditative and inner, by mid-century the imagery of skating, as it became "socialized" and took to cities, was rapidly becoming almost openly erotic and sexual. In the middle of the nineteenth century ice-skating is everywhere, far more than it is today; in every major European and North American city, people skate and someone makes pictures of them skating. Winslow Homer, the greatest of American artists, as early as the 1860s, on furlough from the Civil War, devotes himself to skating scenes in the newly created Central Park. Jules Chéret, the greatest of French poster-makers — and, through his creative dialogue with Georges Seurat, a contributor to Post-Impressionist style — cannot make enough posters for the Palais de Glace in Paris.

There's this incredible wealth of metropolitan urban skating activity from the middle of the nineteenth century, much more of it than we would now think. People skate in Central Park today, but you only have to look at the images to see on how much smaller a scale we skate now than our great-great-great-grandfathers and grandmothers did. There is no Palais de Glace, no ice palace left in Paris at all, and when the city fathers installed a little skating rink a few years ago outside the Hôtel de Ville, it was a five days' wonder. (Even a flat-footed Canadian in hockey sweater and skates making ice-splashing hockey stops was a sight.)

The reasons for the rise and subsequent fall of skating, I think, are extremely simple. It doesn't have much to do with the idea of the sublime; it doesn't even have very much to do with the idea of sports. It's all about sex. Ice-skating was one of the few things urban people could do in public as an acceptable form of flirtation and sexual display. When Central Park was built by Olmsted and Vaux in 1861 there were two separate areas for skating — one in front of what's now the Dairy and a ladies' pond over on the west side, not too far from where the Dakota is now. The ladies' pond was meant for ladies — it was in operation for about ten years and then was closed and later drained because not enough people wanted to skate there. The idea of there being a separate female pond was so against the purpose of skating that it was left virtually unused. The Great Rink, on the other hand, became a place where, hard as it is to believe, as many as thirty thousand people were said to come on a Saturday afternoon to skate or to watch.

And you only need to look at Homer's skating images from that time, his great woodcuts published regularly in *Harper's Weekly*, to see how much they are about fashion, how much they are about flirtation, how entirely they are about sex. Two women turn on skates, catching that Wordsworthian wind — only now they compare each other's fashionable hats and turn away in disdain. Men show off; women pretend to be impressed — the eternal circle of the selective lek. There's a wonderful Homer woodcut of a single girl on skates turning her head to look back over her shoulder in perfect come-hither seduction, made respectable by her neat little muff. That's a recurrent theme of ice-skating imagery in the nineteenth century: the girl looking back over her shoulder with a come-hither half-smile. It's the exact opposite, if you think of it, of Goethe's lofty stare in the early part of the century. Goethe was saying, *I'm above it all*; she's saying, *Come join me down here.*

To glide is to escape the normal bonds of the body, but it also makes us body-conscious. Skating, like ballet, is a virtuous stylization of sexual poses that subliminally restates them. Skating rinks in the nineteenth century served the purpose that health clubs and gyms serve now — they're places where, with impeccable motives, you can go and engage in wild flirtation and open body display. A sexual display is always acceptable when it's billed as hygienic and salubrious. Erotic acts and invitations are innocent when they're called exercise. (Even today, still photos of pairs skaters tend to be far more daringly and explicitly erotic than almost anything else that would be considered family entertainment.)

It's almost a rule: when overt sexuality is repressed, it finds a theatrical, public, stylized form for its expression. Suppression puts the enactment of desire on blades, whether it's the sexuality of young women in the nineteenth century or the sexuality of homosexual men in the twentieth. Toller Cranston, skating in a way that seemed flamboyant and even "effeminate," forced his desire on our attention without crying out its name: surreptitiously presented, it then became sanctioned by its beauty. It is no accident, as historians say, that so many of the great skaters of the mid-twentieth century were gay. As long as homosexuality was disapproved of, oppressed, or persecuted, homosexual flirtation got expressed in ice skating—just a part of the understood code of what skating was in the twentieth century. When the erotic impulse is suppressed, it puts itself on skates and offers as art what it is denied as affection. Once public show was allowed, however, and men could hold hands on the Mall, skating became just another sport. And once actual sex between unmarried people became socially acceptable, sometime in the 1920s, the energy fell away from ice-skating and the skating rink got moved to the periphery of the park—in every sense. Skating became again a thing the kids did.

This double move—away from sex and ever closer to it—is inevitable, as Freud would have said. We dam up the libido in wools and furs and steel and then release it in lengthened legs and heightened movement. This double action of the ice, which Pushkin recognized in his erotic poetry of winter, is a crucial part of our winter legacy. Winter cools us down, and then its energy heats us up.

THE INTERTWINING OF sex and skating has a third component: sport as an alternative to sex. Skating by the middle of the nineteenth century was being divided into two schools: the English style and the international style. The English style, long lost to us, was based on the forms of military drill and was an expression of military values and military discipline. The apotheosis of the English style was what was called "combination skating," which was an attempt to imitate on skates pure drill, the kind of thing we see in palace courtyards and parade grounds. It was stiff-legged, correct, and correctly attired; its goal was perfection of the figure traced on the ice and its practitioners went through the austere cadences of their routines with unsmiling dignity — a sort of militarized version of the Romantic reverie. As someone wrote at the time, the English skaters, even in romantic Switzerland, skated "for all the world, as though they were changing the guard at Buckingham Palace." Photographs of that sort of skating have an unintended *Monty Python* Ministry of Silly Walks look to them now: the tension between English stiffness and English will to action becomes a source of English eccentricity.

Then a man named Jackson Haines changed everything. A young American trained as a dancer, in the middle of the nineteenth century Haines took up skating, and he went to Europe to demonstrate a newly musicalized version of it. He invented the stunts and skills we associate with figure skating now: jumps, spins, arabesques, and pirouettes. He was never, curiously, much welcomed in America, in part because there weren't sufficient arenas for him to play in, and he was certainly never welcomed in England. But he became a sensation in Europe, particularly in Vienna and Germany, for this new style that we now call figure skating. Although "perfect control of the body and limbs is what is aimed at" in the English school, he thought that skating, as he wrote once, "should become an art rather than a science." The English school persisted alongside the new school that Haines had founded—but it went in a very separate direction; in 1892, when a guide to skating was published in London, it was divided neatly into two parts, one about British style and the other devoted to Haines's international school.

By the end of the century the urge towards team sports and spectator sport becomes very, very powerful. People begin to pay to watch other people compete. And that's true all throughout the West: it's true about the invention of organized soccer in Britain, the spread of rugby in France, and the growth of baseball from cricket and rounders to Big Sport in the United States. Now we take this so much for granted—sports 'r' us—that it is difficult for us to see how peculiar, how unusual, this new thing was. As the great Caribbean thinker C. L. R. James reminds us in his seminal study of cricket and national feeling, *Beyond a Boundary*, for almost fifteen hundred years, since ancient times, sport as a national or civic adhesive had largely vanished. Then, very suddenly, in the last part of the nineteenth century it returns: "Golf was known to be ancient [but] the first annual tournament of the Open Championship was held only in 1860. The Football Association was founded only in 1863. It was in 1866 that the first athletic championship was held in England . . . in the United States the first all-professional baseball team was organized in 1869." And on and on: team sport is an entirely and thoroughly *modern* phenomenon.

Many social forces had to come together to make the transformation of team sports happen. In one way it was a sign of increased "solidarity" among working people and of the birth of that other new thing, the weekend. People who labour together on Friday play together on Sunday. Department stores sponsored team sports, factories sponsored team sports, newspapers sponsored team sports. In other ways it was a mirror of the new mass militarism. Even the move against professionalism and spectator sports — the cult of Olympic amateurism sponsored by Baron Coubertin — involved an appeal not to pleasure but to morality. There was a whole rhetoric of purification and renewal attached to team sports, specifically anti-sexual. The Winter Olympics, which began in its current form in the 1920s but was foreshadowed by "Nordic games" at the turn of the twentieth century, with its cult of amateurism, with its insistent national regimentation, also involved a cult of implicit militarism. Organized team sport was a way of escaping this dangerous flirtation with freelancing that you could find in the middle of the century. You lost yourself not in your inner self but in a common cause.

And so you even begin to get a kind of rebound Romanticism — a rebound Romanticism in which people begin to go back to the idea of winter sport not as an arena for social engagement but as a place to test your morale, to test your endurance, to test, in short, your courage. One sees this, for instance, after the First World War in Ernest Hemingway's dispatches on winter sports for the *Toronto Star*. All the rhetoric that Hemingway soon after imbues the bullfight first shows up in his writing on luge and sledding. That cult of the lonely individual, the courageous individual, taking up sports in winter takes an ugly turn in the 1930s, when it becomes essential to the ideology of Nazism. One of the images that occurs in Nazi propaganda posters is that of the solitary skier or solitary skater, the Nordic man who, braving the elements, is able to find himself as a singular figure outside the corrupting influences of the cosmopolis, the corrupting influence of the Jewish city.

But for the most part team sports involved finding a complex balance between solidarity, bringing people together in a common culture, and rivalry, dividing people through a common cult of competition. Above all it was moved by that curious and fragile but utterly real thing we call identity. We play and watch sports above all to connect — with our friends, our neighbours, our city, and even our country. In a modern time, when those things are uncertain, up for definition — Who are our neighbours? What's the nature of our city? What is our country all about? — a game is the easiest way to say what our identity is, who we really are. Team sports are always a form of mock warfare, but with both terms having equal weight. Sports are a form of warfare, clan against clan and city against city and nation against nation. But we play them because, well, they're play. They're also a parody of warfare. They mock the passions they exemplify. Their intensities and energies stop just short of murder, just this safe side of rage. The whistle blows and we shake hands and plan to play again tomorrow. Where politics highlight social difference and try to end it, sports dramatize social difference and then perpetuate it — the Habs need the Leafs in order to persist as the Habs. Stylizing tribal passions, team sports help us transcend them, or at least treat them as a game, as in every sense a sport. And that leads us at last, and blessedly, to ice hockey.

Ice hockey is a peculiar passion among the world's sports. In America , it is regarded as having a "dross of brutal messiness," in John Updike's phrase – as a blue-collar sport, most notable for its toothless warriors and its acceptance of fist-fights as a normal part of the game. Outside America and the Northern countries, it

is one of the most minor of team sports, a chilly footnote to association football. Only in Canada, and in Russia, the Czech
Republic, and to some degree in Sweden and Finland, where it
vies with the other winter sports, does it have any primacy. In
Canada, to be sure, it is close to a national religion.

Its rules are simple and easily explained. Played with a puck
– a rock-hard disk of frozen rubber – it is also played with sticks,
like field hockey. As with association football, it has two opposing
goals, a mix of forwards and defenders; the forwards, or strikers,
are expected to be fast and skilled; the defenders large and rug-
ged. Goalkeeping is even more essential to the ice game than it is
in football – since the goal is smaller, and the scoring is higher,
the presence of a skilled or just lucky goalkeeper, more usually
called a goalie, most often makes the difference, in championship
play at least.

Its professional history is simple. The National Hockey League
began to coalesce from a number of amateur teams just before the
First World War, and for more than fifty years remained a closely
held six-team league, with franchises only in the two capitals of
Canada, Montreal and Toronto, and four northern American cities
– Detroit, Boston, New York and Chicago – and the players
almost without exception all Canadians. Only in the late 1960s
did ice hockey teams begin to proliferate throughout the Sunbelt
regions of the United States, as part of a constant, only fitfully
successful effort to create a larger "footprint" for the game in
America – with the end the none-too-worthy goal of getting a
bigger television contract for the league's owners. Meanwhile,
"amateur" hockey had grown in Eastern Europe, particularly in
the old Soviet Union, after the Second World War, and by the
nineteen sixties, the Russians dominated Olympic play. Only in

1972 was there a confrontation between the Russians and the Canadian pros – the so-called eight-game Summit Series – and though Team Canada eventually won the series on a last second goal by a previously obscure player named Paul Henderson, there was no question that the fast-paced, expertly-timed Russian game was the superior version. (The series had the effect in Canada that the Hungarian victory in football in 1953 did in England; it was a clear sign that the game had altered irrevocably, to the disadvantage of the inventing country.) With the fall of the Iron Curtain, Russian and Czech players, trained in the more precise European style, began to populate, and even dominate, North American professional hockey. The finest North American players – Wayne Gretzky, generally though to be the finest player ever to enter the game, is a good instance – played an ever-more European game, dependent more on having superior vision of the ice and intelligent passing than on the end-to-end rushes and inspired physical play that had distinguished great Canadian players of earlier generations, among them Gordie Howe and the great Maurice " The Rocket" Richard.

IN SOME WAYS ice hockey is just one more of those team sports that emerges in the 1860s and '70s, in the orbit of the British Empire. The first recorded games are played in the 1870s, typical of the British imperial cult of sports that spreads cricket to Trinidad and soccer to South Africa. Field hockey, one might think, but iced over. No more moving or positive story of imperialism exists than the spread of sport: most hallucinatory with cricket, where the white trousers and gentlemen's manners now decorate a sport enlivened by Caribbean energy and Indian passions; most universal with soccer; most amateur with rugby.

Ice hockey is also a peculiar hybrid, many sports brought together into one. One thing seems certain: far from being a simple rural sport, a kind of pastoral child of winter and ponds, it is above all a city sport, and it's made in the strange crucible of the growing Canadian cities. Through city pressures and city privileges, the game we know gets made, and in particular it gets forged from the melting pot of Irish, English, and French attitudes in my hometown of Montreal.

Now, I'm well aware that other towns claim hockey for their own, including Kingston and Halifax. So I assure you that it is pure coincidence, forced on me by fact, that I claim the birth of hockey for Montreal, and also claim the particular stable of that birth to be my own alma mater, McGill University — and, more narrowly, also call the labour bed of the birth of hockey the six-square-block area between Sherbrooke and St. Catherine streets and Stanley and Drummond, where I happened to grow up. What can I say? It happens to be so, and there is nothing to be done about it. (Seriously, the most persuasive account of this moment points to its home there, and we owe it to the Laval University historian, Michel Vigneault, who has shown in detail how it happened. Obviously hockey grew up in many niches and in many parts of the country, but if modern hockey was born in any one place, it was in Montreal, and the game still bears many marks of the forceps.)

The earliest records we have of a game of ice hockey come from the 1870s and '80s around McGill, but it seems quite possible that the winter game was brought there from Nova Scotia. (There is a whole other argument that it began in Kingston, but people from Kingston who wanted to have the Hockey Hall of Fame there seem to have invented that one.) Certainly it was a young Nova Scotia–raised engineer, John George Alwyn

Creighton, working in Montreal as the Grand Trunk Railroad was being built, who first consolidated the rules of hockey at McGill in 1873.

The strange thing about ice hockey is that, while it looks as if it belongs to the larger family of games that share its name, it doesn't. It looks like lawn hockey; it must be like field hockey; it has something in common with polo — it's one of those games you play by knocking a ball around with a stick until it goes into a goal. It even seems to belong to the same family of sports as association football, what we call soccer.

But Creighton was not a field-hockey player, nor was he a soccer player (soccer was a workingmen's sport in any case). He was a *rugby* player, and hockey for him was a way of extending the rugby season into the winter months. The scene of his invention was the old Victoria Skating Rink in Montreal, the first large purpose-built rink in Canada, between Drummond and Stanley, where on a cold March day Creighton is said to have been heard hollering out rugby rules to the players of the new sport. (Lord Stanley saw his first ice hockey game at the Victoria Rink.)

As someone once said, the central point of rugby is to survive it. And that's where an ambiguity begins. Ice hockey is a hybrid, even a freak — what botanists call in a very different sense a "sport" — seeming to belong to the association football family, it also belongs to the rugby family, while the other contact sport that feeds into it is lacrosse — also an "association" game, one in which team play in passing is paramount, and it is also the other acceptably violent sport of the time. (The hockey rule, not held in common with association football kinds of games, that there is space behind the goal is a carryover from lacrosse, and it gives hockey a distinctly strategic character.) The DNA of hockey, its combination of being the most flashily brilliant and speedy of games and at the same time the most brutal of contact sports, comes from that doubleness — from the reality that what Creighton was trying to create when he first codified the rules of hockey in 1873 was a form of rugby on ice, played according to rules inflected by lacrosse.

Hockey's rules have changed and evolved since then. When Creighton first invented (or consolidated) those rules, there were no forward passes — just like rugby, where you can carry the ball or shift it backwards but can't pass it ahead. Not only its explicit rules but also its implicit spirit recall that brutal and yet most gallant of games. And, like rugby, hockey is (or pretends to be) a self-policing sport. Rugby is brutal, but pointed as much to the shared party after as the triumph of one team. It rewards comradeship, penalizes selfishness, and has its own unwritten internal rules to mitigate its violence. There are right ways to tackle and wrong ways, and since the point of the sport is that after-party, the rules are enforced by the social group. So hockey — both grim and graceful, brutal as much as balletic — belongs both to the family of association sports, of control sports, and to the rugby family of collision sports. Its history, in a sense, is the struggle to see which of its two parents will determine its legacy.

TWO PARENTS . . . AND two solitudes? We think of that time and that place — Montreal at the end of the nineteenth century — as one of two parallel encampments, of a British and a French establishment living apart from each other in a kind of gloomy splendour, the French establishment dominated by an extremely hidebound pre–Quiet Revolution Roman Catholic Church, while the English-speaking Scottish establishment, gloomier even than its counterparts back in Scotland, has McGill University at its centre. As a boy I recall the twin grey cathedrals of those cultures — the Dominion/Sun Life Building and St. Joseph's Oratory — dominating the skyline of that beautiful mountain-island city. (Both were built a bit later, but they still exemplify the embattled bulwark culture of those who made them).

In one way we expect sports to mirror the social arrangement of their society. But sports are a hammer as much as a mirror, breaking social conventions as they invent them. Baseball was shaped by nineteenth-century Irish and German immigrants to the United States, who gave the game its character, but it later acted as a conduit for Jews and Italians, who entered the game to take on Americanness. Sports preserve the pressures of the era that they're made in, but they alter some of them too. Hockey reflected the social order of late-nineteenth-century Montreal, but it disturbed that order too, in healthy and invigorating ways.

For there was a kind of free-valence atomic shell at play in Montreal life at that time. Between the pious French and the prosperous English stood the Irish, who occupied two positions at once, in a way that would prove potent for the making of the winter game. As English-speakers they were in one way aligned with the anglo elite. But they were also Roman Catholics, and that meant they were educated with (and sometimes married to and buried alongside) the French. To be Irish was to have a kind of double identity. On the one hand you belonged to the English-speaking minority and on the other hand you despised your masters in the English-speaking minority; you were a fellow worshipper with the French-speaking majority but at the same time you were reluctant to identify with the French underclass.

When you played hockey, you wanted to beat the Brits at McGill . . . but the way to do it might be to look for help from the francophones across the hall. And so the Irish played a central role, in some ways *the* central role, in the invention of ice hockey. The old flag of Montreal, which showed an impress quartered among the French, Irish, Scots, and English, was exclusivist (we would now need to include Greeks and Portuguese and Jews and Haitians) but it was not false. Ethnic rivalry, and coalitions of convenience, made a city culture.

Hockey, as we've seen, is first played by the students of McGill as winter rugby, and as members of the anglo elite in Montreal, they begin with a monopoly on it. But then the Irish kids down in Pointe Saint-Charles need a winter sport to play as well, and so they form an Irish hockey club called, naturally, the Shamrocks. At this time the idea of Catholics playing sports with non-Catholics is one that the Catholic Church in Quebec tries hard to discourage. Indeed, the whole idea of sport is frowned on by the Church hierarchy, who actually try to ban tobogganing in 1885. As a consequence, organized hockey is slow to spread among the francophone majority. Yet, because there is a kind of implicit alliance between the Irish and the French in Montreal, based on their common Catholic education, you begin to get French-Canadian kids playing hockey for Irish teams.

It's not at the street level that hockey gets passed to the francophone community — the neighbourhoods are still too separate for that — but at the Catholic college level, at Collège Sainte-Marie and Mont-Saint-Louis and Saint-Laurent, and then largely through the tutelage of the Irish students. In 1894 and 1895, though the student body at Collège Sainte-Marie is heavily francophone, the hockey team at Sainte-Marie is entirely Irish, and only slowly does it begin to become more and more francophone. The first kids who come to play are from mixed marriages, and even today historians have a hard time being certain if a name represents a francophone, mixed, or Irish family background. The Kent brothers, Stephen and Rosaire, for instance, play for various teams at the beginning of the century, but Rosaire, with his French first name, seems to play exclusively for French teams, while his brother Stephen goes back and forth. The circumstances, at least the sporting ones, are more mixed than the clichés of solitude quite allow for.

Although hockey is passed from the Irish to the French in the colleges, the game seems in francophone neighbourhoods to have some of the aura of a street sport: a game played at high speed for fun with an emphasis on individual skill — much like African-American street and playground basketball in U.S. cities in the 1940s and '50s. An awareness grows that on the French-Canadian side people play with a particular kind of flair, and eventually two teams, the National and the Montagnards, emerge (the Montagnards began as a snowshoeing club, which gives them their name). The new clubs are successful enough to get their own rink in the East End — at the corner of Duluth and Saint-Hubert, just north of Sherbrooke Street — and become the first Quebecois hockey teams.

One of the fascinating things that happens in the history of hockey in Montreal through these crucial crucible years is that there is a constant awkward dance among the Shamrocks, the Montagnards, and the National for the allegiance of their players. In 1898 the Montagnards include a Proulx and a Mercier, but also a Cummings and a Conrad. If anyone wanted to make a great Canadian movie — *the* great Canadian movie — it would be all about the hockey love triangle among the Montagnards, the

Thomas Nast invented our modern image of Santa Claus as the presiding deity of the Union cause, as seen in his 1865 illustration for *Harper's Weekly, Image of Santa Claus and St. Nicholas.*

For Nast, Santa brought comfort to the northern troops, toys to northern children, and a reminder of joyous abundance in a time of brutal loss. Above, Nast's *Christmas Eve* (1862); below, *Santa Claus in Camp* (1862).

Ice-skating is a test of masculine poise, as seen in Gilbert Stuart's *The Skater, Portrait of William Grant* (1782). Keep your dignity on skates and you can keep it anywhere.

It's hard enough to keep your dignity on skates — Henry Raeburn's Presbyterian preacher, seen here in *Reverend Robert Walker Skating on Duddingston Loch* (c. 1795), actually keeps his divinity.

Goethe on ice: the great German poet skates away in smug certainty, demonstrating his superiority to the things of the world, especially sex and snowballs, in J. I. Raab's *Johann Goethe Ice-Skating in Frankfurt, Germany* (c. 1850s).

Skating on the Ladies' Skating-Pond in the Central Park, New York

Winslow Homer saw New York's exciting new Central Park as a lek for flirtation, fashion competition — see those flying ribbons! — and unimpeded sexual display, as shown in his 1860 wood engraving *Skating on the Ladies' Skating-Pond in the Central Park, New York* (above) and 1866's *Our National Winter Exercise — Skating* (below).

Homer's *Cutting a Figure* (1871) shows a woman on skates with a come-hither glance over her shoulder — an image central to the advance of the idea of women as knowing creatures in control of their own allure.

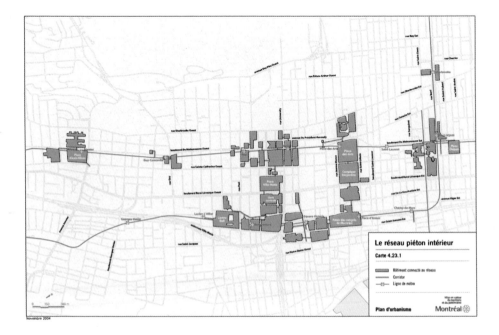

By our own time, the underground city of Montreal, spurred by its brutal winter and godfathered by the planner Vincent Ponte, has become a vast, alternative urban universe.

Shamrocks, and the McGill Redmen in Montreal between 1900 and 1903. On the one hand all the prejudice and bigotry that kept these communities apart still existed, and at the same time there was an irresistible attraction, through the medium of this new sport of hockey, towards assimilation and joint effort—towards collaboration, in every sense. Sport, as I said, acts as a mirror for our divisions, but it also acts as a hammer that destroys them, if for no higher reason than that the tribal urge to defeat the enemy in surrogate warfare is stronger even than ordinary social bigotry.

At a crucial moment in 1903, two of the stars of the Montagnards, Louis Hurtubise and Théophile Viau, were incited to "cross over" and play with the Irish Shamrocks, who were in a senior, professional league while the francophone team continued to play in the intermediate league. The potential betrayal was a six days' wonder in Montreal. Could these kids leave the Montagnards for the Shamrocks—a much more visible team, playing as they did in the Victoria Arena—and do so without betraying their national identity? True, they would help the Shamrocks beat the rival English teams, but they would also be crossing over from one allegiance to another, from east to west. For a week or two Hurtubise and Viau, a speedy winger and a rock-solid defenceman, had the whole weight of national identity on their shoulders: if they left the Montagnards they would in effect become symbolic Irishmen; if they stayed with the Montagnards they would remain ghettoized within the narrow precincts of the French-Canadian, Church-dominated culture and remain intermediates forever. We can only imagine the pressure on these two kids—improve your lot or declare your loyalty?

If you were making this movie in anglophone Canada, you

would have Hurtubise and Viau play with the Shamrocks, where they would Overcome Obstacles, and then all would band together to beat some American team. And if you were making the movie in Quebec you would have Viau and Hurtubise, after their flirtation with false anglo Irish glory — room here for a lovely Franco-Irish romance — go back to the Montagnards to assert their national identity in face of the temptations of assimilation. And if you were making a real documentary about what actually happened . . . they would take turns, playing on both teams at once, in the best Canadian way. For that seems to be what did actually happen: the best surmise in a murky story seems to be that they played a bit for one team and then a bit for the other. Canadianly, they found a compromise that involved never actually having to choose, keeping a dual identity and playing occasionally for both sweaters. The controversy does not so much come to a crisis and climax as just drift away in the cold winter air.

And in a broader sense, this sinuous unfolding compromise of styles and skaters sneaking back and forth across lines, never resolved but routinely companionate, is what gave hockey its identity. It was the merging of manners — the rugby-based style of the McGill team; the very rough-and-tumble, brutal, and in some ways brutal style of the Shamrocks; and the increasingly pass-oriented creative style of the Montagnards (what we call river hockey, though really born on frozen back-alley rivulets) — that gave composite hockey its strong identity.

In 1909, when my own beloved Montreal Canadiens are invented, they are, I will say to my great disappointment, far from being a kind of growth upwards from the Montreal street, a straightforward commercial enterprise on the part of English

businessmen who want to find a way of getting the dash and allegiance of the Montagnards without actually having to pay the
kids who are on the Montagnards. So the Canadiens are invented
as an imitation national team, as a kind of exploitation of the
loyalty and allegiance that the indigenous team has already
invented. (The Habs do wear, briefly, the striped rugby-style uni-
forms that were associated with the Montagnards; these were
later revived in their centennial season, perhaps as a tribute. I
wear one now to their games.)

That's how pro hockey is made, with all the elements that we
can still see today. It is in part an improvisational game played on
a frozen street, in part a brutal game of rugby at high speed, in
part a form of soccer on ice. All these elements get mixed with
residual British ideas of fair play and self-policing schoolyard justice, which produce both the long handshake lines at the end of
playoff games and the sometimes ugly sense that the players
should settle it themselves — a sense unknown to the supposedly
more anarchic but actually more authoritarian American games,
where one punch gets you thrown out by the ref. Hockey is both
a city sport and a clan sport, a modern melting-pot sport that
retains an archaic tang of *my gang here versus your gang there.* The
most creative of sports that a single original mind can dominate,
it is also the most clannish, most given to brutal tribal rules of
insult and retribution. And it is the play — the compromise, one
might say — between clan and creativity that still gives it its character now. It's still this game, with its tightly wound strands of
tripartite DNA, that we love.

WHY DO WE love it? Why is this game so good when it's not being
degraded and diluted by greed, violence, and stupidity? Hockey is

not in my blood, but it is in my sense of the beautiful.

Now, I am a sports fan. Those who know me best will tell you that I am a sports fan almost before I am anything else, before I am a scholar or student, almost before, or more than, I am a writer. I would play every sport if I could, though I can't, and I watch all sports because I can. If it moves, has a score and a man in stripes with a whistle following it, I am there. I was at every Montreal Expos home opener for twenty years; my first piece in *The New Yorker* was about them, and there is still a hole in my heart where they once lived. I have followed the New York Jets in American football for forty years and blog about them intensely every week during the season. Basketball, the native sport of my adopted city of New York, is one I've followed since I moved there, and I would say unhesitatingly that the most spectacular athletes I have ever seen are Julius Erving and Michael Jordan. Nor do my passions end at the ocean's edge. For me the most thrilling walk in the world is along London's King's Road from Sloane Square to Stamford Bridge on a grey Saturday in early spring to watch Chelsea play. My heart follows the French national football team from World Cup failure to World Cup triumph, and certainly if I were asked to name the most amazing game of my experience, I would unhesitatingly answer that it was watching France beat the New Zealand All Blacks in the World Cup of rugby in 1999.

So, I like sports. I really do. But of all these games to watch and play — to play by proxy, which is what true watching is — the most interesting, rewarding, consistently entertaining, difficult, and beautiful is the winter game, ice hockey — when it is played well, as it is too rarely. This estimation, I recognize, of the primacy of ice hockey as spectacle and sport is rare, pretty much limited to Canadians and Russians and adulterated, it must be said, by what John Updike called a "dross of brutal messiness" that hangs onto the sport too. So I want to take a few minutes to show why in this odd judgement I am right, and also why, on the whole, no one else knows it. (That dross of brutal messiness that the great golf-lover saw in it is, as I hope we've seen, in part the echo of old city-clan rivalry, made salubrious by being stylized.)

It seems to me there are two things that make hockey the greatest of all games. One is rooted in what it gives to the players and the other in what it gives to its fans. For the player — and for us as vicarious players — it offers the finest theatre in the world to display the power of spatial intelligence and situational awareness. *Spatial intelligence* is a term that the Harvard psychologist Howard Gardner was the first to popularize. His point was that body is inseparable from mind, attitude from analysis, and that there are many kinds of smartness. There is the familiar IQ-test analytic intelligence, but there are also emotional intelligence, social intelligence, and spatial intelligence: the ability to grasp a changing whole and anticipate its next stage. It's the ability to make quick decisions, to size up all the relationships in a fast-changing array and understand them. A related notion is that of situational awareness: a heightened consciousness of your sur-roundings and both the intentions of the people around you and their anticipated actions.

Well, hockey, obviously, which is played at incredibly high speed, reveals and rewards situational and spatial intelligence at a degree of difficulty that no other sport possesses. So much so that the greatest of all hockey players, Wayne Gretzky, had, besides his other significant skills as a fine-edge skater, almost nothing else that he's specifically good at. That is his gift — the gift of spatial and situational intelligence: knowing what's going to happen in three seconds, anticipating the pattern approaching by seeing the pattern now, sussing out the goalie's next decision and Jari Kurri's or Luc Robitaille's eventual trajectory in what would be a single glance if a glance were even taken. Gretzky is the extreme expression of the common skill the game demands.

To watch him behind the net was to see stasis rooted in smarts. I recall games (one in particular, late in his career, against the Canadiens stands out; you can still find it on YouTube) in which he would position himself there, waiting for the other team to make a move. If you went after him he would put the puck perfectly on the stick of the open man. If you left him there he would wait, and perhaps try a wraparound or find a free winger as the patterns of the power play wove and unwove in front of him. It depended on supreme skill held in tactful abeyance — and it was a demonstration that he also scores who only stands and waits.

Anyone who has kids who play hockey knows the phenomenon: there are big, strong kids and smaller, weaker kids — and then there is always one kid who "sees the ice," who, in the midst of all the flubbed passes and scraped shins and sudden falls, grasps where the play is going next. Hockey is the one game in which, as a hockey-playing savant of my acquaintance says, a good mind can turn a game upside down.

In no other sport can a quality of mind so dominate as in the supposedly brutal game of ice hockey. Hockey is the one game where an intelligence can completely overthrow expectations. (When Gretzky recognized his successor in the still-adolescent Sidney Crosby, it was exactly that quality he was recognizing: not athleticism, but insight.) Yes, no doubt soccer rewards similar skills. A Johan Cruyff or an Eric Cantona has similar situational awareness and spatial intelligence, while we grow disgusted with superior players — like the shoulda-been-great Brazilian Ronaldo — who lack it; but there are eleven men on a soccer pitch and maybe two goals in a game, and the whole thing, despite the sporadic show of "pace," proceeds at a walk, sometimes accelerating to a jog.

ALL SPORTS ENTERTAIN us in part because of the thrill of watching a great athlete do what we can't, even if what he or she's doing is in part a mental exercise. Our empathetic engagement — what a close female friend of mine (whose uncle is actually in the Hockey Hall of Fame) calls "pitiful vicarious identification" or "the sad armchair act of pretending you're doing what you're actually watching" — with the players is key. But sports also entertain us as forms of drama. We get engaged, even in the absence of a single great player or performance, with the way the game tells a thrilling and unpredictable narrative woven by ten or twenty players at once. A great game is a great show, and it's also a great story. What makes those stories great is when they're unpredictable but not unjust — uncharted enough that there's no certainty of the result but organized enough that the result does not seem to be pure chance.

I think by now most of us have heard, however vaguely, something about the branch of mathematics called game theory. It's a way of understanding competitions that began with the great mathematician John von Neumann at the end of the 1940s and has since spread and conquered the world, or at least many academic disciplines, particularly economics and some of the more hard-ass parts of political science. Game theory attempts to mathematically capture behaviour in strategic situations, games, in which an individual's success in making choices depends on the choices of others. Anyone who has seen the movie *A Beautiful Mind* knows about John Nash and his equilibrium, and the more general notion that you can understand many social phenomena in the world if you see them as simple games rooted in guessing and outguessing your opponent's plans.

The funny thing about game theory is that, though it has been used to explain everything from economics to nuclear warfare, it's very rarely used to explain *games* — or at least not sports. And yet when you think about it, part of the pleasure we take in sports has everything to do with game theory, which has exactly to do with questions of how much we know, how much our opponents know, how much they know of what we know, and so on.

I am far too innumerate to even attempt a rigorous analysis of this sort, but I do think it can be enlightening to play with a few of its key concepts. One concept opposes open-information (or perfect-information) games against ones with closed, or imperfect, information. Chess is probably the most famous instance of an open-information game. When you're playing chess, you have all the information the other player has; nothing is concealed from you, and so there are truly never any surprises in the strategic sense. There are no hidden rooks.

On the other hand, old-fashioned five-card draw poker is a completely hidden or closed-information game. You don't know what's in your opponent's hand, so you have to guess on the basis of their behaviour and your knowledge of their past playing patterns what they might be holding in their hand right now. It's a game of deduced intention but also of inferred information. The best games — the games that people seem to enjoy most — offer some kind of equilibrium between a small sum of hidden information and a larger sum of open information held in tension. In

Texas hold-'em, the most popular of poker games, there are five shared cards — a lot of open information — and a crucial two cards' worth of closed information.

Team sports, which are both athletic contests and strategic ones, can be ranked along the same dimensions. Basketball, for instance, in some ways comes closest to being an open-information sport. Plays are limited, surprises are unimportant — no one basket is so significant that it is worth over-planning to achieve it, and even if you could, it wouldn't matter that much. What matters are trends, tendencies, and small tactical victories — real strategic surprise is relatively limited. The great basketball coach Phil Jackson ran his famous triangle offence with the Lakers, and with the Bulls before them. It requires tactical discipline, but the other team always knows what he's doing; it's a question of whether they can do it more efficiently and consistently than you can defence it. (The key event in basketball, foul shooting, is purely mechanical, and a matter, not trivial, of consistency alone.)

Pro football, on the other hand, is a good example of something closer to a closed-information sport: you have a series of particular strategic plans that you invent in secret and that you then spring on your opponent. That's why football rewards coaches like the great Bill Walsh, whose genius was not for tactical stability but for strategic innovation and surprise — half the playing time is actually spent watching people plan in secret. In the '82 Super Bowl, Walsh pulled a single play, designed to freeze a Bengals linebacker, from his script for a winning touchdown. That he had a script is proof of the partly closed nature of the game. And baseball is more like hold-'em poker: everything's evident except the hole card of the pitch that's about to be thrown.

Now, hockey looks, when you watch it with an unpractised eye, like an open-information sport. It looks like wild improvisation with no strategic plan underneath — a series of instinctive reactions to bouncing pucks and sliding players. (When people say they can't see the puck, I think what they really mean is that they can see it but they just can't see its *point*, its purpose in travelling. The game appears to be simply a brutal series of random collisions in which the invisible puck somehow sporadically ends up in the net.) But the more closely you observe the game, the more you see that it's kind of the Texas hold-'em of the world's spectator sports: there's a great deal that's open, but crucial elements are buried or cloaked and are revealed only afterwards to the eye of experience and deeper knowledge. There are hole cards in hockey, and some of the fun of being a fan is learning to look for them.

Some of this is plain in the inordinate effect a man with a plan can have on a hockey team; the defensive system that Jacques Lemaire installed with the Devils could take a mediocre team and make it into a champion. The trap, or shell, is tedious but it's wonderfully effective, and unlike the triangle offence it's hidden, in the sense that it takes place so quickly, and demands so many rapid adjustments, that I have found even experienced hockey fans have a hard time describing the way it works. The tension between the obvious givens and hidden hole cards is true as well at a more granular level of the game.

Just think about the difference between taking a penalty in soccer and the shootout in hockey. The penalty in soccer is something that academic game theorists have actually looked at in detail: what's the best technique, they ask, the optimal strategy for the shooter in soccer to pursue when he's got a penalty shot to take? It's a play of minds, because the goalkeeper has to anticipate what the shooter will do, and the shooter, the goalkeeper. Shoot left? Shoot right? High? Low? And the theorists have discovered that the optimal strategy is . . . just to blast away. The goal is so big and the goalkeeper so small that the shooter is much better off just blasting to the middle rather than trying to pick a corner.

So, predictably, the optimal strategy for the goalkeeper in the soccer shootout is just to stay in place, not dive to either corner — though it's very hard for a goalkeeper to summon the discipline to do that. And so you have this situation in soccer where basically any kind of strategic planning doesn't pay. In the shootout in hockey, you have exactly the same confrontation between shooter and goalkeeper, but the shooter just blasting away or the goalie staying in place is never going to work. There are just too many dimensions in play — the shot takes place in depth and in motion, not from a fixed spot — and the odds between goalie and shooter are too closely matched. The shootout in hockey puts a premium on having a hole card: an idea, a strategy, a plan in advance, unknown to the opposition. And the goalie needs to respond to that kind of strategic initiative, that kind of creativity, with aggressive anticipation. The obvious play, which benefits you in a sport such as soccer, penalizes you in hockey.

Though it may seem as if the great goals in hockey history were chance events, stray moments seized by opportunistic players, the truth is that as you understand the sport more deeply you can see that there is a kind of hidden strategic reservoir, almost a morality play, a *history*, behind every great goal in the game. When I think about the great goals that have been scored in hockey, the famous goals in my own lifetime, I see an element of historical pattern and strategic consequence in each of them. I think, for instance, of probably the most famous goal in my own fanship, the goal that Guy Lafleur scored in 1979 in the famous "too many men on the ice" game, the Montreal Canadiens and the Boston Bruins in the seventh game of the Stanley Cup semi-finals. What's remarkable about that goal, if you watch it now, is not only that Lafleur takes a terrific shot but also how much else is going on around it, pointing towards past and future alike. Seeing it now, we're stunned by the sheer incompetence of Gilles Gilbert, the Boston goalie, who is playing a stand-up-and-kick style that now looks antediluvian — a very old-fashioned kind of upright goaltending whose futility, so evident on this shot, would make it extinct within a decade. The shot invalidates a style, not just a moment.

But one also notices that the man actually carrying the puck is Jacques Lemaire, Lafleur's centre, and that Lemaire draws the defence towards him before he makes a quiet drop-pass to set up the shot. Now, Lemaire was only promoted to the top line after an up-and-down career as a one-dimensional player, famous for his heavy shot. (He in effect won the Stanley Cup eight years before, by taking a more or less random shot from centre ice that happened to stun and elude the Chicago Blackhawks goalie, Tony Esposito.) But in this case Lemaire doesn't take the shot, and we're reminded that Lemaire was schooled for five years by Scotty Bowman, the Canadiens coach, who patiently trans-formed him from an offensive-minded player into a defensive-minded player, first demoting him to the second line, then eventually putting him back on the first line after he under-stood the virtues of an all-over game. And it's Lemaire, as we've seen, who then takes Bowman's regimen and, in his years with the dull but effective New Jersey Devils, turns it into the modern trap, an ice-clogging reactive defensive game plan that demands more self-discipline than style. So the pass, in a sense, is more potent than the goal. What Lemaire has learned matters as much as what Lafleur has done — a whole history compressed into a back pass and a shot.

Part of the joy of understanding the game is being able to read it well enough to spot when those pivotal moments take place. The fine hockey writer Michael Farber has analyzed Sidney Crosby's goal in the most recent Olympics in that spirit: six seconds that subsume twenty years. One could do the same with Mario Lemieux's great goal in the '87 Canada Cup — seeing, for instance, how in that goal Gretzky identified himself as primarily a playmaker, not a scorer — but it's enough to say for now that each of these goals is the result of a plan and history unknown to or beyond the control of the opposition, shared among the players through their common spatial intelligence, each taking place at such high speed that the plan is invisible to all but the tutored eye. Each is crucially significant to the outcome of the contest but is not the only such moment in the contest, and each has long-term consequences for the way the sport evolves.

Hockey approaches a more perfect balance between planning and reading, idea and improvisation, than any other sport. Runs in baseball are information; in basketball, baskets are events; in soccer, goals are exclamations. But goals in hockey are *punctuation* — they end sentences that can be traced through phrases to make long chains of meaning. And so great goals, like great aphorisms, repay any amount of after-the-fact analysis. How did so much get packed into one phrase, or play? Ice hockey looks like a reflex, rapture sport but is really a rational, reasoned one. Spotting the patterns amid the quick plunges is part of the fun. I often go to sleep at night running through great goals I have seen — there is a weighting towards the seventies Habs, but only because they were the greatest team of all time, not because I was a teenager then — and what astonishes me is that, no matter how often you rewind them, they still play back beautifully, and in your mind's eye (or on the YouTube screen) you always see more. Hockey offers drama at first viewing, meaning on the second, and learning on the third and fourth, even forty years on. The tradition that began a hundred years ago in Montreal, of a game that combined the collisions of rugby with the beauty of ice-skating, has, if only for a moment, been realized, and it lingers in your head.

SO ICE HOCKEY is both a clan sport and a craft sport — even an art sport — in the sense that it tends to achieve a level of equilibrium that demands a new frontier of invention and strategic innovation. The game gets stuck and then has to unstick itself — or rather, someone has to unstick it. The history of Russian hockey is illustrative here. Far from being the robotic, top-down, totalitarian exercise of our frantic North American paranoia, the classic Russian teams of the sixties and seventies were very much the product of a couple of eccentric and original imaginations: Anatoli Tarasov, the greatest Russian coach, and Vsevolod Bobrov, the greatest Russian athlete of his day. As Paul Harder writes: "Soviet hockey succeeded not because it was an efficient totalitarian institution, but because it was so atypical." Just as Canadian hockey got made in Montreal by a collision of three groups, the Irish and the French and the English, Russian hockey was made entirely in Moscow through a collision of three distinct intelligences: Tarasov, Bobrov, and Nikolay Epstein, who invented what we now call the trap. Mostly working outside the Soviet system, which concentrated on soccer and field sports, they saw ways of reintroducing soccer style with a higher-level passing game and brought hockey to a level of finish that it has since largely lost. Yet our present expectation that a Russian player will have superior skills is a testament to the enduring insight of the three coaches.

The game can change. A craft sport and a clan sport, hockey is uniquely able both to win our admiration and to anchor our allegiances. If I am one patriotic thing more than any other, I am a fan of the Montreal Canadiens, but if I am one sports-loving thing more than any other, I wait every four years to see the Olympics, where hockey is played as it ought to be played. I love my clan; I ache for a higher craft.

Now I must make another confession: the game as it is played on a professional level has become so adulterated by a dross of brutality, and by brutality's mental twin stupidity, that I have at moments been inclined to abandon it. The game without its clannishness of *your group against mine*, of *let's settle it here*, would lack the authenticity that still clings to it even after every cynical quaver is accepted. Mere violence, simple thuggery left unpunished, does not extend hockey's traditions; it sells out its soul, and to the worst instincts of contemporary entertainment — to Xtreme sports and cage fighting and all the other dumb spectacles made for young men with an appetite for violence and an insulation from its effects. In hockey this has begun to so disfigure the game as to make it at times almost ugly.

Some of the violence of the game is, as I hope I have suggested, intrinsic to it — part of its footprint, its DNA, the mud it tracks in from history. But more of it is imposed and unnecessary. That hockey has a violence problem is beyond all dispute; in fact, for most non-fans of the game, hockey simply is a violence problem.

And always has been. Throughout its century-plus history, some who love the sport — including Ken Dryden and, more recently, Mario Lemieux — have been trying to cure it, while those who actually like the violence are enraged that anyone would want to see it changed. For many, I sadly realize, among the base of hockey fans, the truth, however bizarre it may seem, is that skill, creative and stylish play of the kind that Tarasov and Bobrov brought to Russian hockey, is seen as essentially passive and feminine, and so somehow threatening; anyone who plays that way should be humiliated, as with Brad Marchand assaulting a helpless Daniel Sedin. (There's a famous Canadian story, "The Drubbing of Nesterenko" by Hanford Woods, that tries to look deep into the heart of this hockey psychosis, and the sexual insecurity that lies at its base: the villain, by the way, is a Montreal Canadien, John Ferguson, and the bad actors all Habs fans.) Again and again, we hear on television the brutal words of every bully in every playground in the world: Well, why didn't he fight back when I hit him? Well, because fighting isn't his job, not what he came to do, not what he *ought* to do . . . Sadly, it never seems to be enough. It would be nice to blame once again the degradation of the sport on American hucksterism and the American cult of violence-as-spectacle that disgusts the world. But this would be, in hard and simple truth, a variant of the lost-pond theory of hockey's history. Canada is implicated too (and, more narrowly, if passively, the Russians and Swedes and Finns, who've joined in the rampage). The truth is that the real problem is the troubling alliance between the Canadian weakness for a pure clan ethic — rooted in the old ethnic jockeying through which hockey made its first footprint, and in the British myth of self-policed sport — and the American urge to degrade anything if the degradation will sell.

Does it matter? The meaning of all modern sport, from the late nineteenth century on, is that it connects us; it is the easiest form of history we have, and the one place where the politics of identity play out as play. At their worst, sports encourage our violent and voyeuristic instincts — the players are acting out our anger. At their best they encourage our analytic and communal inclinations — see, even quick, bright things can happen in patterns and for a reason. So, with our selves invested in our games, we have to save the game to save ourselves. It can be done. British soccer was a source of repulsion for decent Europeans because of the cult of violence that tainted its atmosphere well into the 1980s; then intelligent people acted and it was largely cured. If we do not do the same about the brutality and thuggishness inside the game we love, we don't deserve better.

THERE — A CHANCE to talk about hockey, seized and taken! Dared and done, as Robert Browning once said. And I hope that, as much as with Schubert or Mary Shelley, this story echoes with our single recurring theme. We might think, naturally enough, that this will be a story about nature, about rivers iced over and bodies in motion, that the truth of winter sports will be one of nation and purity, of the mountain and the lake and the frozen pond, things set apart from the city and its contests and its corruptions.

But the reality of recreational winter is that it is cosmopolitan too, and city-made — hybridized and mongrelized and made up of the deepest demands and needs of mixed-up people for mixed-up pleasures. The escape from the mind and its anxieties leads us back to . . . the mind and its anxieties. Throughout these chapters the single thing that I've tried to emphasize most is that the modern idea of winter begins with an idea of Romantic escape; it begins with an idea of release from the too rationalized, the too Cartesian, the too reasonable systems of the French Enlightenment and takes us instead into a world of natural purity and natural authority. And this escape takes place in different forms, from painting to *patinage*.

Yet every time we've looked more deeply into that idea, it turns out to be partial, incomplete, inadequate to lived experience. Just as you can expel nature with a pitchfork and she'll always return, so you can flee your culture on skis or skates but she will always eventually catch you. You make up dreams of pure pond hockey, then its history turns out to be a truth about ethnic rivalry in the heart of a cosmopolitan city. There is no escape from sexuality, from the struggles of clans, from social life. We race into the corners of the pond and find there the corners of our own minds. The philosophical skater may have found his solitude, but there is a girl with a snowball waiting in her fist. The pattern we see in the story of recreational winter is just like the pattern we saw in those of Romantic and recuperative winter — that the most cosmopolitan, urban, even, if you insist, corrupting ambiguities of modern culture are all present in each step the skater takes on his way to that white pond in the woods, onto the face of that blue five-dollar bill. When we choose the solitary path of spinning at evening, we sense intimations of the social life that will begin again in the morning. As that great skater William Wordsworth knew in every chilly Lake District winter, a time of rapture is the end result of a sequence of reasons. As we throw our bodies to the wind, our minds open up to the world.

FIVE

REMEMBERING WINTER
The Season in Silence

ICE WINE, AS every drinker knows, is sweetness made from stress. That's not news, or not exactly. All good wine takes its essential sugar from the stress of its circumstances: pinot noir, the grape of the cold country of Champagne, gets flabby and soupy as the climate warms. But ice wine is extreme sweetness made from extraordinary stress. Every winter the grapes on the Niagara Peninsula are left not merely to chill but to actually freeze — the worst thing that normally can happen to fruit — and then the brutal cold forces all the natural sugar into the core of the grape, where it waits to be pressed out.

And in that simple paradox — the hardest weather makes the nicest wine — lies a secret that gives shape to the winter season, and to our feelings about it. Without the stress of cold in a temperate climate, without the cycle of the seasons experienced not as a gentle swell up and down but as an extreme lurch, *bang!* from one quadrant of the year to the next, a compensatory pleasure would vanish from the world. There is a lovely term in botany — *vernalization* — referring to seeds that can only thrive in spring if they have been through the severity of winter. Well, many aspects of our life have become, in the past several hundred years, "vernalized." (Even those who live in warmth recognize the need for at least the symbols of the cold, as in all that sprayed-on snow in Los Angeles in December.) If we didn't remember winter in spring, it wouldn't be as lovely; if we didn't think of spring in winter, or search winter to find some new emotion of its own to make up for the absent ones, half of the keyboard of life would be missing. We would be playing life with no flats or sharps, on a piano with no black keys.

Winter stress makes summer sweetness — and the stress of warm times makes us long for the strange sweetness of cold ones. Not a bad place to start, perhaps, especially if coupled with the most beautiful of all stressed-out-by-summer, longing-for-winter songs. We've started every chapter with imagined music, and let's begin this one with "River," Joni Mitchell's great song from her ever-more-classic album *Blue*, whose subject is really that of a girl from Saskatchewan finding herself adrift in love and celebrity, in the islands of the Caribbean and the deserts of southern California, and of memory turning at that moment to winter, to a memory of skating on a river in Saskatchewan long ago and long before. (In fact, Joni turned that into an entire album of memories about Saskatchewan just two years ago.) The song is about one river and one woman — but it's also about so much we've touched on: about the myth of the hockey pond, about solitary skating, above all about Christmas, about the loss of winter in a warm climate. How shall we sing the songs of winter in a warm climate?

There is a literature of exile from the South, one that ordinary literate readers know well. The great Australian critic and poet Clive James's most recent book of poems is called *Opal Sunset*, and it is all about remembering Australian youth and Australian sunshine from chilly Cambridge. "Go back to the opal sunset," he implores himself, where there's wine and avocado and sun all day. There's an important literature from the Caribbean too, about remembering the South from exile in the North. Derek Walcott turns to that subject again and again, with twin themes of lost pleasure and of the apparent (though only apparent) lack of "seriousness" one must feel in a sunny land without four seasons, with its superficial joys (or at least our too superficial sense of them). "Winter adds depth and darkness to life as well as to literature, and in the unending summer of the tropics not even poverty or poetry . . . seems capable of being profound because the nature around it is so exultant, so resolutely ecstatic, like its music. A culture based on joy is bound to be shallow," Walcott said in his Nobel acceptance speech. The southern writer envies or is frustrated by the assumption of "that seriousness that comes only out of culture with four seasons." How can there be a *people* down there? he asks — knowing full well that there are but that the pleasure we take in their idyllic surroundings conspires to suppress, or simplify, their real existence.

Well, in return, there is a smaller but equally strong literature written in the South, remembering the North — whether made by expatriate nineteenth-century Russian poets in France or expatriate Canadian singers in Los Angeles. And where the southern writer expatriated to winter lands tries to explain that there are people down there, the banished writer from the winter countries tries to explain (or sing) that there are *pleasures* up there. "I wish I had a river to skate away on . . ." Joni sings. And so their thoughts and songs turn again and again to the pleasures of recollection itself — to the reality that winter seems to act as a kind of magical place of memory, a storehouse of things recalled.

Stress makes sweetness, and snow and ice are the frosting of loss. In all of these chapters, so far the one obvious text that I haven't cited, that I haven't referred to at all and have been saving for this last descant, is in one sense the best text, the most important single poetic text about winter that we possess. And that's François Villon's beautiful fifteenth-century love poem, "Ballad of Yesterday's Beauties," as it's sometimes called, with its lists of long-lost belles and its repeated refrain: "*Mais où sont les neiges d'antan?*"

The line seems to leap right out of its Renaissance setting to become a permanent modern refrain. Dante Gabriel Rossetti's famous translation — "Where are the snows of yesteryear?" — is, I think, misleading, because it gives the poem an archaizing tone, false to its real emotion. A simpler translation would be better: "Where have the snows gone?" Or better yet, "Where are the snows we knew?" Or even, as one more acerbic translator has offered, "Well, where are yesterday's snows?" For the refrain is double-packed: both sardonic and, in the best sense, sentimental. On the one hand, we *know* where the old snows are — they've melted, and for good. On the other hand, they linger strongly in memory, like great beauties who have aged or passed away. And in that line's double sense is an intimation (evoked, we know, at the height of that little ice age) that somehow winter — the dead season, the off-season, the bleak season, the null season — is actually and secretly the season in which we store our own sense of the past.

My subject in this last essay is *remembering* winter, and I want to talk about the loss of winter in three different but entangled senses. First in the simple, largely positive sense in which, as architecture changes and technology grows, we are capable of being further and further removed from the season. (We walk around in the subterranean city in Montreal and think, *Oh my God, it's* cold *outside?*) Second, in the objective, if ominous and even cosmic, sense that winter may be passing away from us as the result of man-wrought global warming, and that our relationship to it has changed and is still changing. (We walk in the Arctic — at least, some do — and think, *Is it* still *cold outside?*) And finally, and most mysteriously — and I may risk getting lost here in philosophical snowdrifts from which my frozen body will someday be recovered, a risk I shall have to take, stiff-lipped as a British polar explorer — but not least important, in the sense in which winter and the idea of memory remain almost mystically entangled in the modern mind.

These are three very different senses of remembering winter, but they group around a common meditative norm: how do we incorporate a mechanical, mineral act — the fact of a season not made for us and indifferent in every sense to our existence — into our sense of time and order? How does a season produced by the tilts of poles and the presence of climate cycles that are going on in every uninhabited planet in the solar system, how could these simple physical events engage and attach themselves to our lives?

Now, all of nature is in one sense indifferent to our selves; there'd be summer too if no one were here to see it. There is a July on Venus, a spring on Mars, all with no one there to witness them. But with winter we approach this truth more starkly. In spring and summer our sense of harmony comes more easily, with less stress: we were made in, and made for, times and weather like this. We have at least the illusion of being woven into the climate. We were made for the temperate ease of the savannah, and we constantly have to build savannah boxes around ourselves just to survive. Nobody's at home above the

Arctic Circle — and yet, somehow, we are. Nobody is even "natur-ally" at home in Canada — "a few acres of snow" — and yet, somehow, here we are. To *make* winter, to distinguish and dis-criminate its pleasures and terrors, requires an effort of mind and memory as great as any modern people have attempted.

YOU'LL RECALL THAT in the early nineteenth century the invention of central heating — of steam heat and the radiator — played a large role in making a newly Romantic idea of winter. Winter became emancipated from its threat, something that you could look at and talk about rather than something that you simply had to seize up about. Warm people like to look at cold scenes. And, doubting their nerve, they like to go out into them too, as hot people like to jump into frigid swimming pools.

But you'll recall that there was also a deeper idea present at the birth of central heating in nineteenth-century Britain, and that was the idea that central heating was tied to a new conception of architecture: an architecture not of brick and stone alone, not simply of mass, but of air — an envelope of warm air. Every new practice of building has a new idea of living implicit in it, and the new idea of living implied by central steam heat was of man freed to live (semi-naked, if he liked) within a space where heat was evenly distributed, where the old divide between hugging the hearth and standing by the window would slowly disappear. We really had achieved, or were on the verge of achieving, full real-ization of the savannah box in the middle of a Glasgow winter. Natural man, even the naked savage, could be reborn *indoors*. And that idea is one that has grown, changed, and transformed in our own time; you could create a whole alternative universe inside that could be an antidote to the world outside.

And so central heating, as much as it brought us into a new relationship with winter, changed our urban experience of winter. Now, one of the odd things about winter and urbanism is that in many ways nineteenth-century people were more successful at incorporating winter experiences into city places than we are. If you look at nineteenth-century engravings, if you trace nineteenth-century city history, you'll see that there is an incredible richness of urban life designed to explore and increase the joy of winter. My beloved adopted city of Paris is a wonderful instance of this. In the late nineteenth century Paris had six or so working ice rinks, an "ice palace," and a wonderful kind of dance bar called the North Pole. When MGM made Colette's *Gigi* back in the 1950s, a key scene was set at an ice rink; on location in Paris, since none any longer existed, the movie crew had to counterfeit one of their own. Visit Paris now and try to go skating: you have to wait for them to set up a little rink outside the Hôtel de Ville around Christmastime, and if you actually have hockey skates you're a phenomenon. In Ottawa, the capital of Canada, there was a Crystal Palace with a toboggan chute that apparently used to run all the way down to the Ottawa River.

Many elements played a part in this change; there are no mono-causal phenomena in life, save perhaps for sex and lingerie. What happened to cut off the urban experience from winter was of course the same thing that happened to the city in every other way, the introduction of the ultimate small-scale combined confessional booth and savannah box: the car. It would be, I suppose, something of an exaggeration to say that the past century was shaped beyond all other things by a constant, losing fight between the soul-destroying demands of the car and the soul-enriching values of the city for the inner life of modern man and woman, but it would not really be much of an exaggeration. The truth is that what cars need is almost the exact opposite of what cities need. Cars need places to park, and those places, in their scale and single purpose, are inherently antihuman. Cars need drawers to lodge in, wide-spaced feet to run on; they lame street movement and create cross-town paralysis. Cities, by contrast, need corners to live on, narrow streets to easily cross, squares and piazzas — a whole array of architectural arrangements that enable the gift of density to blossom and for life to become interconnected and interchanged. What the car buys you in convenience it kills in civic capital. A parking lot is a cemetery of civil society. (It is, perhaps, not entirely an accident, or at least a good grim joke, that the Victoria Rink in Montreal, where hockey was born, is now a parking garage, and the game is mostly learned and played far away from the centre of town.)

The winter city would seem to be the *last* place where the car-and-city problem can be solved. Winter drives people off the streets into cars, and the worse the winter, the graver the continuing crises of cities and cars. But, by a series of contingencies — the usual mix of the imaginative individual who plants a seed and the lucky terrain it falls on — it turns out that the worse the winter, the more ingenious the urban solution can become and the more revived city life can be. Stress burrows down and makes another kind of sweetness. This is evidenced all over the world in winter cities — and, indeed, in what is called the "winter cities movement," which stretches from Finland to Minneapolis and Calgary — but I think is best evidenced in my own hometown of Montreal.

WHEN I WAS a mostly miserable adolescent, my one keen pleasure was to do what we called "juking" from school; I would cut class and go walking in the underground city in Montreal. You could begin at Place Ville Marie, which in those days had wonderfully uniform signage and two little movie theatres (both gone now) and proceed down an inviting cavern into Central Station, which still held, as Canadian railway stations mostly do, the sense of bustle and purpose that a railway station should. (American railway stations have all become bus stations or graveyards.) There were wonderful art deco bas-relief murals there, showing gravely stylized scenes from winter sports: hockey players staring down the puck like costumed dancers in a Fred Astaire chorus, lacrosse players right out of an RKO set. (Puzzlingly, the frieze seemed to change colours regularly, from red to blue and back again. I have never been able to discover if this was a trick of the lighting or a hallucination of my adolescence.)

And from there you could proceed into the gloomier but still impressive brutalist spaces of Place Bonaventure. Or else, proceeding in the opposite direction, you could pick up the Metro there and, quickly enough, head out to the western part of downtown, where the corridor would take you to funky Alexis Nihon Plaza (they hadn't made it a *place* yet), dense with the smell of doughnuts and hot dogs — *chiens chauds*, as the then perfectly reasonable French translation had it — and very nearby the Montreal Forum, where the greatest of all hockey teams past and present, the Canadiens of the seventies, still reigned; and continue down a tiled corridor with a bend and a mirror, if I recall, to the most elegant of Montreal developments, Westmount Square, which had an American-style coffee shop and entrancing women's clothing stores. All of this was nothing like a mall, for malls are

made to wander up and down in and cunningly — or shame-
fully — designed to keep the visitor on a constant turning hamster
wheel of big retail. This was purposeful wandering, a boy's foot-
steps, happy and, in the dead of winter, warm. There were odd,
stale smells then, but you could weirdly waltz right through a
whole world. I had to read the English writer Keith Waterhouse's
wonderful memoir, *City Lights: A Street Life*, about walking on
similar illicit grounds in Leeds in the 1930s — his happy wanderings all above ground, of course — to be reminded of my own
sense of the joys of a proud provincial capital for a teenage boy.

I took the freedom of that underground city for granted — as
every denizen takes his burrow — as just the natural and logical
consequence of a cold city, but of course it was nothing of the
kind. Instead, a generation of planners, fairly called visionary,
and in particular another émigré, American-born but a long-time
resident of Montreal, named Vincent Ponte, had shaped my
school-free afternoons. Cities, as the urban philosopher Jane
Jacobs taught us, are self-organizing, but they are not (as in her
lesser moments she sometimes seemed to imagine) self-starting.
The entirety of this subterranean system was the result of conscious decisions, envisioned and executed by a generation of
urbanists who, for once, got it mostly right, and they have gone
on getting it righter since. Forty years after my wanderings,
Montreal now has a huge indoor network of tunnels, walkways,
atriums, and above-ground extensions within sixty separate real
estate complexes, some public and most private. It's almost twenty
miles long, and still growing. Within the Big Burrow there are
office, retail, institutional, cultural, hotel, residential, recreational, and transportation services, including ten Metro stations,
two commuter rail stations, and two regional bus stations. By

now eighty percent of the entire downtown's office space can be accessed without stepping into the cold air, and more than half a million people a day are citizens of the subterranean city. There are two thousand stores, almost two thousand housing units, two hundred restaurants, forty banks, forty movie theatres, a cathedral, an exhibition centre, and a convention centre. It's a model of urbanism in a cold climate, the ultimate winter city.

There's a plaque in ground zero of this complex, Place Ville Marie, dedicated to the late Vincent Ponte, naming him as the godfather of this underground winter world. Ponte was a young architect who came to Montreal with the Chinese-American I. M. Pei in 1959, at the urgings of the developer William Zeckendorf, to rebuild the big gash in the middle of the city where the railway had run and make it into a new development, a cruciform high-rise unlike anything seen in the city until then. Now Ponte, like Pei at the time, was in many respects a classic Corbusian thinker and architect, someone who had absorbed the then-governing rhetoric of the mega-block, the enormous tower set in a plaza. He was a "master planner," a type that right-thinking architectural critics now reject. But parts of his plan *were* masterly, and he seems to have had a special gift for making master plans seem seductive, irresistible; one later client, a Dallas realtor named Jack Gosnell, said that listening to him was like attending a concert by Elvis Costello: "horn-rimmed glasses, a shock of black hair, and a hypnotic sound."

It hadn't yet become quite so evident as it soon would that the big, open plaza in which the ideal skyscraper was always placed would for the most part, and wherever one found it, become an urban wasteland. Without corners or small stores, without the necessities of collision and bump and interchange that cities demand, those plazas, from Anchorage to Albany, became spiritual ashtrays. But though Ponte may not have known that the big plaza would never work in a winter city — well, they never work anywhere, but they work least well when the wind blows cold — he did see something else: that one could look down and dig down and make a second city there.

And so his master plan for Montreal in 1961 was one of the first "multidimensional" city plans, inspired by Renaissance ideals, insisting on street life at several levels, and beginning — by a simple, baby-step series of connections between the train station, the new Place Ville Marie, and the Queen Elizabeth Hotel across what was then Dorchester Street — to build the city below. And on that basis there began a kind of organic growth; one tunnel met another, and one crossing crossed one more, and soon a kind of small Italian hill town was rolling along underneath Montreal.

Two simple changes — and who exactly spurred them is a matter of some small debate — helped and were hugely important. One assured that everything in the city below a certain point would be public property. In New York City, by contrast, if you own a property you own it, as the saying goes, all the way down to China. (Of course, in China you own the opposite building right through to Manhattan; at the moment the smart money is on the Chinese to take possession of the earth between the two points if there were a conflict.) If you want to tunnel underneath the Empire State Building you have to defer to the people who own it. In Montreal, somewhat uniquely, you have a complicated lease arrangement where everything below ground belongs to everybody: you can tunnel by right, if not quite at will. Ponte also seems to have rightly envisioned the new Montreal subway, the Metro, as the real spine and bloodstream of an underground city, to have seen that the below-ground city spreads naturally from the existence of a more familiar city thing: the below-grade train. The multidimensional city depends on a subway to serve as its nervous system, and a series of tunnels and walkways to serve as its connective tissue.

The idea of an underground city, of digging deep for space denied above, is an ancient one, and usually ambiguous in feeling. Ideas of fear and caution inflect the below-ground living space. The Jews of the Middle Ages were not allowed to let their synagogues rise above, or anywhere near, the local church steeple, so they had to dig down for more space. In our own time, the idea of going below ground seems especially unappealing — it puts us in mind of the Morlocks in H. G. Wells' *The Time Machine*, forced by the Eloi to live in a sunless subterranean wasteland — and, to be sure, the very first substantiation of that underground world in Montreal had its dank passages and smelly subsections. But over time and with experience, it became apparent that if you create light wells, and if you have a kind of permeable membrane of stairs and escalators leading you below ground and above ground and back again, you can create a fully heated, massive below-ground city that will be as appealing as the city above.

Everyone could arrive in the centre of the city by train and leave their car at home — or never have one. The underground city helped midwife a remarkable rebirth of the central city (but not always and not everywhere — the western edge of St. Catherine Street in Montreal has been laid waste). On the whole a kind of virtuous circle begins that Ponte, for one, seems to have anticipated: when people are brought in below ground they are eager to come up above ground. You create a permeable membrane between the underworld and the overworld, all based on foot traffic — on the pedestrian, the walker, who is the city's red blood cell, without whom the city pales and sickens and dies of anemia.

Early last March I had the great good fortune to walk through the subterranean city with the architect Peter Rose, one of the builders of modern Montreal in its formative years. It was a bitterly cold day — the kind of day in Montreal that makes you believe that spring will never come, bringing my Haitian cab driver on the way in from the airport to something close to tears as he considered the climate of his exile. Peter and I trod from one end of the underground city pretty much to the other, stopping for lunch and coffee along the way. The first thing Peter asked me to note about the underground city now is that it isn't really any longer underground, and the other thing is that it is not a separate city but a *second* city, beneath the skin, that feeds and sustains the city streets above. Where the underground city of my youth still had something a touch stale about it, smelling of the tunnel and the burrow, the new one — stretching east to entangle the vast basements of the vast developments with which provincial and federal governments have warred for the heart of Montreal and the allegiance of Quebecers — is now a subtle, mutable space well lit by intermittent pools of light amid the foot traffic of office buildings, creating exactly the atmosphere that Ponte dreamed of, in which the inner world becomes an artificial Serengeti. One walks, coat on arm, quite literally for miles, without stopping to think that outside it is bitter and hostile.

Once again, the possibility of walking below, in comfort, gives the city back to the walker, whose natural mode is curiosity. We have learned that even very small elevations towards the sun can make a big difference in feeling and temperature. Even in the dead of winter on a bitter day, the street life above our starting point at Place Victoria had a density equal to that of the life going on below. Density tends to produce, and reproduce, density. The underground/above-ground spaces create a permeable membrane of civility where life tilts easily up or down. Like ant colonies in the best sense, the overflow outside is a sign of the teeming life inside.

Successful cities are never mono-causal; there is no one master plan. (The most beautiful city in the world is built on and around water, and demands, of all things, boats.) Ponte made a parallel plan for Dallas that was an absolute disaster, simply because tunnels alone — in the absence of a subway and winter — don't work. Ponte is as hated in Dallas as he is honoured in Montreal. There the multidimensional underground plan is decried, derided — exactly because it killed the life of the streets, "stripping them of their humanity." The trouble is that the Texas city was rooted in the car and its parking places; Ponte's vision could not be applied without the spine of the metro. ("The tunnels these days have got to be dealt with in a compassionate, thoughtful, and fair way," one urbanist says of the Dallas tunnels waiting for destruction.) In Montreal the choice is not between the street and the tunnel but between the winter street and the underground city. The greatest nervous system in the world is no good without blood circulating, and clean arteries are no use at all without clear neural networks.

I think there is also a subtler asymmetry at work between winter and summer cities that may miss even the architect's and planner's eyes. It is the difference between being very hot and very cold. When you're very cold, you can almost always get warmer; the first and most effective savannah "box" is still a fur coat. In very hot weather there are sharp limits to how cool you can get, and you can't get much cooler, at least not decently, on a city street. In cold weather, with the right clothes on, you can walk out and around the city happily, if a bit briskly. The city "works" for walkers on two levels and temperatures. But in ninety-degree weather there is really nothing to do save gasp and go inside where it's air-conditioned; there is no equivalent portable temperate box, save an air-conditioned car (most Americans are already in shorts and T-shirts). "We cannot walk in hotness," my then four-year-old daughter declared one day in the ever-hot Roman Forum, and it is true.

So there is an essential irony in this story. The stress of the winter city makes it sweet. The multidimensional plan is not an all-purpose solution to anything, but it is an ideal solution to one thing, and that is winter. Where the tropical city resists the underground solution in both senses — both the metro and the purposeful non-mall — and retreats to air-conditioning units that shuffle from barred space to gated community to fenced enclosure, the winter city invites the walker in. Winter cities can become close to ideal cities because, in escaping the cold, they defeat cities' real enemy — the car — and let cities' real necessities — the pedestrian and the small store — intermingle on several levels, even in the most resistant season.

Winter acts on the city as a positive stressful and shaping presence. It is no accident, none at all, that the cities that feel most successfully urban, that have kept the cosmopolitan spirit alive through the long assault by the car, are almost all northern cities: the towns of northern Europe, Paris (yes, it is), the cities of Scandinavia, the cities of Canada. It is not just that these cities thrive in spite of the weather, but rather that the weather, met by a resourceful enough architect's response, makes them better cities. Winter is not a barrier the city has to overcome but a pressure that makes it better — the ice-wine principle. Extreme stress forces compression, and it's compression that makes things sweet. The winter city is alive for walkers in a way that the tropical city is not. The more winter, the more walkers; the more walkers, a richer world. It's a simple but immensely potent formula.

YET THERE ARE losses in the conquest of winter, and they are real — losses that I think have to do with the relationship between the indoor city and the outdoor world. The first loss has something to do with that prime experience of the watcher and the window, the experience that shaped the nineteenth century, the Romantic apprehension of what winter is and could be. That feeling that only the thinnest of membranes, the simple pane of glass separating the onlooker — the poet or the painter or the ordinary child — from the threat beyond is one that has receded from our immediate experience. There is a great difference between the experience of winter before our eyes and of winter above our heads. The artificiality of the underground or indoor city — this ability of ours to make an artificial environment, to turn those little bubbles from the savannah into larger tempered sheds — means that we escape winter where we once engaged it.

This alteration to what I call Romantic winter is, of course, still more acute in the case of radical winter, where the great frontier of the Far North, and South, is now colonized, domesticated, fixed. (Richard Panek's book *The 4 Percent Universe* has wonderful descriptions of the base station at the South Pole as it exists today, in all its slightly claustrophobic comfort. On "warm" days people run outside in sneakers and jeans; on colder ones they snuggle inside with DVDs. Neither hopelessness nor heroism infects their circle.) I think that we feel this loss, this alienation, this divorce from the experience of winter, and everything we connect with winter, in our literature and in our art.

Though it may seem a lurch to pass in a paragraph from city planning to verse making, it shouldn't. What else is poetry for, save to memorialize an everyday emotion, to build tunnels between common life and common space? Two poems by my two favourite mid-century American poets, Elizabeth Bishop and Randall Jarrell, certainly began to hint at how that kind of trans-formation of winter imagery has taken place in our minds and, indeed, in our souls: part of our increasing alienation from nature is our distance from winter.

You'll recall that all the nineteenth-century poetry that has littered our path — Cowper and Wordsworth and Coleridge — and all of its art — from Friedrich to Lawren Harris — rested on the sense that the seeming pain of winter, whether experienced tem-porally in one place or spatially in pursuit of a pole or two, provided a deeper pleasure. Meaning lay in the pursuit, in singing skates or pressing icebergs. In the second half of the twentieth century, winter is experienced in poetry of disillusion rather than of renewed illusion. I think of Bishop's wonderful poem "The Imaginary Iceberg," which begins:

> We'd rather have the iceberg than the ship,
> although it meant the end of travel.
> Although it stood stock-still like cloudy rock
> and all the sea were moving marble.
> We'd rather have the iceberg than the ship;

we'd rather own this breathing plain of snow
though the ship's sails were laid upon the sea
as the snow lies undissolved upon the water.
O solemn, floating field,
are you aware an iceberg takes repose
with you, and when it wakes may pasture on your snows?
. . .
The iceberg cuts its facets from within.
Like jewelry from a grave
it saves itself perpetually and adorns
only itself, perhaps the snows
which so surprise us lying on the sea.
Good-bye, we say, good-bye, the ship steers off
where waves give in to one another's waves
and clouds run in a warmer sky.
Icebergs behoove the soul
(both being self-made from elements least visible)
to see them so: fleshed, fair, erected indivisible.

We would rather have the iceberg, even as a destructive knell and portent of our own disillusion. Remember the myth and meaning of the iceberg that we looked at in the paintings of Lawren Harris? They were all about transferring human consciousness into the icebergs. Now Bishop's imagery becomes, on the whole, inanimate as the last vestiges of the Romantic faith in a living, spiritual nature pass away. Now the iceberg is the one thing into which consciousness *can't* pass, even if we will it to, for the iceberg "cuts its facets from within." It saves itself perpetually and adorns only itself. The iceberg is alluring because it's self-sufficient; that's why we'd rather have it than a ship that's as

certain to sink as we are. It's a full stop at the end of consciousness — and we prefer it because of its stubborn, resolute blankness.
The iceberg, once a dangerous, half-sinister, half-benign, pulsat-
ing, living deity, is now an emblem of self-sufficient indifference.
The ship sinks; the icebergs don't care.

Randall Jarrell's winter poem, "90 North," set as a childhood
fantasy, is similarly disillusioned about the old straight, hard path
between pain and meaning. Where Bishop writes an epitaph for
Romantic winter, Jarrell writes one for radical winter.

> At home, in my flannel gown, like a bear to its floe,
> I clambered to bed; up the globe's impossible sides
> I sailed all night — till at last, with my black beard,
> My furs and my dogs, I stood at the northern pole.
> . . .
> Where, living or dying, I am still alone;
> Here where North, the night, the berg of death
> Crowd me out of the ignorant darkness,
> I see at last that all the knowledge
>
> I wrung from the darkness — that the darkness flung me —
> Is worthless as ignorance: nothing comes from nothing,
> The darkness from the darkness. Pain comes from the darkness
> And we call it wisdom. It is pain.

The search for radical winter now ends as a metaphor not for
stoic courage but for nothing: "I see at last that all the knowledge /
I wrung from the darkness / . . . is worthless as ignorance . . . /
Pain comes from the darkness / And we call it wisdom. It is pain."
Though Bishop's iceberg is more nobly enigmatic and mysterious,

and Jarrell's is simply the name we give to death, both begin with the awareness that neither divinity nor an occult secret resides in cold, in winter. The secret winter is keeping is that there is no secret, just the resistant, obstinate fact of matter. Pain can be called wisdom — that was the foundation, the story, or myth, of the nineteenth-century Pole — but now we know it's just pain.

That sense still filters into our contemporary polar art and winter poetry. Not courage but the claustrophobia of safety and the too-oft-repeated history of lost lore haunt our hearts. There is, for instance, a fine recent memoir by the British writer Jenny Diski, called *Skating to Antarctica*. Published in 1997, it's about a trip to the Antarctic, counterpoised with a memoir of her parents and of her parents' miserable marriage. But what's significant is that the Antarctic is no longer a symbol of exploration, of going beyond, of the unknown, the unknowable. Just the opposite: it's a symbol of confinement, a background for claustrophobia; it represents the bad memories we can't escape and the buried life that drags us down. When Diski goes to the South Pole, she knows just where she is going — and she knows that the essential challenge it will present to her is just to get through it.

It may seem a long reach from the cheerful burrows of underground retailing to these sad polar prose poems. But they evoke in us a common intuition that our withdrawal from winter fear brings with it a numbing of winter feeling. As safety grows, the sense of the seasons flees from us. A sense of security is excellent for civic capital, bad for sensibilities. This sense that even a polar voyage in the dead of winter is perfectly comfortable, but newly *narrow*, seems evocative of the limits of our lives. It has less to do with fear and the physical compression of fear, and more to do with the boredom of life lived in a sterile environment.

The world was once haunted by Titus Oates's self-made epi-taph: "I am just going outside and may be some time." Well, *we* are going inside and may be some time; we *are* inside, and have been for a while. The poetry of courage is replaced by the poetry of confinement, the art of the endless open channel overtaken by the art of the perpetually retold tale. Our successful withdrawal from the risks of winter makes for a lessening of its intensities. We have all gone inside, and may be some time.

THESE WINTER LOSSES are emotional — spiritual, if you like to ele-vate them, "merely" aesthetic and architectural if you intend to deprecate them. Yet surely this sense of loss is deepened and made more urgent by our knowledge that winter might be lost to us, that winter is something that is simply disappearing.

For the other, bigger loss that has us remembering rather than experiencing winter is real and hard-edged. Obviously I'm thinking about the desolation of the North and the coming of man-caused climate change, and with it the actual loss of winter. This threat — perhaps, now, this inalterable fact — has been artic-ulated and itemized far more frighteningly and effectively by others than I can hope to do now. The catalogue of what we stand to lose, in cities swamped and icebergs melting and environ-ments irrevocably altered, has all been written about and prophesied.

The literature on global warming and the North is complex and immense, but several recent books put the phenomenon — or catastrophe — in sharp journalistic perspective. My brother-in-law, Edward Struzik, the Arctic writer and explorer, is the man in our family who actually goes out and looks at these places, where most of us stay home and talk about them. Edward has itemized

all the fears and all the possibilities of the loss of winter very elo-
quently in his book *The Big Thaw*.

Although I'm sure the threat and the fears of the coming of
global warming are present in the forefront of all our minds, let
me just itemize a few things. Melting ice sheets in the Arctic are
already adding one hundred cubic miles of ice to the oceans.
That means that by the end of the century — this century — the
millions of people who live within three feet of sea level may all
have to move, possibly including the entire island of Manhattan.
There seems already to be no stopping the advance of the
treeline into the vast tundra regions of the Arctic. You recall
how I talked in the second chapter about how you can experience
winter as a fundamentally spatial phenomenon, one that begins
at about the treeline every summer and then fights its way like
a Civil War general farther and farther into the south, and then
goes back up? Well, that treeline, behind which winter has
always hidden, is now extending farther and farther north; it
seems likely now there will be spruce trees within the Arctic
Circle and on the Arctic islands in the next quarter-century. The
exile of First Nations peoples from low-lying shores is already
taking place: five coastal communities are already being evacu-
ated. We may already have passed a Gladwellian tipping point:
in 2007, for the first time, the frost of winter above the Arctic
Circle could no longer keep up with the melt of summer. The
anticipation now is that the Arctic will be seasonally free of ice
not in fifty years, as people feared only ten years ago, but in
something more like five years.

The facts, and their images, are all terrifying, but the one that
I think is most redolent with the sense of catastrophic change is
that polar bears are now taking to cannibalism. As temperatures

warm and the habitat of their traditional prey vanishes, polar bears are eating other polar bears. And somewhere soon along this loop, the tundra will start heating up as the permafrost melts and all the carbon escapes; instead of being a great cooling force in nature, the tundra will become one more source of warmth. We may not be coming to the end of the planet, but we may truly be coming — and sooner than we might expect — to the end of winter as we have known it.

The human response to this threat, to this sense of the loss of winter, is already taking place. In 2005 Sheila Watt-Cloutier, the Canadian Inuit activist, coined a startling phrase and presented it before the Inter-American Commission on Human Rights: what was being violated, she said, by the polluters who were causing the world to warm, was "the right to be cold." This phrase, strange-sounding or even comical to southerners, does point out an ethical imperative. It insists that one of the fundamental human rights for all people who live in northern climates is the right to be cold, exactly because their culture cannot go on in its absence. As we warm the world, entire peoples are being deprived of their weather, a right as fundamental as a seafaring nation's right to access the ocean, or a Venetian's right to be wet. That phrase may put a smile on the lips of those of us who are plenty cold enough already without asserting a right to be so forever, but the sense of cultural dislocation that it sums up, that sense of a total remaking of our expectations — not just of what life is like but of what nature is like, what the planet is like — is real and radical and profound.

The end of winter! Of course, it's likely that these prophecies will not come wholly true, because that is the usual way with prophecies, or it may very well be that they will come true in ways we cannot yet imagine — just possibly for the better, more likely for much worse. (One possible twist in the story of climate change is that it will make for more severe rather than less severe winters down here in the once-tempered seasons.) But that we will lose much of the familiar physical world and its familiar fixed cycles seems likely, perhaps certain.

I can't speak with any expertise to that, except to say that people who spend their lives going to see what's happening all say that it's going to happen. But I can speak to another, lesser, but in its way more immediate kind of loss — a cultural loss, or, if you like, an aesthetic one, in the higher sense that all our choices beyond the merely animal are finally aesthetic. If winter passes, or if it changes radically, the world will adjust. But will we? Conceivably a world without winter might even in the very long run be a greener place. But Demeter without her mourning is someone else; she inhabits a more facile and fatuous planet.

For the idea and imagery of winter has long been bound up with our ideas of memory and the past. We will not lose our sense of these things, of course, if winter changes, any more than those who live in torrid climates have lost theirs. But the apparatus, the affect, the folklore, the mythology of memory and the mineral world will go — the *feel* of the thing will alter, and we will ask where the snows of yesterday went all the time, and forever. Without our memory of winter, the North, the snow, the seasonal cycle, something will be lost to our civilization too, a loss as grave in its way as that of the Inuit.

It is hard not to be haunted at this moment in history by that heartbreaking story of the Greenland Inuit's loss of their three meteorites — the Tent, the Woman, and the Dog, from which for centuries they wrought their knives and harpoons — at the hands of the American explorer Robert Peary, who sold them to the natural history museum in my adopted city of New York for forty thousand dollars. I've said that the tale of the three clans in Montreal would make the great Canadian film; well, this story would make the great northern Schubertian song cycle, if anyone still wrote such things. I often go to look at the three meteorites now and touch their cool surfaces. It seemed to the people who stole them — well, bought and sold them — a neat enough bit of imperial collecting. Now it surely seems an act of cultural vandalism as cruel as any on record. The Greeks who lost the Parthenon frieze had other friezes to keep. It is true that afterwards the Inuit would find trading for iron far easier. But the meteorites were theirs — their place, their legend. The fact of the Woman and the Tent and the Dog was central to the Inuit sense of who they were. When the stones were hauled away, the necessary useful acts were no longer tied to a cosmic purpose, or even, to our more knowing eyes, a happy cosmic accident. They were only what they were. In every sense, their stones were what bound them to the stars.

Well, the seasons are our three (or four) meteorites. We chip at them for our history. The relationship between winter and memory is complex and can seem inarticulate, something sensed more than spoken, so let me try to unwrap a few of those connections here. First there's a simple biological sense, in which winter holds the past in place: roots and tubers that are buried throughout the winter months have their genetic memory locked within them, tied up within them, waiting to bloom again. That simple botanical fact has become a much richer cultural idea in the hands of those like Caspar David Friedrich and Franz Schubert and Alexander Pushkin, who found national memory there. That idea of national memory may have its sinister shadings, but the notion that the true character of the Germans or the Scandinavians or the Russians — or the Canadians — was suddenly revealed in winter was a rich counter-Enlightenment idea, one at the heart of the Romantic rebellion against arid reason. Everybody has got a warm summer, but we in the North have a winter, and we know ourselves and see ourselves best then. It was a big idea. And that idea of memory presses deep, extending from racial or national memory to planetary memory among the glaciologists, and memories of the Nativity as we imagine it to be — or merely of childhood as we had hoped it might be — among the makers of modern Christmas. Sports too are memory bound — the next period, the season's statistics.

YET THERE ARE two different ways in which winter touches memory: there is memory *in* winter and memory *of* winter. In the first sense we use winter as a blank slate, the place where everything is scrubbed away. From the most mystical German vision to the most obvious folk use, winter is the climate of the imagination. Winter displaces us from the normal cycles of nature — nothing's growing — and with our disjunction from nature comes our escape into the mind, which can make of nature what it will. We talked before about how snow and ice, the elements of winter, are all immensely labile. And one of the things that the Romantic imagination from Coleridge onwards seized on is this ability we have to project our dreams onto winter forms, to see in the frozen lake that Coleridge glimpsed in 1799 the forms of the Israelites parting the Red Sea.

At a simple, practical, everyday level, that's our experience of building a snowman. That's why we send our children out on the first day of a snowstorm — exactly because they are in a newly labile environment where the imagination can not only project but can construct anew from something given. We see the world through the lens of the window, and even when the window is not frosted — remember the great debates between Goethe and his contemporaries about the meaning of hoarfrost? — it still has two sides, one for the world and one for our mind. Start with snow and a snowman is what you'll get. A snow day, in the simplest sense, is a day a child spends outside normal time.

And in each of the great winter fables and in all of the great winter art, we've glimpsed again and again a more sublime version of that temptation of timelessness. Think again of Hans Christian Andersen's "The Snow Queen." Think about how the seductive power of the Snow Queen for Kay is that she offers him immortality of a sort — not immortality through endlessly renewed youth, but immortality in the possibility of stopping time completely. That's what happens when Kay goes to live with the Snow Queen and forgets everything that made him human — it's the ability to stop time dead that she gives him. And that timelessness is related to the eternity of mineral life. At that very moment, in the company of the Snow Queen, the snowflake, its crystalline form, looks far more beautiful to Kay than natural, organic forms. The snowflake looks more beautiful than a flower. At that moment he potentially escapes from the cycles of natural time into a timeless world, represented by the Snow Queen and the winter empire she superintends. Winter keeps us forever frozen.

Now, Andersen has Gerda rescue Kay from his false rejection of organic life, with its cycles of growth and decay; that's why they'll get married. But the possibility of entering a timeless world represented by winter is exactly the temptation that

Andersen wants us to feel. Of course, in Andersen's hands this notion becomes an entirely mystical — if you like, allegorical — construction. But it's an allegorical construction that is rooted, I think, in our actual, immediate experience of what it is like to live through a cold winter. It's exactly that sensation, that feeling of potential serenity and escape, that I knew at twelve years old, watching the endless snows fall outside on a late November day in Montreal. It's that actual, real, tangible, pit-of-the-stomach sensation that time has somehow stood still even as the snow falls that is the ultimate source of this beautiful, allegorical, mythical fable.

The second sense of memory and winter involves not memory working within winter but our memory *of* winter, after it is over. The snows of winter become the tangible sands of the memory clock. Summer, and tropical islands, supplies the illusion of *same time* over and over — the "day of our life" we once had — and of the warm, good place we once lived and were made to leave. Winter and cold places instead supply, I think, a sense of past time, and an urge to think about time passing. We use winters as our clock. *Où sont les neiges d'antan?* Once again there's a simple root, everyday sense in which memory is keyed by, set off by the coldest season. We set our inner clocks by the storms we've known. I know 1968 by the snow it brought. We recall the storm of '87, the storm of '61 — a snowstorm marks our memory, in a way that a seaside only vaguely casts a shadow over our minds. What year did that happen? The summers all bleed together. What year was the Forum closed and the car covered over by snow for four days? Ah, that was the storm of '96.

This core common sense can be raised to art. It's one you find all over twentieth-century literature, as in the beautiful moment in *The Great Gatsby* when, after the disillusionment of Nick Carraway's summer in Manhattan, he remembers — the thing he chooses to remember from all his experience — the moment when, coming home from college for Christmas, he changed trains in Chicago to go to St. Paul. It's exactly the moment of escape from the corruption of the East to enter the remembered winters of the West, which represent the possibility of purification, the possibility of recuperation, the possibility of recovery. Intertwining the idea of winter, the representation of winter, with the idea of memory and the idea of restoration is, I think, an enormously powerful theme in modern art.

Or just look at the movies, and particularly the best black-and-white movies of the 1940s. In cinema there is no more powerful metaphor for recapturing lost time than the idea of remembered winter. With Orson Welles, of course, it takes an almost kitsch form in *Citizen Kane*, when the one thing that can revivify the dying tycoon's life is the memory of his sled. It's done much more beautifully in his *The Magnificent Ambersons*: the snow scene becomes the one place where the onrushing modernity of the car is stilled and held off for a brief time. Winter is even more effectively present in Max Ophüls' beautiful film *Letter from an Unknown Woman*, where the lovers are finally able to break into the Prater, an amusement park in Vienna, in the dead of winter and recapture a piece of their lost youth in this otherwise abandoned and snow-covered fairground. "Genius," Nabokov once wrote, "resembles an African imagining snow." And memory, he might have added, looks like an amusement park in winter.

Though our setting for all these essays has been winter, our true subject has been time. We share a sense of a timeless winter, of eternal winter, of winter as the place where time stands still, the poles as places permanently outside our dailyness, the snow as nature's secret — all this is at the heart of the idea of winter in the modern mind. Christmas comes but once a year, but the cycle of renewal it celebrates promises to set us free of aging. We look at something as simple as the skaters in Central Park and we see that the particulars of a period — of time passing, fashion changing — seep into their image in a way that it might not if we were writing a cultural history of summer, with summer's ideals of unchanging weather and the summer island's promise of permanent lull. Winter is our nostalgic moment, and nostalgia is just the vernacular of history, the demotic of memory, the slang of time.

Winter, in seeming to end the cycles of fertility, offers the promise of escape from time's cycle, of which the seasonal cycle is merely an expression. Deep, deep in winter ritual and winter myth is the idea of this escape: in "The Snow Queen," where the "dead" forms of crystals are as alive as the living forms of flowers; in the chosen monasticism of the polar expeditions, where escape from news — *we are at war!* — is part of the pleasure; even in the transformation of Santa Claus from an avatar of old Father Time to an ageless wild man of the North Pole, industrialist and imp at the same time. In all these myths and moments winter has been our clock, and winter has supplied the setting for the theatre of our memory. Lose winter and we won't lose our sense of these things, any more than those who live in torrid climates, as I said, have lost theirs. Summer does not bring amnesia — but it symbolizes it, as winter does memory. The *feel* of the thing will alter, and we will all ask with François Villon where the old snows went, and why they've gone forever.

TIME PASSES, INEXORABLY, and the hold we have on it is often simply the distinctions we make within it — the names we give each moment. And so winter has been a testing ground of that Adamic act, the simple act of naming. No effort at naming, discriminating, enduring, explaining, mystifying, fabulizing has been keener than ours with winter over the past two centuries. Even if we were to lose our season, we would not lose all our meanings for it. We could lose the polar icecaps but we would not stop hearing winter music. We could lose the muse and keep the music, since the music makes the muse: our desire for meaning creates the imaginary persona who gives it to us, even though this leaves us adrift in a world of perpetual regret and loss, where we prefer the iceberg to the drifting ship.

But perhaps perpetual regret and loss is the price we pay for our knowledge of time. Our effort at making winter lives, our mind for winter — from the poems of Wallace Stevens to the underground mall — has some of the simple dignity of naming things. We sense this in every effort, by poet or polar explorer, not just to prevail in the face of pain but to create in the face of chaos, of mere blankness — to make something, if no more than a name. For me there is no more comic and moving artefact than the Arctic maps of the nineteenth century, with their carefully chosen colonial names for coves and passages and bays that before were just wastelands out there somewhere.

I sometimes stop and wonder at the reality of the geological and biological world, that the things we see, though certainly existing, have none of the intense sequence, the personifications, the character we give them; without us they would just fall back into the world of nothing. I have a hard time expressing this, though it is one of the strongest emotions I know: this sense that somehow the entirety of the universe could have been made — was made — without purpose, that it is cold, spinning, unconscious, neither kind nor cruel, just following laws that are in the end not even laws, just regularities produced by the cycling of chances. A vast, empty room, with no one home.

There are moments in painting when you get a glimpse of the vast indifference of nature — not only that nature doesn't care about us but that it doesn't care about itself. I'm aware there are those who insist on a sense, half mystical and half material, that the planet protects itself — the idea of Gaia — but I think we are seeing that one with our hearts. We are inside, naming and making, while outside the world doesn't give a damn; yet we persuade ourselves that it's a season bound by many symbols, a Christmas card picture, a thing, a state, a friend. It's winter.

I recall once when I got word that my best friend was dying and I happened to pass a paint store where all the shades of yellow were laid out and named, quite cleverly and precisely — lemon zest and buttercup and canary, each shade given a personality — and I thought, *This is all a lie.* The spectrum of light is as indifferent as the rest of the universe. "Buttercup" and "lemon zest" were not labels but just lies, hopeful names given to arbitrary swatches in a physical phenomenon of light, which is not only indifferent to our existence but without any kind of neat internal structure at all, with no more charm or colour than the indifferent hum of a radio on the wrong station.

There are moments when we can experience winter as, in effect, the universe experiences it: loveless and emotionless and just *there*, an endless cycling of physical law that is not just indifferent to our feelings but in some sense so arbitrary that it doesn't even have the quality of being elemental. There are moments when I almost think that I sense, with fear, the reality of the cosmos as it is: just this big, huge *nothing*, billions of years old, without segments or seasons or anything in it, where the truth of the universe is just that it brutally *is*. We live in a cold world.

But instead we give the coldness names, we write it poetry, we play it music, we experience it as a personality — and this is and remains the act of humanism. Armed with that hope, we see not waste and cold but light and mystery and wonder and something called January. We see not stilled atoms in a senseless world. We see winter.

I know there is something arrogant and imperial in this idea, and I am well aware that Eastern forms of meditation, for which I have great respect, in effect try to extinguish our efforts to name and distinguish and discriminate, and to return us to the choiceless void that is the reality in which we dance, in which these too-neat oppositions — North and South, winter and summer, Canada and the United States, even me going on and on and you reading patiently — don't exist. That way, we escape the cycle of need. I get it, I admire it. But my heart is with the opposite, humane effort to pretend that what we see is not blank cold but real *winter — l'hiver*, Persephone's mourning, Vivaldi's *inverno*, Schubert's wasteland, even Krieghoff's peasant dances and Monet's elegant *effets*. That we have extended this act of lending human feeling where there isn't any is a mistake, I don't doubt, but it makes it possible to welcome the end. It gives Demeter's mourning meaning.

I said that I had deliberately left out and saved two winter touchstones, two true meteorites from which ore has been flinted, until now. One was Villon's poem and the other is the famous myth of the Inuit having thirty or more words for snow. The "Eskimo vocabulary hoax" it's called disparagingly by its debunkers — Inuit languages are agglutinative, we now know, so they have no more "words" for snow than English does; they just compress their sentences more, for the sweetness of simplicity. Nonetheless, the story registers as a folk tale with a memorable moral: if you see snow, you'll discriminate snow. When people say the Inuit see so many kinds of snow because they have so many words for it, they don't really mean that the Inuit are prisoners of their tongue; they mean that their tongues are like "Snowflake" Bentley's microscopic eye, able to make tiny, fine discriminations lost on the rest of us. It's a compliment, however misstated. And the compliment is that where we see and name only one thing, they see and name many things. Where we see the enormous body of a white whale, they see each whisker on its chin. They don't have more words for snow, but snow finds its way into their words. Snow falls in the Inuit tongues as it falls in the circles where they live. The Inuit have more expressions for snow because they talk about it more.

An obvious idea but not, I think, a fatuous one: without the talk, no differences; without the language, no lore; without the meteorites, no chipping; without the Inuit to do the chipping, no knives; without the knives, no winter civilization; and without that, no winter life. Not thirty labels found for a world already labelled, but thirty or more for a world in need of names, endless efforts at description — melting snow, gathering snow, frosted snow, snow over a layer of ice, snow stretching out, skiable snow, pliable snow, resistant snow. All these words are not labels found at ease but worlds described with effort.

THE LAST MORAL of all these winter stories can be simply summarized: *things have names because acts have authors.* That, for me, is the whole of what we mean, or should mean, by humanism, in one monosyllabic sentence. Winter takes its names from winter people. This is true in a simple way. Shackleton and his companions, crossing Georgia Island from the wrong side in the last, bitter leg of their long journey to be rescued, were disoriented above all because the peaks they crossed had no names on the maps they used. Each name given to a cove or peak or plain created by chance forces is a hook to hang your mental hat on. It took a lot of other explorers a long time to name each feature, and each feature's name reflected the wants and needs of the namer.

But it goes deeper too. Those things that we think of as being big waves of response actually have significant individual authors. Whether it's William Cowper for the first time understanding that the experience of winter by the fireside can be positive and cheering, rather than depressing and forbidding, or Vincent Ponte seeing that the real life of the city lay not in the plaza above but in the underground below, each of these moments turns out to have a specific author. From naming the thousand kinds of icebergs to finding the individual shapes of snowflakes, from the rules for icing in hockey to the invention of the Christmas card, each thing exists because one individual gave form to something that had been unformed and unnamed before. It didn't happen by osmosis; it didn't happen by consensus; it didn't happen, God knows, by divine creation. Osmosis may have helped, and consensus happens for a reason, but finally each one of these acts can be broken down into the strange lives and stifled longings of our neighbours.

Things have names because acts have authors. For many, that kind of humanism is hubris. To describe is to dominate, to name is to numb, to explore is to exploit, and certainly to explain one thing is to extinguish another — to map is to oppress the islands left uncharted. Certainly, in any history, we see and are glad when the things left out find a way to be put back in, whether it's Fanny Mendelssohn or the overlooked Inuit at the polar moment. But either this claim is always true — if to describe is to dominate, then that is true of any description, even remedial ones — or else trivial: we can only do our best.

Winter started as this thing we had to get through; it has ended as this time to hold on to. A cycle becomes a season; a season becomes a secular holiday; the solstice becomes feasts. I don't know what sound a tree makes when it falls and there's no one to hear it. None, I think. But I do know that the cycle of seasons on Mars or Jupiter, lacking witnesses, is not a cycle at all, neatly shaped with four distinct faces, but just a slow shading, a flat, uninflected turning, as dumb and dull as any other purely physical inexorable cycle repeated into eternity. Noise in the forest without someone there to hear? Maybe. Summer and winter on Mars without people there to name them? I'm certain not. Deeper than the question of why there is something rather than nothing is the truth that *something* has a shape that only we can give it, the neat segmentation that gives us an illusion of order.

Where are the snows we knew? Where are the winters we recall? Locked inside us, in an idea about time and space that we can hardly accept but can tag with names and nostalgia, so that they are not quite lost. We go down deep and we miss the window; the passage clears and we miss the ice in California as Joni Mitchell dreams of the frozen river. We suffer and we long for memory, we draw a glacier and we draw ourselves, we make up Christmas and the bleak midwinter is suddenly no longer bleak but beautiful. We end up like Friedrich's French soldier in the snow, lost in the forest, counting snowflakes, seeing how they differ, right to the point of death. What the winter journey of the modern imagination teaches us is not that God is in the details but that our ability to grasp and discriminate the details gives us something to put in place of God.

I write these lines on a tiny island in the Caribbean where, like so many winter people, I have gone with my family to seek a week's refuge from March's bite. When I was young, watching snow fall by the window, I thought the idea of fleeing south was a kind of madness, or at least a kind of weakness — who except the exhausted would go to Florida, or Jamaica, or the little isle of Nevis? Well, now I am in what we politely call middle age (though it is further along the spectrum than that) and the lure of the South seems real to me. Who needs another winter? Then I think of spending Christmas here or of living here for good — and I cringe a little.

I realize that these chapters, in the guise of cultural observations and a kind of amateur's cultural anthropology, are really a composite list of things that I like and that I don't, like those of a Playmate of earlier vintage: her turn-ons and turn-offs. I hate cars, concussions, hockey violence generally, southern California at Christmas, Carlyle's politics, postmodern condescension to pre-modern peoples as much as postmodernists hate pre-modern condescension to alien ones . . . I love Christmas carols, *A Christmas Carol*, Dickens and Trollope, free-skating and fast-passing Russian and Quebec hockey, and courage of the kind that drove people towards the poles, which I wish I had more of.

Above all, I suppose, I love snow, in all its forms, and though I am sure I would lose this taste if I had to endure enough of it, so far I've endured a lot and lost not a bit. Winter is, once again, the white page on which we write our hearts. They would look different on a greener page. We name things in Hawaii; people remember in Tahiti; the Serengeti plain in torrid Africa was the first site where people thought as people still do. When we lose a powerful symbol of order, some other symbol comes to take its place. Human beings are matchlessly good at making them. But when we lose, through the vagaries of life or history, some powerful symbol of order, we feel the loss, and we should spend a minute mourning it. In our time, for instance, we have lost the idea of the naked human body as an image of divine order, seen it either pushed into fractured form or else made merely a revivalist symbol, or poked to the happy but less edifying margins of erotic art. We can't remake the nude, because the forces that unmade it are too strong and tidal to be resisted. But we can mourn the loss of the tradition it made and the values it embodied. Without winter, our sense of memory would be different, not over — but different is a kind of over. Life is always different, not over, and it is *different* that we really mind. When it is over, we won't be around to notice, but we know when it is different, and we feel sorry for the loss.

"I wish I had a river I could skate away on," Joni Mitchell tells us, lost in Los Angeles as she longs for snows once known. *Où sont les neiges d'antan?* Where are the old snows? Inside us, where they remain compressed, perhaps frozen, but still capable of being forced out from memory and finely articulated, or at least sweetly sung. Where did they go? Inside us, where they remain, as winter remains my favourite season. I still see the boy at the window, my own otherwise lost self, and feel him thinking, *Oh, a new place, the ice palace, the river, my home — my new home — look at the snow falling, hear how quiet it gets!* For the time being, at least, the snow still falls, and the world, like this speaker, is given the winter gift of silence.

BIBLIOGRAPHY

THE BOOKS AND articles listed in this bibliography are my sources for most of the information contained before — drawn from these diligent scholars who dig weird data from the hard ice of time, and then have them packed into soft snowballs by delinquent essayists. Those that I have used at particular length I have tried to shout out in the right, specific moment in this book, as well. Special thanks also to Ian Bostridge, who set me right on Schubert; to Jane Hirschfeld, who told me so much about the Japanese idea of winter; and to Leland de la Durantaye, who suggested and supplied the epigraph from Frye.

There are many other people to thank. For diligent fact-checking, thanks to Nathaniel Stein at *The New Yorker,* and to Daniel Aureliano Newman and Letitia Henville at Massey College. And thanks, too, to Assistant Editor Kelly Joseph and Editorial Assistant Meredith Dees at Anansi, who worked so hard, particularly on the photo research and acquiring permissions. And my gratitude as well to Sarah MacLachlan, overseeing at Anansi, and Bernie Lucht and Philip Coulter of the CBC's still matchless

Ideas series, and to my friend and lawyer, Michael Levine.

Let me praise at length three more: editor Janie Yoon of Anansi, who, with quiet wit and careful intelligence, helped me work and rework these chapters; it's the first time we have gone to war together and I can only say I hope we find another occasion to put on our armour. Next, my research consultant David A. Smith, without whose matchless grasp of the resources of the New York Public Library I would never have been able to write this book at all; he found source after source with a persistence nearly magical — to name a problem was to be provided with a book, and to worry about an issue was to be given a reference. And Ariel C. Knutson, my invaluable assistant and apprentice, who prepared the bibliography below for publication — and who also collated passages, shared lunches, transcribed the living-room lectures, read texts, offered notes, kept my spirits up, shared Justin Bieber pictures with my daughter, and generally offered more aid and comfort to an over-committed and often frantic writer than anyone should ever have to. She has my deep (and frankly slightly awestruck) gratitude.

ONE: ROMANTIC WINTER

CANADIAN ART AND CULTURE

Adamson, Jeremy. *Lawren S. Harris: Urban Scenes and Wilderness Landscapes, 1906–1930. Art Gallery of Ontario, January 14–February 26, 1978.* Toronto: Art Gallery of Ontario, 1978.

Barbeau, Marius. *Cornelius Krieghoff: Pioneer Painter of North America.* Toronto: Macmillan, 1934.

Cameron, Elspeth, ed. *Canadian Culture: An Introductory Reader.* Toronto: Canadian Scholars' Press, 1997.

Catalogue of an Exhibition of Contemporary British Water Colours: Wood

Engravings by Clare Leighton, A. R. E., Arctic Sketches by Lawren Harris and A. Y. Jackson, R. C. A., May 1931. Toronto: Gallery, 1931.

Cavell, Edward, and Dennis R. Reid. *When Winter Was King: The Image of Winter in 19th Century Canada.* Banff, AB: Altitude Publishing and Whyte Museum of the Canadian Rockies, 1988.

Christensen, Lisa. *A Hiker's Guide to the Rocky Mountain Art of Lawren Harris.* Calgary, AB: Fifth House, 2000.

Davis, Ann. *The Logic of Ecstasy: Canadian Mystical Painting, 1920–1940.* Toronto: University of Toronto Press, 1992.

Glickman, Susan. *The Picturesque and the Sublime: A Poetics of the Canadian Landscape.* Montreal: McGill-Queen's University Press, 1998.

Harper, J. Russell. *Cornelius Krieghoff: The Habitant Farm/La ferme.* Ottawa: National Gallery of Canada, 1977.

_____. *Krieghoff.* Toronto: University of Toronto Press, 1979.

Harris, Lawren. *In the Ward: His Urban Poetry and Paintings,* edited by Gregory Brian Betts. Toronto: Exile Editions, 2007.

_____. *Lawren Harris: Paintings 1910–1948.* Toronto: Art Gallery of Toronto, 1948.

Hulan, Renée. *Northern Experience and the Myths of Canadin Culture.* Montreal and Kingston: McGill-Queen's University Press, 2002.

Hunter, Andrew. *Lawren Stewart Harris: A Painter's Progress.* New York: America's Society Art Gallery, 2000.

Important Paintings, Drawings, Watercolours, Prints and Sculptures by Canadian Artists. Montreal: Christie, Manson & Woods (Canada), 1973.

Jameson, Anna Brownell. *Winter Studies and Summer Rambles in Canada.* Reprint. Toronto: New Canadian Library, 1972.

Jameson, Anna Brownell and Stuart Erskine, eds. *Anna Jameson Letters and Friendships (1812–1860).* London: T. F. Unwin, Ltd., 1915.

Jouvancourt, Hugues de. *Cornelius Krieghoff.* Toronto: Musson, 1973.

Lambert, Richard Stanton. *The Adventure of Canadian Painting.* Toronto: McClelland & Stewart, 1947.

Murray, Joan. *The Best of the Group of Seven.* Toronto: McClelland & Stewart, 1993.

_____. *Lawren Harris: An Introduction to His Life and Art.* Toronto: Firefly, 2003.

———. *Water: Lawren Harris and the Group of Seven.* Toronto: McArthur, 2004.

Murray, Joan, and Robert Fulford. *The Beginning of Vision: The Drawings of Lawren S. Harris.* Toronto: Mira Godard, 1982.

Newlands, Anne. *Canadian Art: From Its Beginnings to 2000.* Toronto: Firefly, 2000.

Reid, Dennis R. *Krieghoff: Images of Canada.* Vancouver: Douglas & McIntyre, 1999.

Robb, Nesca Adeline. *Four in Exile.* London: Hutchinson, 1948.

Silcox, David P. *The Group of Seven and Tom Thomson.* Toronto: Firefly, 2003.

Vezina, Raymond. *Cornelius Krieghoff: Peintre de moeurs (1815–1872).* Ottawa: Éditions du Pelican, 1972.

GERMAN ART AND CULTURE

Behler, Ernst. *German Romantic Literary Theory.* Cambridge: Cambridge University Press, 2005.

Beiser, Frederick C., ed. *The Early Political Writings of the German Romantics.* Cambridge: Cambridge University Press, 1996.

———. *Enlightenment, Revolution, and Romanticism: The Genesis of Modern German Political Thought, 1790–1800.* Cambridge, MA: Harvard University Press, 1992.

Berman, Antoine. *The Experience of the Foreign: Culture and Translation in Romantic Germany.* Albany: State University of New York Press, 1992.

Boyesen, Hjalmar Hjorth. *Essays on German Literature.* Freeport, NY: Book of Libraries Press, 1972.

Brunschwig, Henri. *Enlightenment and Romanticism in Eighteenth-Century Prussia.* Chicago: University of Chicago Press, 1974.

Chaouli, Michel. *The Laboratory of Poetry: Chemistry and Poetics in the Work of Friedrich Schlegel.* Baltimore, MD: Johns Hopkins University Press, 2002.

Durrani, Osman, ed. *German Poetry of the Romantic Era: An Anthology.* London: Berg, 1986.

Gwinner, Thomas. *As Often the Moon May Shine.* Leipzig: Engelsdorfer, 2006.

Hamilton, Paul. *Coleridge and German Philosophy: The Poet in the Land of Logic*. London: Continuum, 2007.

Hanak, Miroslav John. *A Guide to Romantic Poetry in Germany*. New York: Peter Lang, 1987.

Hofmann, Werner. *Caspar David Friedrich*. London: Thames & Hudson, 2001.

Koerner, Joseph Leo. *Caspar David Friederich and the Subject of Landscape*. London: Reaktion Books, 2009.

Kuzniar, Alice A. *Delayed Endings: Nonclosure in Novalis and Hölderlin*. Athens: University of Georgia Press, 1987.

Lacoue-Labarthe, Philippe, and Nancy Jean-Luc. *The Literary Absolute: The Theory of Literature in German Romanticism*. Albany: State University of New York Press, 1988.

Lussky, Alma Elise. *German Romanticism*. New York: G. P. Putnam's Sons, 1932.

Manfred, Frank. *The Philosophical Foundations of Early German Romanticism*. Albany: State University of New York Press, 2004.

McNiece, Gerald. *The Knowledge that Endures: Coleridge, German Philosophy, and the Logic of Romantic Thought*. London: Macmillan, 1992.

Millán-Zaibert, Elizabeth. *Friedrich Schlegel and the Emergence of Romantic Philosophy*. Albany: State University of New York Press, 2007.

Novalis [Georg Philipp Friedrich Freiherr von Hardenberg]. *Novalis: Notes for a Romantic Encyclopaedia (Das Allgemeine Brouillon)*. Translated and edited by David W. Wood. Albany: State University of New York Press, 2007.

Peucker, Brigitte. *Arcadia to Elysium: Preromantic Modes in 18th Century Germany*. Bonn: Bouvier, 1980.

Pierce, Frederick E., and Carl F. Schreiber, eds. *Fiction and Fantasy of German Romance: Selections from the German Romantic Authors, 1790–1830, in English Translation*. New York: Oxford University Press, 1927.

Rose, William. *From Goethe to Byron: The Development of "Weltschmerz" in German Literature*. London: G. Routledge and Sons, 1924.

Siegel, Linda. *Caspar David Friedrich and the Age of German Romanticism*. Boston: Branen Press, 1978.

———. *Music in German Romantic Literature: A Collection of Essays, Reviews and Stories*. Novato, CA: Elra, 1983.

Simpson, Patricia Anne. *The Erotics of War in German Romanticism*. Lewisburg, PA: Bucknell University Press, 2006.

Stopp, Elisabeth, ed. *German Romantics in Context: Selected Essays, 1971–1986*. London: Bristol Classical Press, 1992.

Tymms, Ralph. *German Romantic Literature*. London: Methuen, 1955.

Vaughan, William. *German Romantic Painting*. New Haven, CT: Yale University Press, 1980.

Ziolkowski, Theodore. *German Romanticism and Its Institutions*. Princeton, NJ: Princeton University Press, 1990.

SCANDINAVIAN ART AND CULTURE

Andersen, Hans Christian. *The Diaries of Hans Christian Andersen*, edited by Patricia L. Conroy and Sven Hakon Rossel. Seattle: University of Washington Press, 1990.

———. *Hans Christian Andersen: The Maker of Fairy Tales*, edited by Jean Hersholt and Fritz Kredel. New York: Limited Editions Club, 1942.

———. *The Nightingale*. San Francisco, 1934.

———. *The Stories of Hans Christian Andersen*, edited by Jeffrey Frank, Diana Frank, Vilhelm Pedersen, and Lorenz Froelich. Boston: Houghton Mifflin, 2003.

———. *The Story of My Life*. Boston: Houghton Mifflin, 1871.

Andersen, Jens. *Hans Christian Andersen: A New Life*. Woodstock, NY: Overlook, 2005.

Barry, Sebastian. *Andersen's English*. London: Faber, 2009.

Böök, Fredrik. *Hans Christian Andersen: A Biography*. Norman: University of Oklahoma, 1962.

Boyd, Louise Arner, and John Kirtland Wright. *The Fiord Region of East Greenland*. New York: American Geographical Society, 1935.

Bredsdorff, Elias. *Hans Christian Andersen: The Story of His Life and Work*. London: Phaidon, 1975.

Brust, Beth Wagner. *The Amazing Paper Cuttings of Hans Christian Andersen*. New York: Ticknor and Fields, 1994.

Godden, Rumer. *Hans Christian Andersen*. London: Hutchinson, 1955.

———. *Hans Christian Andersen: A Great Life in Brief*. New York: Knopf, 1955.

Greenaway, Kate. *Kate Greenaway's Original Drawings for the Snow Queen.* New York: Schocken, 1981.

Greene, Carol. *Hans Christian Andersen: Teller of Tales.* Chicago: Children's Press, 1986.

Grønbech, Bo. *Hans Christian Andersen.* Boston: Twayne, 1980.

Heltoft, Kjeld, and David Hohnen. *Hans Christian Andersen as an Artist.* Copenhagen: Christian Ejlers, 2005.

Lederer, Wolfgang. *The Kiss of the Snow Queen: Hans Christian Andersen and Man's Redemption by Woman.* Berkeley: University of California Press, 1986.

Manning-Sanders, Ruth. *Swan of Denmark: The Story of Hans Christian Andersen.* New York: McBride, 1950.

Meynell, Esther. *The Story of Hans Andersen.* London: Methuen, 1949.

Prince, Alison. *Hans Christian Andersen: The Fan Dancer.* London: Allison & Busby, 1998.

Rowland, Herbert. *More than Meets the Eye: Hans Christian Andersen and Nineteenth-Century American Criticism.* Madison, NJ: Fairleigh Dickinson University Press, 2006.

Spink, Reginald. *Hans Christian Andersen and His World.* New York: Putnam, 1972.

Yolen, Jane, and Dennis Nolan. *The Perfect Wizard: Hans Christian Andersen.* New York: Dutton, 2004.

OTHER ART AND CULTURE

Azarian, Mary and Jacqueline Briggs Martin. *Snowflake Bentley.* Boston: Houghton Mifflin, 1998.

Bruegmann, Robert. *Central Heating and Forced Ventilation: Origins and Effects on Architectural Design.* University of California: *Journal of the Society of Architectural Historians*, Vol. 37, No. 3, October 1978.

Coleridge, Samuel Taylor. *The Letters of Samuel Taylor Coleridge.* London: Grey Walls Press. 1950.

Cowper, William. *The Complete Poetical Works of William Cowper.* London: Humphrey Milford, 1913.

Dortmann, Andrea. *Winter Facets: Traces and Tropes of the Cold.* (Ph.D. Diss.) New York University, 2003.

Engell, James. *The Creative Imagination: Enlightenment to Romanticism.* Cambridge, MA: Harvard University Press, 1981.

Gourmont, Remy de. *Simone: Poème Champêtre.* Paris: Mercure de France, 1901.

Gray, Camilla, and Marian Burleigh-Motley. *The Russian Experiment in Art, 1863–1922.* London: Thames and Hudson, 1996.

Johnson, Samuel. *The Winter's Walk.* London: C. Taylor, 1787.

Kroitor, Harry Peter. *William Cowper and Science in the Eighteenth Century.* (Ph.D. Diss.) University of Maryland, 1957.

Lurie, Alison. *Boys and Girls Forever: Children's Classics from Cinderella to Harry Potter.* New York: Penguin, 2003.

Moffett, Charles S. *Impressionists in Winter: Effets de Neige.* Washington, DC: Phillips Collection and Philip Wilson, 1998.

Montesquieu, Charles de Secondat. *The Spirit of Laws.* Chicago: Encyclopedia Britannica, 1952.

Nabokov, Vladimir, ed. *Pushkin, Lermontov, Tyutchev: Poems.* London: L. Drummond, 1947.

Ruskin, John and John Hayman. *John Ruskin and Switzerland.* Waterloo: Wilfrid Laurier University Press, 1990.

Sarabianov, Dmitri V. *Russian Art from Neoclassicism to the Avant-Garde, 1800–1917: Painting, Sculpture, Architecture.* New York: Abrams, 1990.

Stevens, Wallace. *Harmonium.* London: St. James Press, 1975.

Vivaldi — Concerto for Violin, Strings and Basso Continuo Op. 8 No 4, Rv 297 Winter. Dowani Ag, 2006.

THE SCIENCE OF ICE

Agassiz, Louis. *Geological Sketches.* Boston: Ticknor and Fields, 1866.

Agassiz, Louis, and Albert Carozzi. *Studies on Glaciers: Preceded by the Discourse of Neuchâtel.* New York: Hafner, 1967.

Bailey, Ronald H. *Glacier.* Alexandria, VA: Time-Life Books, 1982.

Balch, Edwin Swift. *Glacières; or, Freezing Caverns.* Philadelphia: Allen, Lane & Scott, 1900.

Ball, Robert S. *Cause of an Ice Age.* New York: D. Appleton, 1891.

Bonney, T. G. *Ice-Work, Present and Past.* New York: Appleton, 1896.

Coleman, Arthur Philemon. *Ice Ages, Recent and Ancient*. New York: Macmillan, 1926.

Cruikshank, Julie. *Do Glaciers Listen?: Local Knowledge, Colonial Encounters, and Social Imagination*. Vancouver: UBC Press, 2005.

Dyson, James Lindsay. *The World of Ice*. New York: Knopf, 1962.

Faber, Monika, ed. *Infinite Ice: The Arctic and the Alps from 1860 to the Present*. Ostfildern, Germany: Hatje Cantz, 2008.

Fagan, Brian. *The Little Ice Age: How Climate Made History, 1300–1850*. New York, NY: Basic Books, 2000.

Gosnell, Mariana. *Ice: The Nature, the History, and the Uses of an Astonishing Substance*. New York: Knopf, 2005.

Gresswell, R. Kay. *The Physical Geography of Glaciers and Glaciation*. London: Hulton Educational, 1958.

Grove, Jean M. *The Little Ice Age*. London: Methuen, 1988.

Hambrey, M. J. *Glaciers*. Vancouver: UBC Press, 1994.

Hobbs, William Herbert. *Characteristics of Existing Glaciers*. New York: Macmillan, 1911.

Hoel, Adolf, and Werner Werenskiold. *Glaciers and Snowfields in Norway*. Oslo: Oslo University Press, 1962.

Hubbard, Bernard Rosecrans. *Mush, You Malemutes!* New York: American Press, 1932.

John, Brian Stephen. *The Ice Age: Past and Present*. London: Collins, 1977.

Kingery, W. D., ed. *Ice and Snow: Properties, Processes, and Applications*. Proceedings of a conference held at the Massachusetts Institute of Technology, February 12–16, 1962. Cambridge, MA: MIT Press, 1963.

Moore, W. G. *Glaciers*. London: Hutchinson, 1972.

Paterson, W. S. B. *The Physics of Glaciers*. Oxford: Pergamon, 1994.

Shaler, Nathaniel Southgate. *Illustrations of the Earth's Surface: Glaciers*. Boston: R. Osgood, 1881.

Sharp, Robert P. *Glaciers*. Eugene: Oregon State System of Higher Education, 1960.

———. *Living Ice: Understanding Glaciers and Glaciation*. Cambridge: Cambridge University Press, 1988.

Souchez, Roland. *Ice Composition and Glacier Dynamics*. Berlin: Springer, 1991.

Stratz, Rudolph. *Where Snow Is Sovereign: A Romance of the Glaciers.* New York: Dodd, Mead, 1909.

Tufnell, Lance. *Glacier Hazards.* London: Longman, 1984.

Tutton, Alfred Edwin Howard. *The High Alps: A Natural History of Ice and Snow.* London: Kegan Paul, Trench, Trubner, 1927.

Tyndall, John. *The Forms of Water in Clouds and Rivers, Ice and Glaciers.* New York: J. A. Hill, 1904.

———. *The Glaciers of the Alps: Being a Narrative of Excursions and Ascents, an Account of the Origin and Phenomena of Glaciers and an Exposition of the Physical Principles to Which They Are Related.* London: Longmans, Green, 1911.

Vial, A. E. Lockington. *Alpine Glaciers.* London: Batchworth Press, 1952.

White, Frank, and Paul A. Mayewski. *The Ice Chronicles: The Quest to Understand Global Climate Change.* Hanover: University Press of New England, 2002.

Wilson, Eric. *The Spiritual History of Ice: Romanticism, Science, and the Imagination.* New York: Palgrave Macmillan, 2003.

Wright, Charles S. *Glaciology.* London: Harrison and Sons, for the Committee of the Captain Scott Arctic Fund, 1922.

TWO: RADICAL WINTER

POLAR EXPLORATION (GENERAL)

Anderson, Harry S. *Exploring the Polar Regions.* New York: Facts on File, 2005.

Andrist, Ralph K. *Heroes of Polar Exploration.* New York: American Heritage, 1962.

Arcangues, Michel d'. *Dictionnaire des explorateurs des pôles.* Biarritz, France: Séguier, 2001.

Barrett, Andrea. *The Voyage of the Narwhal: A Novel.* New York: Norton, 1998.

Bruce, William S. *Polar Exploration.* London: Williams and Norgate, 1911.

Capelotti, P. J. *By Airship to the North Pole: An Archaeology of Human Exploration.* New Brunswick, NJ: Rutgers University Press, 1999.

Cherry-Garrard, Apsley. *The Worst Journey in the World*. New York: Carroll & Graf Pub., 1989.

Diski, Jenny. *Skating to Antarctica*. London: Granta Books, 1997.

Fleming, Fergus. *Barrow's Boys*. New York: Atlantic Monthly Press, 2000.

———. *Ninety Degrees North: The Quest for the North Pole*. New York: Grove Press, 2001.

Hobbs, William Herbert. *Evolution in the Travel Technique of Polar Exploration*. Lwów, Poland: Towarzystwo Geograficzne we Lwowie, 1934.

Imbert, Bertrand. *North Pole, South Pole: Journeys to the Ends of the Earth*. New York: H. N. Abrams, 1992.

Jones, A. G. E. *Polar Portraits: Collected Papers*. Whitby, UK: Caedmon, 1992.

Klink, Amyr. *Between Two Poles*. London: Bloomsbury, 1995.

Markham, Clements R. *The Arctic Navy List, 1773–1873*. 1875. Reprint. Dallington, UK: Naval and Military Press, 1992.

Maxtone-Graham, John. *Safe Return Doubtful: The Heroic Age of Polar Exploration*. New York: Scribner, 1988.

Mills, William J. *Exploring Polar Frontiers: A Historical Encyclopedia*. Santa Barbara, CA: ABC-CLIO, 2003.

Moss, Sarah. *The Frozen Ship: The Histories and Tales of Polar Exploration*. New York: BlueBridge, 2006.

Murphy, David Thomas. *German Exploration of the Polar World: A History, 1870–1940*. Lincoln: University of Nebraska Press, 2002.

Osgood, Cornelius. *Winter*. Lincoln: University of Nebraska Press, 2006.

Parmer, Jean M. *Polar Books: Bibliography and Price Guide*. San Diego, CA: J. Parmer, 1990.

Pease, Francis K. *To the Ends of the Earth*. London: Hurst and Blackett, 1935.

Rémy, Frédérique. *Histoire des pôles: Mythes et réalités polaires (XVIIe–XVIIIe siècles)*. Paris: Éditions Desjonquères, 2009.

Sandak, Cass R. *The Arctic and Antarctic: Exploration in the 20th Century*. New York: F. Watts, 1987.

Scott, J. M. *The Private Life of Polar Exploration*. Edinburgh: W. Blackwood, 1982.

Snowman, Daniel. *Pole Positions: The Polar Regions and the Future of the Planet*. London: Hodder and Stoughton, 1993.

Spufford, Francis. *I May Be Some Time: Ice and the English Imagination*. New York: St. Martin's Press, 1997.

Stam, David H. *Books on Ice: British and American Literature of Polar Exploration*. New York: Grolier Club, 2005.

Streever, Bill. *Cold: Adventures in the World's Frozen Places*. New York: Little, Brown and Co., 2009.

Struzik, Ed. *Northwest Passage: The Quest for an Arctic Route to the East*. Toronto: Key Porter Books, 1990.

———. *Ten Rivers: Adventure Stories from the Arctic*. Toronto: CanWest Books, 2005.

Willis, Clint, ed. *Ice: Stories of Survival from Polar Exploration*. New York: Thunder's Mouth Press/Balliett and Fitzgerald, 1999.

SPECIFIC POLAR EXPEDITIONS

Amundsen, Roald. *The Amundsen Photographs*. New York: Atlantic Monthly Press, 1987.

Bomann-Larsen, Tor. *Roald Amundsen: En biografi*. Oslo: Cappelen, 2003.

Cox, Lynne. *South with the Sun: Roald Amundsen, His Polar Exploration, and the Quest for Discovery*. New York, NY: Knopf, 2011.

Hartley, Catharine. *To the Poles Without a Beard: The Polar Adventures of a World Record–Breaking Woman*. Oxford: Isis, 2004.

Heimermann, Benoît, and Gérard Janichon. *Charcot: Le gentleman des pôles*. Rennes: Éditions Ouest-France, 1991.

Janichon, Gérard, and Christian de Marliave. *L'aventure polaire française: Des baleiniers aux expeditions de Paul-Émile Victor*. Paris: Arthaud, 1997.

Kløver, Geir O. *Cold Recall: Reflections of a Polar Explorer*. Oslo: Fram Museum, 2009.

Kubnick, Henri. *Charcot et les explorations polaires*. Tours, France: Mame, 1938.

Mabire, Jean. *Roald Amundsen: Le plus grand des explorateurs polaires*. Grenoble, France: Glénat, 1998.

Mills, Leif. *Men of Ice: The Lives of Alistair Forbes Mackay (1878–1914) and Cecil Henry Meares (1877–1937)*. Whitby, UK: Caedmon, 2008.

Orphelin, Catherine. *Paul-Émile Victor: Mémoires et rêves d'un humaniste*. Marseille, France: AGEP, 1992.

Owen, Russell. *The Conquest of the North and South Poles: Adventures of the Peary and Byrd Expeditions*. New York: Random House, 1952.

Partridge, Bellamy. *Amundsen: The Splendid Norseman*. New York: Frederick A. Stokes, 1922.

Pool, Beekman H. *Polar Extremes: The World of Lincoln*. Fairbanks: University of Alaska Press, 2002.

Ross, M. J. *Polar Pioneers: John Ross and James Clark Ross*. Montreal: McGill-Queen's University Press, 1994.

Rouillon, Gaston. *Jean-Baptiste Charcot: Sa vie, son oeuvre, leurs prolongements 50 ans après*. Talloires, France: G. Rouillon, 1986.

Shackleton, Ernest Henry. *South: The Story of Shackleton's Last Expedition*. New York: Konecky, 1999.

Smith, Michael. *Captain Crozier: Last Man Standing?* Cork, Ireland: Collins Press, 2006.

Vaeth, J. Gordon. *To the Ends of the Earth: The Explorations of Roald Amundsen*. New York: Harper and Row, 1962.

Victor, Paul-Émile. *Dialogues à une voix*. Paris: Laffont, 1995.

————. *L'iglou*. Paris: Payot et Rivages, 1995.

OTHER

Bradfield, Elizabeth. *Approaching Ice: Poems*. New York: Persea Books, 2010.

Carroll, Lewis. *The Hunting of the Snark*. Champaign, IL: Book Jungle, 2008.

Mailer, Norman. *Of a Fire on the Moon*. Boston: Little Brown, 1970.

Poe, Edgar Allan. *The Narrative of Arthur Gordon Pym of Nantucket*. London: Penguin Books, 2006.

Shelley, Mary Wollstonecraft. *Frankenstein*. New York: Viking, 1998.

THREE: RECUPERATIVE WINTER

COMMERCIAL CHRISTMAS

Abelson, Elaine S. *When Ladies Go A-Thieving: Middle-Class Shoplifters in the Victorian Department Store*. New York: Oxford University Press, 1989.

Bowlby, Rachel. *Carried Away: The Invention of Modern Shopping*. New York: Columbia University Press, 2001.

Devorkin, Joseph. *Great Merchants of Early New York: "The Ladies' Mile."* New York: Society for the Architecture of the City, 1987.

Dickens, Charles. *The Annotated Christmas Carol*. New York: W. W. Norton, 2004.

_____. *Christmas Books and Stories*. New York: P. Collier and Sons, 1870.

Eckstein, Bob. *The History of the Snowman*. New York, NY: Simon Spotlight Entertainment, 2007.

Hamlin, David D. *Work and Play: The Production and Consumption of Toys in Germany*. Ann Arbor: University of Michigan Press, 2007.

Harris, Leon A. *Merchant Princes: An Intimate History of Jewish Families Who Built Great Department Stores*. New York: Harper and Row, 1979.

Hendrickson, Robert. *The Grand Emporiums: The Illustrated History of America's Great Department Stores*. New York: Stein and Day, 1979.

Hower, Ralph M. *The History of Macy's of New York, 1858–1919: Chapters in the Evolution of the Department Store*. Cambridge, MA: Harvard University Press, 1943.

Moss, Mark Howard. *Shopping as an Entertainment Experience*. Lanham, MD: Lexington Books, 2007.

Phenix, Patricia. *Eatonians: The Story of the Family Behind the Family*. Toronto: McClelland and Stewart, 2002.

Samuelson, Sue. *Christmas: An Annotated Bibliography*. New York: Garland Publishing, Inc. 1982.

Whitaker, Jan. *Service and Style: How the American Department Store Fashioned the Middle Class*. New York: St. Martin's Press, 2006.

RELIGION, POETRY, AND CUSTOMS

Auden, W. H. *For the Time Being: A Christmas Oratorio*. London: Faber and Faber, 1944.

Abrahams, Roger D. *Christmas and Carnival on Saint Vincent*. California Folklore Society, 1973.

Chesterton, G. K. *Avowals and Denials: A Book of Essays*. LaVergne, TN: Barton Press, 2010.

_____. *The Thing: Why I Am a Catholic*. New York: Dodd, Mead, 1944.

Coffin, Tristram Potter. *The Book of Christmas Folklore*. New York: Seabury Press, 1973.

Comfort, David. *Just Say Noel!: A History of Christmas from the Nativity to the Nineties*. New York: Simon and Schuster, 1995.

Crashaw, Richard. *Steps to the Temple*. Cambridge: Cambridge University Press, 1904.

Dawson, W. F. *Christmas: Its Origin and Associations*. London: E. Stock, 1902.

Farjeon, B. L. *Christmas Angel*. London: Ward and Downey, 1885.

_____. *Shadows on the Snow: A Christmas Story*. New York: Harper and Brothers, 1877.

Foley, Daniel J. *The Christmas Tree: An Evergreen Garland Filled with History, Folklore, Symbolism, Traditions, Legends and Stories*. Philadelphia: Chilton, 1960.

Golby, J. M. *The Making of the Modern Christmas*. Stroud, UK: Sutton, 2000.

Hervey, Thomas Kibble. *The Book of Christmas: Descriptive of the Customs, Ceremonies, Traditions, Superstitions, Fun, Feeling, and Festivities of the Christmas Season*. Whitefish, MT: Kessinger, 2006.

Jekels, Ludwig. *Selected Papers*. New York: International Universities Press, 1953.

Johnson, Sheila K. "The Christmas Card Syndrome." *New York Times Magazine*, December 5, 1971, 38–29.

Jones, Ernest. *Essays on Applied Psychoanalysis*. London: International Psycho-Analytical Press, 1923.

Kelleher, Daniel Lawrence, ed. *An Anthology of Christmas Prose and Verse*. London: Cresset Press, 1928.

Lévi-Strauss, Claude. "*Le Père Noël supplicié.*" *Les Temps Modernes*, 7 (1952), 1572–90.

Mabie, Hamilton W. *The Book of Christmas*. New York: Macmillan, 1909.

Miles, Clement A. *Christmas Customs and Traditions: Their History and Significance*. New York: Dover Publications, 1976.

Nissenbaum, Stephen. *The Battle for Christmas*. New York: Alfred A. Knopf, 1996.

O'Neil, Sunny. *The Gift of Christmas Past: A Return to Victorian Traditions*. Nashville, TN: American Association for State and Local History, 1981.

Paru, Marden D. "Tannenbaum and the Jewish Problem." *Jewish Social Studies* 35, no. 3/4 (1973): 283–89.

Reid, Robert Ewen. *Infantile Crises Associated with Christmas: A Psychoanalytic Interpretation*. (Ph.D. Diss.) Claremont, California: School of Theology, 1968.

Samuelson, Sue. *Christmas: An Annotated Bibliography*. New York: Garland, 1982.

Sansom, William. *Christmas*. London: Weidenfeld and Nicolson, 1968.

Snyder, Phillip V. *December 25th: The Joys of Christmas Past*. New York: Dodd, Mead, 1985.

Spicer, Dorothy Gladys. *46 days of Christmas: A Cycle of Old World Songs, Legends and Customs*. New York: Coward-McCann, 1960.

Steiner, Rudolf. *The Festivals and Their Meaning*. Vol. 1, *Christmas*. London: Rudolf Steiner, 1955.

Stokker, Kathleen. *Keeping Christmas: Yuletide Traditions in Norway and the New Land*. St. Paul, MN: Minnesota Historical Society Press, 2000.

Trollope, Anthony. *Anthony Trollope: The Complete Shorter Fiction*, edited by Julian Thompson. New York: Caroll and Graf, 1992.

Wallis, Wilson D. *Culture and Progress*. New York: McGraw-Hill, 1930.

Weiser, Franz Xavier. *Handbook of Christian Feasts and Customs: The Year of the Lord in Liturgy and Folklore*. New York: Harcourt, Brace, 1958.

CHRISTMAS IN THE UNITED STATES

Barnett, James Harwood. *The American Christmas: A Study in National Culture*. New York: Arno Press, 1976.

Benney, Mark, Rolf Meyersohn, David Riesman, and Robert Weiss. *Christmas in an Apartment Hotel*. Chicago: *American Journal of Sociology* and University of Chicago Press, 1959.

Bye, Roger. *How Christmas Came to Hawaii*. Honolulu: Dilligham, 1967.

Cure, Karen. *An Old-Fashioned Christmas: American Holiday Traditions*. New York: H. N. Abrams, 1984.

Lankford, Mary D. *Christmas USA*. New York: Collins, 2006.

Marling, Karal Ann. *Merry Christmas!: Celebrating America's Greatest Holiday*. Cambridge, MA: Harvard University Press, 2000.

Rawlings, Kevin. *We Were Marching on Christmas Day: A History and Chronicle of Christmas During the Civil War*. Baltimore, MD: Toomey Press, 1995.

Restad, Penne L. *Christmas in America: A History*. New York: Oxford University Press, 1995.

Richards, Katharine Lambert. *How Christmas Came to the Sunday-Schools: The Observance of Christmas in the Protestant Church Schools of the United States, an Historical Study*. New York: Dodd, Mead, 1934.

SANTA CLAUS

de Groot, Adrianus Dingeman. *Saint Nicholas: A Psychoanalytic Study of His History and Myth*. New York: Basic Books, 1965.

Nast, Thomas. *Thomas Nast: Cartoons and Illustrations*. New York: Dover, 1974.

Paine, Albert. *Thomas Nast: His Period and His Pictures*. New York: Chelsea House, 1980.

Siefker, Phyllis. *Santa Claus, Last of the Wild Men: The Origins and Evolution of Saint Nicholas, Spanning 50,000 years*. Jefferson, NC: McFarland, 1997.

Standiford, Les. *The Man Who Invented Christmas*. New York: Crown, 2008.

FOUR: RECREATIONAL WINTER

WINTER SPORTS (GENERAL)

Bass, Howard. *Winter Sports*. South Brunswick, NJ: A. S. Barnes, 1968.

Berlioz, Hector. *The Memoirs of Hector Berlioz*. New York: Knopf, 2002.

Cereghini, Mario. *5000 years of Winter Sports*. Milan: Edizioni del Milione, 1955.

Chadwick, Henry. *Handbook of Winter Sports*. New York: Beadle and Adams, 1879.

Cleaver, Reginald. *A Winter-Sport Book*. London: A. and C. Black, 1911.

Devlin, Iseult. *Winter Sports*. Camden, ME: Ragged Mountain Press, 2001.

Dier, J. C., ed. *A Book of Winter Sports: An Attempt to Catch the Spirit of the Keen Joys of the Winter Season*. New York: Macmillan, 1912.

Flower, Raymond. *The Story of Skiing and Other Winter Sports*. London: Angus and Robertson, 1976.

Gogol, Nikolai Vasilievich. *Dead Souls*. New York: Everyman's Library, 2004.

James, C. L. R. *Beyond a Boundary*. New York: Pantheon Books, 1983.

Jessup, Elon Huntington. *Snow and Ice Sports: A Winter Manual*. New York: E. P. Dutton, 1923.

Liebers, Arthur. *The Complete Book of Winter Sports*. New York: Coward, McCann and Geoghegan, 1971.

Loiseau, Gilbert G. *Bobsleigh: Technique, entraînment, compétition*. Paris: Éditions Amphora, 1968.

Lytton, Neville. *Winter Sports*. London: Seeley, Service, 1930.

Macy, Sue. *Freeze Frame: A Photographic History of the Winter Olympics*. Washington, DC: National Geographic, 2006.

McWhirter, Norris, ed. *Guinness Book of Olympic Records*. New York: Bantam Books, 1979.

Putnam, Harold, ed. *The Dartmouth Book of Winter Sports*. New York: A. S. Barnes, 1939.

Syers, E., ed. *The Book of Winter Sports*. London: E. Arnold, 1908.

White, William Dustin. *The Book of Winter Sports*. Boston: Houghton Mifflin, 1925.

Wordsworth, William. *The Prelude*. Harmondsworth: Penguin, 1971.

EUROPE

Achard, Michel. *Histoire du ski et des sports d'hiver dans le massif du Pilat (Loire-Forez) de 1892 à nos jours*. Le Bassat, France: M. Achard, 1989.

Benson, E. F. *Winter Sports in Switzerland*. London: G. Allen, 1913.

Colburn, Henry. *Colburn's Calendar of Amusements in Town and Country for 1840: Comprising London Seasons and Sights; Balls, Masquerades, Theatres; Winter, Summer, and Harvest Sports*. London: H. Colburn, 1840.

Dupays, Paul. *L'hiver: Ses joies, ses sports, ses caprices*. Paris: Argo, 1934.

Lang, Andrew. *Lost Leaders*. New York: Longmans, Green, 1889.

Massot, Claude. *Guide des sports d'hiver en France*. Paris: Stock, 1970.

McDermott, F. *How to Be Happy in Switzerland (Winter Sports)*. London: Arrowsmith, 1928.

Meijerman, A. M. *Hollandso winters*. Hilversum, Netherlands: W. de Haan, 1967.

Perrin, Henri. *Les stations de sports d'hiver: Création et gestion, rôle des collectivités locales*. Paris: Berger-Levrault, 1971.

Root, Waverley. *Winter Sports in Europe: A Comprehensive Guide*. New York: Grove Press, 1956.

———. *Winter Sports in France: A Comprehensive Guide*. New York: Grove Press, 1956.

CANADA

Beers, W. George. *Over the Snow: or, The Montreal Carnival*. Montreal: W. Drysdale and J. Robinson, 1883.

Bryden, Wendy. *Canada at the Olympic Winter Games: The Official Sports History and Record Book*. Edmonton: Hurtig, 1987.

Corbet, Elise A., and Anthony W. Rasporich, eds. *Winter Sports in the West*. Calgary: Historical Society of Alberta, 1990.

Ellis, David W. H. *Canada at the Olympics, 1988*. St. Albert, AB: Ellis Sports Equipment and Consulting, 1989.

Le Moine, J. M. *Historical and Sporting Notes on Quebec and Its Environs*. Quebec: L. J. Demers & Frère, 1889.

Quebec Winter Carnival: January 29th to February 3rd, 1894. Montreal: Sabiston, 1894.

UNITED STATES

Cruikshank, James A. *Spalding's Winter Sports*. New York: American Sports, 1917.

Harris, Fred Henry. *Dartmouth Out o' Doors: A Book Descriptive of the Outdoor Life in and about Hanover, N.H.* Boston: George E. Crosby, 1913.

James, George Wharton. *Winter Sports at Huntington Lake Lodge in the High Sierras: The Story of the First Annual Ice and Snow Carnival of the Commercial Club of Fresno, California*. Pasadena, CA: Radiant Life Press, 1916.

Larson, Paul Clifford. *Icy Pleasures: Minnesota Celebrates Winter*. Afton, MN: Afton Historical Society Press, 1998.

Lewin, Josh. *Getting in the Game: Inside Baseball's Winter Meetings.* Washington, DC: Brasseys, 2004.

Ortloff, George Christian. *Lake Placid, the Olympic Years, 1932–1980: A Portrait of America's Premier Winter Resort.* Lake Placid, NY: Macromedia, 1976.

Spalding Catalogue of Fall and Winter Sports. New York: A. G. Spalding and Brothers, 1906.

HOCKEY AND SKATING

Dowbiggin, Bruce. *Of Ice and Men: Steve Yzerman, Chris Chelios, Glen Sather, Dominik Hasek, The Craft of Hockey.* Toronto: Macfarlane Walter & Ross, 1998.

Duhatschek, Eric. *One Hundred Years of Hockey: The Chronicle of a Century on Ice.* San Diego, CA: Thunder Bay Press, 1999.

Hunter, Doug. *War Games: Conn Smythe and Hockey's Fighting Men.* Toronto: Viking, 1996.

Klein, Jeff Z. and Karl-Eric Reif. *Hockey Compendium.* Toronto: McClelland & Stewart, 1986.

McFarlane, Brian. *Proud Past, Bright Future: One Hundred Years of Canadian Women's Hockey.* Toronto: Stoddart, 1994.

Podnieks, Andrew. *Canada's Olympic Hockey Teams: The Complete History, 1920–1998.* Toronto: Doubleday Canada, 1997.

Tarasov, Anatoli Vladimirovich. *Road to Olympus.* Toronto: Griffin House, 1969.

Taylor, Duff. *Skating.* London: Seeley, Service, 1937.

Vaughan, Garth. *The Puck Starts Here: The Origin of Canada's Great Winter Game, Ice Hockey.* Fredericton, NB: Goose Lane Editions, 1996.

Vigneault, Michel. *La naissance d'un sport organisé au Canada: Le hockey à Montréal, 1875–1917.* (Ph.D. Diss.) L'Université Laval, 2001.

Whitehead, Eric. *The Patricks: Hockey's Royal Family.* Toronto: Doubleday Canada, 1980.

FIVE: REMEMBERING WINTER

Bishop, Elizabeth. *Elizabeth Bishop: The Complete Poems 1927–1979*. New York: Farrar, Straus & Giroux, 1980.

Frye, Northrop. *Northrop Frye on Religion*. (*Collected Works of Northrop Frye, Vol. IV*) Toronto: University of Toronto Press, 2000.

Golany, Gideon. *Geo-Space Urban Design*. New York: John Wiley, 1996.

Jarrell, Randall. *The Complete Poems*. New York: Farrar, Straus & Giroux, Sunburst Books, 1969.

Pressman, Norman. *Shaping Cities for Winter: Climatic Comfort and Sustainable Desire*. Prince George, BC: Winter Cities Association, 2004.

Struzik, Ed. *The Big Thaw: Travels in the Melting North*. Mississauga, ON: J. Wiley & Sons Canada, 2009.

Turvey, G. Calum, Alfons Weersink, and Szu-Hsuan Celia Chiang. *Pricing Weather Insurance with a Random Strike Price: The Ontario Ice-Wine Harvest*. Blackwell Publishing: Journal of Agriculture Economics, 2005.

"Underground City, Montreal." *A View on Cities*. July 5, 2011. http://www. aviewoncities.com/montreal/reso.htm

PERMISSIONS

Every reasonable effort has been made to trace ownership of copyright materials. The publisher will gladly rectify any inadvertent errors or omissions in credits in future editions.

ILLUSTRATIONS

Monastery Graveyard in the Snow (Cloister Cemetery in the Snow), Caspar David Friedrich, 1819
© bpk, Berlin/Nationalgalerie, Staatliche Museen, Berlin/Art Resource, NY

The Chasseur in the Forest, Caspar David Friedrich, 1812
© Foto Marburg www.fotomarburg.de/Art Resource, NY

The Sea of Ice, Caspar David Friedrich, 1824
© bpk, Berlin/Hamburger Kunsthalle, Hamburg/Elke Walford/Art Resource, NY

Ice Flowers in Window (photograph)
© Mauri Rautkari/plainpicture/Pictorium

The Blue Rigi, J. M. W. Turner, 1842
© Tate, London, 2011

Bilking the Toll, Cornelius Krieghoff, 1860
© Musée McCord — McCord Museum, Montréal/Art Resource, NY

One Hundred Famous Views of Edo #99, Kinryūzan Temple, Asakusa,
Utagawa Hiroshige, 1856–1858
Image provided courtesy Brooklyn Museum, Gift of Frank L. Babbot Fund

Icebergs, Davis Strait, Lawren Harris, 1930
Courtesy of Mr. and Mrs. H. Spencer Clark
Photo: McMichael Canadian Art Collection

Arctic Sketch IX, Lawren Harris, 1930
Courtesy of the family of Lawren S. Harris
Photo: Heffel Fine Art Auction House

A Dendrite Star, Wilson "Snowflake" Bentley, c. 1885–1931
© Smithsonian Institution Archives, Bentley Snowflake 591 [*A Dendrite Star*]. Record Unit 31, Box 12, Folder 17. Image #SIA2008-1395

Image of Santa Claus and St. Nicholas, Thomas Nast, 1865
Image provided courtesy HarpWeek

*Christmas Eve ,*Thomas Nast, 1862
Image provided courtesy HarpWeek

Santa Claus in Camp, Thomas Nast, 1862
Image provided courtesy HarpWeek

The Skater, Portrait of William Grant, Gilbert Stuart, 1782
Andrew W. Mellon Collection, Image courtesy National Gallery of Art, Washington

Revd Dr. Robert Walker (1755–1808) Skating on Duddingston Loch, Sir Henry Raeburn, c.1795
Image provided courtesy National Gallery of Scotland

Johann Goethe Ice-Skating in Frankfurt, Germany, J. I. Raab, c. 1850s
© Image provided courtesy of Art.com

Skating on the Ladies' Skating-Pond in the Central Park, New York,
Winslow Homer, 1860
Image provided courtesy Brooklyn Museum, Gift of Harvey Isbitts

Our National Winter Exercise — Skating, Winslow Homer, 1866
Image provided courtesy Brooklyn Museum, Gift of Harvey Isbitts

Cutting a Figure, Winslow Homer, 1871
Image provided courtesy Brooklyn Museum, Gift of Harvey Isbitts

The underground city of Montreal
© Ville de Montréal

POETRY EXCERPTS

INDEX